STEP~BY~STEP GARDENING

Compiled by Alan Wilbur

WILLOW BOOKS
COLLINS
St. James's Place, London 1982

Contents

This book is based on material from Practical Gardening Magazine and we would like to thank staff and contributors for their help.

© EMAP National Publications Ltd, Peterborough, 1982

Printed by Pindar Print Limited, Scarborough, North Yorkshire.
Published by Willow Books
William Collins Sons and Co Ltd
London · Glasgow · Sydney · Auckland
Toronto · Johannesburg

First published 1982
ISBN 00 218080 4

Garden design

Colour guide on page 33

GOOD gardens don't just happen. They are planned that way. While there is always room for some manoeuvre and a certain amount of mind-changing, basic planning is essential if the end product is to be just as you want it.

How often have you seen a garden and thought, "I wish mine looked like that"? Perhaps you have given time and energy to making a new garden or altering some part of an established one only to find that you do not like the end result.

Let's see what the gardener, who is prepared to spend some time and effort, can achieve towards making the most of what he has.

Let's assume that, like the vast majority of garden owners in this country, your "estate" is less than one tenth of an acre. If, on the other hand, your "garden" consists of several acres you need the services of a professional designer or landscape architect who is prepared to visit the site and work with you towards a long term design project.

So how and where do you make a start? First of all ask yourself a few simple questions. What sort of garden do you want to make? If the answer is "like Fred's, three doors away", then think again. Find out what it is you like about his garden and analyse it. But do not try to copy it.

Generally speaking **good** gardens are good because they suit the site they are in. Any attempt to copy on a different site would be a disaster of the first order.

How do you use your garden?

Is it a place where the children play football, or where you rebuild old cars, boats and the like? In other words do you need space for outdoor activities, or do you need a garden that is quiet with the maximum amount of space given over to your favourite plants? Maybe it is some-thing in between; space to sit, some lawn and a limited amount of planting to add interest.

Do you wish to incorporate any special features such as a pool, rock garden, good lawns, "barbeque", formal rose garden?

However small your garden may be, careful planning will enable you to include many, or even all of these features.

Careful planning is needed to include all these items without losing the sense of cohesion and ending up with a cluttered mess.

Are there any serious limitations to the site?

Is the garden exposed to wind (or noise), and so needs shelter planting? Is the site shaded for much of the day, making it unsuitable for sitting out on all but the warmest of summer days? Remember the estate agent's line, "In the summer the river looks beautiful at the bottom of the garden," but he doesn't say it is not so hot in the winter when the garden is at the bottom of the river! But you take the point; are there any drainage problems?

Does the land tend to fall away from the house towards distant views? This almost always accentuates and lends an even greater feeling of distance to the view. But when the land falls towards the house it has a foreshortening effect on any views.

Soil type

Try to grow the plants that like your soil. If you are on a heavy alkaline soil and want to grow rhododendrons, sell the house and move! You can grow rhododendrons on such a site but, it certainly isn't easy.

A gardener's life can be difficult enough with unavoidable problems — drought, frost, wind, rain (at the wrong time, of course), and the inevitable plague of aphids that eat everything except weeds, and the weeds that swamp everything except other weeds. So, grow the plants that suit your site and keep it simple. Make out a list of the things that your garden has to do and has to be. Do this before you start to think about the plants than you would like to grow.

Remember that in a well laid out garden with good lines and some thought and organisation in the way it is used, the planting will be comparatively easy. If, on the other hand your garden is badly proportioned, lacks a theme or unity, has no mood or atmosphere, it could be difficult, if not impossible, to put it right with planting alone.

Late autumn and early winter is a good time of year to consider reorganising or replanning your garden. New garden owners will, of course, be thinking in terms of a complete landscape scheme but owners of established gardens will only be considering minor alterations. Whichever situation you are in, it is obviously a good idea to plan the alterations in some detail before the work begins.

The next logical step is to get out into the garden and on with the job. How do you translate a plan on paper into a reality on the ground? Obviously, a professional landscape gardener would have the necessary knowledge, tools and measuring equipment to make this a comparatively simple job. But for most gardeners, setting out a garden from a plan is a "once in a lifetime" operation and, therefore, experience is obviously limited and the only tools available are your normal range of garden implements.

Accurate setting out is the first step in creating a successful garden. The ideas that you have worked out on paper may need slight modification on the ground

A steeply sloping site creates special problems but can be transformed with careful planting.

Where you have taken over a neglected garden it is often better to clear the site.

Mature trees should be preserved wherever possible and the new garden planned around them.

Garden design

Colour guide on page 33

and if you are able to mark out the job accurately before beginning the work, these minor adjustments will immediately be apparent and can be made quickly and easily before any constructional work is undertaken.

Base line

The first and most important requirement is to set out a straight line. On a clear, open site this is comparatively simple. You can stretch a garden line between two fixed points and that is all that is required. But in an established garden there are often obstacles which prevent a line being used.

The simplest method under these circumstances is to use a bunch of ordinary garden canes in the same way that a surveyor would use his ranging poles. Set any two canes in any position along the proposed line. By siting between these two canes, it is possible to position any number of additional canes exactly in line with the original two. Where there is an obstacle in the way, you can usually overcome it by using a taller cane and siting over the top of the bush, wall, fence or whatever.

Having established such a baseline, you can measure accurately from it.

Right angle

The next measurement that you are likely to require is a right angle either marked from a baseline or from the house or an existing path. There are two simple methods of achieving this. The first method, and the one most widely used, is known as the 3-4-5 method. If you form a triangle in such a way that the three sides measure 3 units, 4 units and 5 units respectively, it does not matter whether the units are feet, yards or metres, the angle formed between the lines 3-4 will always be 90°.

The best method of doing this is to insert two pegs at A and B. The pegs are set at 3 units apart. Fix a line to pegs A-B that has previously been marked off to equal 9 units, with a second mark equal to 5 units. Place a third peg (C) on the 5 unit mark and draw the string tight on all three pegs. Insert peg C into the ground and the angle between AB and C will be 90°.

There is a second method, which allows you to mark a right angle on each side of the baseline. Mark out your baseline EF and fix two pegs in these positions. Attach a garden line to one of the pegs and extend the garden line along the baseline for slightly more than half the baseline length. Attach a cane to the end of the garden line and scribe an arc on to the ground in a position roughly approximate to E and F. Repeat this operation from the other peg on the baseline and scribe two more arcs. Where the arcs cross on the ground, insert pegs D and G. The line between pegs D and G will cross lines E and F at right angles.

Levelling

Having marked out a satisfactory baseline from which to take other measurements and mastered the technique of marking a right angle from this baseline or any other feature, the next problem you are likely to encounter will be that of setting levels for paving, paths, lawns or foundations. For this you will require a supply of pegs, a straight edge which can be made from a wooden board about 8in (2.4m) long, 6in (15cm) wide and 1in (2.5cm) thick. It should be straight, not warped, preferably planed to give a smooth surface but, most important, the two opposite edges of the board must be absolutely parallel.

All levels are set from a fixed point. If, for example, you are constructing a paved patio adjacent to the house, where the patio abuts on to the brickwork, set a peg two bricks below the damp-proof course. Where you are constructing a path from a doorway or gateway to some distant point, the level is determined by the door or gate and other levels must be taken from it. Where a new path is to meet an existing path, then the new path is set at the same level as the existing one. There is always a fixed level from which to work and a few moments thought before you begin digging out soil will often save you a lot of unnecessary work.

Slopes

Very often we are required to set paving or pathways on a slope. Let us say, for example, that we are constructing a patio adjacent to the house and we have set our level alongside the house at two bricks below the damp-proof course. It will be necessary to slope the paving away from the wall of the house to prevent water collecting and damage to the foundations, usually about 1in (2.5cm) for every 12ft (3.6m). If you set the paving absolutely level, water will still collect in the joint between the stones and on the stones themselves since paving stones are very rarely absolutely flat.

The best way of marking out the correct fall is to use your spirit level on a straight edge. Put out two marking pegs — peg No. 1 adjacent to the house and peg No. 2 approximately 8ft away. Place a thin strip of wood or other suitable material on top of peg No. 2 and then drive peg No. 2 into the ground. Using the spirit level and straight edge, check that peg No. 2 *plus the block of wood* are now level with peg No. 1. Stretch a line between peg No. 1 and peg No. 2 *with the block of wood removed* and you will have created a slope that can be reproduced elsewhere. By varying the thickness of the wood block, you can vary the degree of slope as required.

The operation can be repeated and extended for an indefinite length by placing the straight edge on peg No. 2, positioning a third peg at the far end of the

Sketch out your ideas, preferably in the garden, using a sketch pad or clip-board.

Then work out the plan more carefully in the house. Work on squared paper to scale.

It helps to visualise the garden features if you cut them out of paper and move them about.

straight edge, reinserting the wood block and repeating the levelling operation. If you then stretch a line between pegs 1, 2 and 3, all pegs will touch the line in an absolutely uniform slope.

Foundations

Marking out foundations often presents a number of problems but this can be reduced to a few very simple lines. First of all, set out pegs or canes to mark the corners of any proposed wall. These pegs are set out by measuring from the plan and by constructing right angles as already described. Join all pegs together by stringing a garden line from peg to peg to mark the outside edge of the wall. It is then a simple matter to put in a second line of pegs parallel to the first to mark the back edge of the wall. All that is now required is to extend the double line that you have formed by driving in two pegs at each corner, well clear of any excavations and you can mark from these pegs and set levels to determine the width and depth of any excavation. Providing that the pegs have been set clear of excavations and the surplus soil — which should always be set well away from the work, you can continually refer to them. Once the wall is higher than the pegs, any further measurements can be taken from the wall itself.

Marking a curve

There is only one other system of measurement that is likely to be required and that is the ability to mark out a predetermined curve or irregular shape. This can be a curved border following a wall or pathway, an island border cut in the middle of a lawn, or a shape for a pond or any similar feature. The basic method of measurement is the same for all. First, set out a baseline. Where the proposed curve is to follow an existing boundary wall, fence or path, use these. With an island bed or a pool, create a baseline which represents the longest axis of the feature. Mark this line clearly on your plan and, working to scale, mark it off in equal lengths of, say, 6ft (1.8m).

From each mark on the plan, draw a second line at right angles to the baseline and extend these until they meet the curved edge of the border or pool. Measure this line and write the measurement on the plan. Repeat the operation on each mark along the baseline. Now we can begin setting out. First of all, insert canes along the baseline in the same way that the plan was marked off in equal units. Then, beginning at one end, systematically insert a second line of canes to form the edge of the border, measuring from the pegs on the baseline the distances previously marked on the plan. Once all the canes are inserted, string a garden line from cane to cane to roughly mark out the edge and make any minor adjustments to the line by eye as digging or excavation work proceeds.

With an understanding of these basic marking out techniques, you can set out any feature in the garden to correspond exactly to your plan. Providing that your basic measurement has been correct, there is no reason why the finished result should not be as accurate as though it had been undertaken with the most sophisticated measuring equipment. It may seem an awful chore to set out a garden in this way, but remember if you build a wall or path and get it wrong, then changing it requires major structural alterations. Accurate setting out at the beginning of the job often identifies potential problems and any alterations that you are obliged to make simply involves a new measurement and moving a cane or level peg. You also have the added advantage of seeing on the ground a full-sized picture of what you hope to construct and this, if nothing else, makes the setting out operation well worth while.

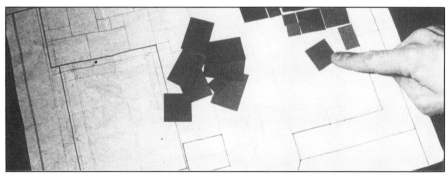

In the same way, paving slabs can be cut out and tried out in various arrangements until the ideal is achieved. This method is easier on the back too.

When building garden features such as walls, always use a line and spirit level.

Site preparation

THIS imaginary site is to the rear of a large terraced house. It is rather long and narrow with numerous existing brick walls and changes of level. There are tall buildings to the northern end of the garden and neighbouring gardens to each side of the site and there is no access other than through the house.

Access from the house is gained on two levels. To the right hand side there is a glazed door leading from a sitting room down a ramp on to a new lawn. To the left-hand side there are french doors from a basement opening on to an existing concrete area, and the garden is approached by a flight of wide stone steps. A second door leads from the concrete area to the boiler room.

In a situation such as this, it is important to make as much use as possible of the existing features. There is little or no opportunity to remove or bring in additional soil. There is an obvious advantage in reducing the amount of constructional materials that have to be carted through the house such as paving or bricks for new walls. Any plants that exist which can be saved and re-used are preserved and protected throughout the structural operations.

This applies particularly to the two trees at the northern end of the garden and the evergreen hedges (yew) on the east and west boundaries. These were in fact amongst the best features of the site as a whole.

A secondary but equally important problem in a situation such as this is the amount of shade cast by surrounding buildings. There is only the centre third of the garden which is in full sun all day. The northern end is shaded by the trees and neighbouring buildings and the southern end is shaded by adjacent houses.

It was decided to preserve existing brick walls and to repair these and add to them where necessary. This eliminated the need for any dramatic changes in soil level and reduced the handling of bulk materials to a minimum.

The concrete area outside the basement flat was impossible to remove. There were too many drains and other services and there was also the problem of disposing of surface water if the concrete was broken.

The steps from the concrete to the lawn at a higher level were completely remade to about double their previous width. This did a great deal to improve the view of the garden from the lower sitting room in the basement. Colour was added to this particular corner by adding annual bedding, geraniums, fuchsias etc planted in pots at the foot of the steps.

A large quantity of Old London Yorkstone paving existed in the garden and had previously been used to form perimeter pathways. This was all lifted and saved to form a new central paved area. Very little additional stone was needed in this particular instance.

It was essential to preserve at least one "long view" from the garden and yet, at the same time, there was a need to create a feeling of privacy and enclosure. Natural changes in level were turned to advantage to achieve this.

Four small sections of new hedging were planted above a retaining wall to create a paved courtyard in the centre of the garden. A table and four chairs in white cast aluminium (copies of a traditional design) are a focal point in this small sitting area.

At the northernmost end of the garden a small figure was sited slightly off centre so that it was always visible from the house. The figure was in fact lit at night on appropriate occasions with two small spot lights and was very effective in this rather dark and otherwise shaded corner.

The main part of the garden consisted of a small lawn and the central paved pathway, the focal point being the pool and fountain. This part of the garden was made as large as the natural changes in level permitted. No heavy planting, trees or tall growing shrubs were sited near the house as this would have created a feeling of enclosure.

Planting

The planting was kept as simple as possible. The tall boundary walls were clothed in suitable climbing plants using roses, clematis and honeysuckle as the principal planting. The narrow borders below the climbers were packed with ground cover material such as *Hosta, bergenia,* lily of the valley and spring bulbs.

The two borders to the side of and behind the small pool contained largely evergreen shrubs including rhododendrons and a number of variegated plants for foliage effect. Inside the paved courtyard area, enclosed by yew hedges, there were two beds of white floribunda roses and the courtyard around the statue consisted of a few good foliage plants such as *Mahonia bealei, Aucuba,* and *Fatsia,* with a ground cover planting of *Vinca Hedera* and again, spring bulbs. The end wall was clothed in *Hydrangea petiolaris.*

The planting was kept as simple as possible since the overall design was rather complex incorporating varying surfaces, levels and building materials.

The simplicity of the planting made a very pleasing contrast.

The overall effect was a very orderly, easy to maintain garden that held interest all through the year.

Obviously this type of garden is very specialised in that it was created as a result of an existing set of circumstances but the same principles can be applied to any site. By careful thought and planning you can make use of what at first sight appeared to be obstacles and turn them very much to your advantage.

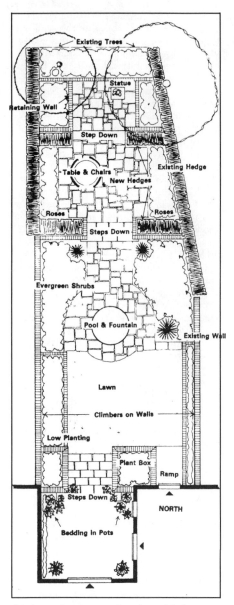

An imaginary garden in which many typical problems are likely to be encountered.

A sloping site

GARDENING on a sloping site brings its own attendant crop of problems. Nevertheless, careful planning can produce very attractive results. When you consider the lengths that owners of flat gardens will go to in order to create changes of level, perhaps one ought to be a little less daunted by the sight of a steeply sloping garden. If you can begin by thinking that the slope is an advantage to be used rather than an obstacle to be overcome, then you are already half-way towards your goal.

Obviously, dealing with a sloping garden can prove more expensive than developing a level site. There is almost invariably a need to construct retaining walls and steps and usually some earth moving, all of which can be expensive and time consuming.

But remember that careful consideration as to the siting of retaining walls will make the slopes so much easier and less expensive to manage in the long term. Almost invariably when faced with a sloping garden, the owners wish to include a rock garden and, of course, this is always so much easier than it would be on a flat site.

There are a number of very obvious difficulties to overcome when dealing with changing levels. First of all, if any part of the site is to be put down to grass, it is an advantage although not always essential to construct a ramp, or at least a very easy flight of steps, which will enable you to transport a mower from one level to the other.

By digging into banks, one can expose springs or old land drains which at some time will run with water and can have a very damaging effect on the lower levels where water is likely to accumulate. Try to intercept such water at its source and carry it away with land drains to a suitable outlet.

Finally, give careful consideration to the angles of the slopes that you are creating. Any sloping surface greater than 35° from the horizontal which is put down to grass would be difficult to mow. A similar slope of bare earth intended for planting will be subject to erosion by wind, rain and frost.

The steeper the angle the greater the incidence of erosion but this is also influenced by soil type. On a light sandy soil, erosion will be fairly rapid and will be continuous until such time as the plant roots have stabilised in the soil. On a heavy clay soil, much steeper angles can be produced and they will hold their formation for a considerable period of time. But there is always the risk of a sudden land slide occurring when the soil is

saturated, often following periods of frost and snow. Do not assume, therefore, that because an existing bank is stable, it will always remain so. Again, clay banks can be stabilised by planting or grassing but always try to reduce them to an angle of 35° or less.

Think of ways in which changes in level can be used and turned to advantage. Make a virtue out of necessity and use the slopes in your garden. It may be a difficult site but you have an opportunity to create a garden that most people would love to own.

Fencing

SOONER or later everyone who owns a garden is faced with the problem of making or repairing fences. It seems appropriate, therefore, to give some thought to the erection of fences at a time of year when either the ground adjacent to the fence is vacant, or the crops there are dormant and not easily damaged.

There are many types of fencing, the most popular of which is the interwoven type of fencing panel. The basic techniques can, however, be applied to most types of panel fencing.

Fencing panels are a very variable commodity and it is worthwhile checking around looking at prices and quality. There are different styles of fence; some are a plain basket weave, others have a peep-proof overlapping design incorporated into the basic weave. A third type has horizontal slats overlapping rather like weather-board fencing.

Obviously the better the quality the more you would expect to pay, but it is worthwhile remembering that the fence is required to last for a number of years so purchase the best that is available.

All interwoven fencing is short-lived with an average life of ten to fifteen years. The heavier, horizontal overlap panels will last longer but are more expensive.

To begin erecting the fence, first of all clear the site to give yourself as much working room as possible. It is an advantage if you can choose a day when there is very little wind since handling fencing panels some 6ft (1.8m) square in half a gale is slightly more than a two-man job! Mark the position of the fence with a garden line or a piece of strong string.

Set in the first new post and again check for alignment, and that the post is vertical, by placing a spirit level on at least two faces of the post. A fence 6ft high will need a minimum of 2ft 6in (76cm) of post below ground level. Keep the hole as small as possible as this makes it easier to fill back around the new post.

Concrete can be used, particularly in soft ground, and this is better concentrated towards the base of the hole rather than at ground level. The concrete mix should be in the region of six parts all in ballast (sand and shingle) to one part cement, and could be mixed dry and rammed in.

Measure the position for the next fencing post and dig the hole to the required depth. Place the panel at the correct height on the first post making sure there is at least 2in (5cm) clearance at the bottom, and drive galvanised nails through the side supports of the panel into the post. Never nail the fencing panels on to the face of the post. In this position, wind

from behind the panel will very quickly force it away from the post.

Check with the spirit level that the post is upright and support the bottom of the panel to keep it at the right height above ground.

The second post can then be nailed to the panel in the same way. Make sure that you leave the same distances between the tops of all the panels and the tops of the posts. The easiest way to do this is to cut a small block of wood, measured from the first post, to use as a guide for all the others.

Once nailed, the second post can be concreted in. The panel should then be supported with a plank of wood. Drive a long nail through the end of the plank and hook it over the top of the panel to prevent it moving either way.

The whole process is then repeated for each subsequent panel.

Many people like to use a base board or "gravel board" to prevent the rotting action of soil on the panels. This is a strip of timber running along the bottom end of the fence at, or near ground level.

The timber usually measures 4 to 6in (10–15cm) in width and about 1in (2.5cm) in thickness and can be heavily creosoted to prevent rotting. This board will take most of the wear and tear at ground level and is easily replaced if damaged, without removing the fencing panel.

When you get to the last panel, the chances are that it won't fit. You'll be very lucky if it does. That means that this one will have to be cut to size.

When the last-but-one panel is up, set

the final post in the correct position. Now measure carefully the distance between the two posts and mark up the last panel on both sides.

Remove the framings at one end of the panel and reposition them on the marks. Make sure that both are perfectly aligned and nail through. The top and bottom rails are then nailed, or better still, screwed, into the end-grain of the side supports.

Then set the panel on a couple of trestles, or on a wheelbarrow, and saw off the excess timber. The final panel can then be nailed in position.

Most panels are provided with capping strips to shed rainwater, though on some these are built in. Caps should be nailed on to both the panels and the posts to complete the job. When the concrete has set hard, the supporting planks can be removed and the site tidied up.

Erecting fencing on sloping ground presents no real difficulty. The method is illustrated below. Posts are set in the manner previously described and the panels placed in position so that each is slightly higher than its neighbour. Remember that on sloping ground you may need slightly longer posts to ensure that there is sufficient length below ground level.

People often have problems with interwoven fencing on wet ground where the posts rot off very quickly. This can be overcome by securing posts to a concrete spur. The same method can also be used to repair a broken post in an existing fence, without the need to remove either the post or the panel.

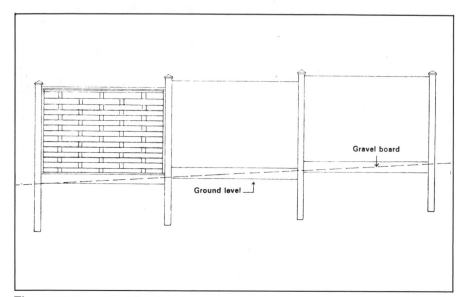

The correct method for fencing a slope.

Square trellis over a solid fence gives good support for climbers.

A close boarded fence for maximum privacy.

Wire mesh is cheap but not a good idea where privacy is wanted.

Wire mesh can be stretched on a frame which increases its life span.

'Ranch-style' but made entirely of rot-proof white plastic.

Bricks and mortar

Colour guide on page 40

BUILDING garden features in bricks and mortar can be carried out at any time of the year. There are, however, certain advantages in undertaking this type of construction during the winter months.

First of all, plants that need to be moved will transplant readily. Secondly, other work in the garden will be minimal and will not interfere with the main construction jobs, and finally, any turfing or seeding where the new work meets existing parts of the garden can be carried out either as the work proceeds or in the spring when the building work has been completed.

On the disadvantage side you will have the inconvenience of working outdoors in cold weather and you will need to protect all newly cemented or concreted work from frost.

This can be achieved by covering with sacks, polythene or any material which will provide a frost-proof barrier. There are also a number of anti-frost additives that can be added to the cement to prevent it freezing. Generally speaking, however, it is better to avoid large scale constructional works involving cement and concrete in frosty weather.

Trenches

Any construction begins with the preparation of a suitable foundation. It is difficult to be specific as to the size, thickness and depth below ground level of concrete foundations.

It is important that any trenches should be dug sufficiently deep to remove any soil containing organic matter. Otherwise, this would gradually decompose and the concrete foundation would settle.

The only real guide is to dig the trenches sufficiently deep to remove any soil that has been previously cultivated or disturbed and so that the base of the trench is formed from firm, well con-solidated earth. If there is any doubt as to the suitability of the base of the excavation then a layer of hardcore should be placed in position and well consolidated before any concrete foundations are laid.

Materials

The materials used in the formation of concrete include:

Sand Sharp sand is generally recommended for most concrete work and for rendering. A mixture of sharp and soft sand is used for brickwork. The important thing is that all sand must be clean, free from dirt, organic matter and other foreign bodies. Sand used for rendering should be sharp but free of coarse grit.

Aggregate Various materials can be used including granite chippings, gravel, broken brick or concrete. Again it should be free from dirt, organic matter and relatively free of dust. Coarse material should only be used for very rough foundations, finer material being used for concrete pillars, gate posts, pathways and slabs.

Cement This is generally Portland cement, although quick-drying and masonry cement are used in special circumstances. Cement must always be stored dry and not used if lumpy or old.

Water Use only clean water, free from silt or chemical contamination. Dirty water can adversely affect the drying process and will affect the ultimate strength of the cement or concrete.

Lime Lime is added to cement mixes to act as a plasticiser. This keeps the mix soft while it is being worked and helps to produce a less brittle joint. It is particularly useful when using stone or natural material and with some soft forms of walling block and paving stone. Masonry cement already contains lime and is specially prepared for use with natural materials.

Where accurate concrete mixes are required, it is better to buy cement, sand, and aggregate separately, but in some areas it is possible to buy a material known as "all-in-ballast", which is a mixture of coarse and fine aggregate plus sand. It is generally good enough for most garden work.

Mixing

Concrete or cement must be thoroughly mixed while dry on a clean hard surface. The quality of the finished product will be impaired if the dry ingredients are *not* thoroughly mixed. The water is added a little at a time, preferably with a watering can or a bucket.

Cement mortar, when mixed, should be wet enough to allow a brick to be placed without undue knocking with the trowel, but not so wet that the mortar runs down the face of the brick work. Concrete is generally much drier; only enough water is added to make the mix workable.

Concrete should be placed in position within half-an-hour and should be firmly rammed to remove air bubbles etc. This also works the "fat" to the surface, giving a smooth finish.

Any shuttering can be removed within 3 or 4 days and the concrete is firm within a week. In very hot weather concrete or brick work should be covered with damp sacks to slow down the drying out process. Generally speaking the slower the concrete dries the harder the resulting concrete will be.

Estimating quantities

To calculate the quantity of concrete required for a footing, multiply the length of the footing by the width, by the thickness of the concrete. If this is calculated in feet, for example 20ft long, 1ft wide

Check levels frequently since mistakes have a way of accumulating as the bricks build up.

Corners are another point where you can hardly take too much trouble to get angles right.

When building garden features always take care over the foundations.

and 6ins deep, the quantity required will be 10cu ft. For this amount of concrete 10cu ft of aggregate (1cu yd = 27cu ft), 6cu ft of sand and approx. 1cu ft (ie 1 bag) cement. The cement and sand do not add to the bulk of the concrete as it simply fills up the spaces between the aggregate.

Stepped foundations

Where a wall or other feature is built on sloping ground it is usual to step the foundation. The height of the step should be equal to the thickness of the building material used. For example; if you are building in ordinary brick, each step in the foundation will be 3in or a multiple of 3in.

It is usual to form the step by casting the concrete at the lowest level and when this has hardened sufficiently, placing bricks across the foundation where the step is required. Then cast the concrete for the second level, leaving the bricks in position as a former.

When stepping foundations in this way it is important to ensure that where one layer of concrete overlaps another, the length of the overlap must be at least equal to the width of the concrete foundation.

If a brick pier or gate post or similar structure is to be built on to the same foundation then the concrete should be thickened at the appropriate place by excavating the original trench to a greater depth. The extra thickness of concrete is required to support the additional weight of brickwork.

It is important to remember that the function of a foundation is to spread the weight of the above-ground structure. At the same time it anchors it firmly to the ground and prevents cracking and sinking. With this in mind all foundations should be of a uniform thickness with no thin or weak spots.

Fill the space with rough rubble and large pebbles for drainage.

Then fill with soil that is weed free and is fairly quick draining.

Pot grown bedding plants can then be planted into position.

The resulting double wall is intended to take plants. Drain holes have been left at intervals.

Lawns from seed and turf

Colour guide on page 34

SOONER or later every garden owner is faced with the problems of making new lawns or repairing and maintaining established ones.

Soil

Once your lawn has been sown or turfed there is very little that you can do that will influence the soil below the grass. So preparation should be thorough and even painstaking to ensure that your lawn has the best possible start.

Ideally, you need at least 6in (15cm) of good top soil and the sub-soil should be broken to a further 6in (15cm) in depth giving a total of 12in (30cm) of good cultivated soil. The drainage must be good and there must be no hard "pan" below the surface, such as is often caused by builders' vehicles, wheelbarrows or even foot traffic that could impede drainage.

The soil should be capable of holding sufficient moisture to sustain the grass during summer droughts but sufficiently free-draining to prevent water-logging during the winter months.

Very rich soils will produce soft grass which requires extensive cutting and are difficult to firm when forming a seed bed. Very light soils will require the addition of organic matter such as peat or farm yard manure to improve their water holding capacity. Heavy soils will benefit from the addition of organic matter to improve the structure and help drainage.

Where time permits it is an advantage if the lawn can be left fallow for one summer and kept in a clean cultivated state either by hand or mechanical hoeing, or by chemical weed control to ensure that the site is free of perennial weeds such as thistle, dock and most important, couch grass.

Light soils are most suitable for fine turf. This is the reason why many golf courses are situated on either high ground where the soil is poor and free draining or on the coast. Often they are actually made on sand dunes. Under such conditions a very high standard of management is required to ensure that there is always sufficient moisture and plant food available for the grass to flourish and to recover from the heavy wear and tear that is common in such situations.

Chalky soils provide the most difficult sites for lawn establishment. The soil is often deficient in plant foods, thin and free draining with an excess of calcium. But with correct preparation adding plenty of organic matter, and careful management, they can produce very fine lawns.

Preparing the site

Let us assume that we are dealing with a new garden that has not previously been laid down to grass. There are certain basic operations that must be undertaken, and it is vital that you do not shortcut any of these operations or you will risk serious problems in the later life of the lawn.

First of all clear the site of all bricks, rubble, rubbish, piles of earth and sub-soil that may have been left by the builders. Strip off any unwanted turf or herbage and cart all these waste materials away from the site. This is also a good time to remove any unwanted trees or other obstacles, which if left to be removed at a later date would result in damage to the lawn surface.

Next, grade out the soil to the approximate levels required. Where extensive grading is required, that is more than 6in (15cm) in depth, first strip off the top soil and pile it up somewhere, grade the sub-soil to the required levels and then replace the top soil to a uniform depth.

It is important that the grading operations do not expose areas of sub-soil as this would result in a very patchy appearance in the established lawn.

After the grading operation has been completed we can begin to think about cultivating the soil and improving its general condition, ensuring that the site is freely drained. Obviously if it is necessary to include a piped drainage system this would be done before the cultivations commence. There are, however, very few private garden situations which require this type of drainage or where such schemes are practicable.

Having levelled and cultivated the ground, the next operation is to reduce the soil to a fine tilth suitable for the preparation of a seed bed. On large areas this can be done with mechanical cultivators and on small areas by hand forking and raking.

Whichever method you use, try to ensure that the cultivations do not disturb the levels set during the grading operations.

Having reached the stage where the soil is finely cultivated you are now ready to begin firming and raking in readiness for the final seed bed preparations. It always seems to be a contradiction that soil has to be cultivated to a considerable depth only to be firmed down again before the seed can be sown. The thing to bear in mind is that loose, unfirmed soil is impossible to level, is filled with air spaces which allow it to dry out too rapidly and creates a situation in which it is impossible to sow seed to a uniform depth.

The type of compaction that you produce is important and it is best achieved by treading over the ground with your weight on your heels. Ideally, tread in two directions at right angles to each other. This firms the lower levels of the soil but leaves the top in a suitable state for raking out and levelling.

All too often the mistake is made in trying to firm the land by using heavy rollers. This has quite the wrong effect on the soil in that it firms up the topmost layers first causing a hard, panning effect and does not penetrate into the lower levels, leaving them loose and subject to further natural settlement. You cannot level land by rolling it. No matter how much weight you apply to soil it will, given time, slowly spring back to take up its original bulk, so that rollers generally tend to have a damaging effect on the soil by destroying its structure. They should be avoided in all but specific circumstances which will be dealt with later.

A perfect if unimaginative expanse of grass.

If you can fallow the site prior to seeding you will have an ideal opportunity of controlling weeds, but remember that any hoeing or other mechanical weed control operations should be very shallow so as not to disturb levels. If you can limit your cultivations to the top 2in (5cm) of the soil you will gain some control of perennial weeds and with time, one hundred per cent control of annual weeds. If you disturb the lower levels and bring up fresh unfallowed soil you would only encourage a new crop of dormant weed seeds to germinate.

About 10 to 14 days before you intend to sow the grass seed, apply a base dressing of fertiliser and thoroughly mix this with the top 2in (5cm) of soil during the final raking operation. This fertiliser should be a compound containing nitrogen, phosphate and potash. For spring sowing, use a proprietary lawn fertiliser, but for an autumn sowing, one lower in nitrogen is better. You are now ready to sow the seed.

Seeding

Generally speaking, grass seed is sown at about 1½oz to the sq yd (45gm per sq m). To ensure even distribution apply the seed in two dressings of ¾oz (20gm) each. Sow the first dressing in a north to south direction and the second dressing at right angles to this in an east to west direction. This will avoid any tendency towards patches in the lawn as a result of uneven seed distribution.

The best time to sow is from mid-August to the end of September while the soil is still warm and there is no shortage of water. Alternatively, you *could* sow from mid-March to April but spring sown lawns are more likely to suffer from drought during the following summer and will almost certainly require watering.

Ideal conditions for sowing the seed would be when the top ½in (13mm) of soil is dry and easy to manage, but below this level there are adequate reserves of moisture.

Grass seed is often left standing in store for some months before it is used and since most seed is sold as a mixture of several species the finer seeds tend to settle towards the bottom of the bag leaving the coarser rye types at the top. It is important to thoroughly shake the bag, turning and shaking several times to ensure that the various seed species are thoroughly mixed before sowing.

When the seed has been applied, lightly rake to partly bury the seed. A wire springtine rake is ideal for this purpose.

If a lightweight roller is available, the ground can be lightly rolled after seeding. The object of this is to firm in the seed, not to compact the ground. If the ground is wet do not roll at this stage but wait until the grass seed has germinated.

Turfing

The basic preparation of the soil is exactly the same as for seeding except that for seed you require a very fine surface tilth free from large stones and other unwanted material. For turf the final degree of finish need not be quite so exacting.

The application of a fertiliser can be omitted if the soil is in good condition or you could use a high phosphate fertiliser such as bone meal or super-phosphate for autumn turfing to encourage root development without the disadvantage of stimulating excessive top growth.

Turf is usually bought cut into strips 1ft (30cm) in width and 3ft (1m) in length and about 1½–2in (4–5cm) in thickness. They are usually delivered either rolled or folded in half, grass to grass.

If the turf cannot be used within twenty-four hours, ideally it should be

Features help to break the monotony of flat green if they are placed carefully.

Avoid too many curves otherwise the result is irritating to the eye.

Curved beds create more interest at the lawn's edge.

Lawns from seed and turf

Colour guide on page 34

laid out flat, grass uppermost and kept watered until required. Turf left in a stack will begin to sweat, and under normal spring and autumn conditions can discolour within about 3–4 days. Turf received during frosty weather will need to be protected by covering with sacks, tarpaulin or even straw. Under such cold conditions turf can be left in the stack for much longer periods without deteriorating.

The best time to lay turf is between October and the end of February, but it can be laid at almost any time of the year providing sufficient water is applied after laying to prevent the turf from shrinking and drying out.

Begin laying the turf at any convenient point on the lawn and lay one straight line of turves end to end. The next row should begin with half a turf so that no two short joints are ever exactly opposite each other. The finished effect is rather like bricks bonded in the face of a wall.

The correct procedure for laying turf is to work from boards placed over the turf that you have already laid so that you do not walk on or otherwise disturb the levelled soil surface. However, for rough work, it is often more convenient to work from the soil surface but it is still better to use boards adjacent to the immediate working area or for wheeling barrow loads of turf on to the site.

While you are placing the turves keep a bucket or barrow load of finely sifted soil conveniently to hand and use this to pack under the turf to fill up slight hollows or undulations that would otherwise occur. Make up the soil level if you have to lay a thin turf and rake away excess soil if you find one piece of turf that has been cut too thickly.

On very fine lawns such as bowling greens the individual turves may be "boxed". This involves placing the turf grass side downwards in a shallow tray or frame and drawing a double ended knife across the base of the soil to a uniform depth determined by the depth of the tray so that all turves are cut to an even thickness. Each individual turf can be inspected for weeds, stones and other debris which are also removed at this stage.

The turf should be lightly beaten into place as it is laid and all joints should be tightly butted. You can make a beater with a flat block of wood ideally about 18in (45cm) long, 1ft (30cm) wide and 3in (7.5cm) thick, fixed to a stout wooden handle. Alternatively, the back of a heavy garden rake will do perfectly well.

Turves are beaten to a uniform level but not to the extent that individual ones are

For the very best turf lawns the turves should be 'boxed'.

At the same time carefully remove all weeds and stones.

compressed out of shape or are unduly spread. Turf that is over beaten will often shrink back to its original size and cause excessive cracking of the lawn surface.

Never beat the turves into place with the back of a spade. The back of a spade is curved and you will not make the turves level with a curved beater. Indeed, even the wood block beater should be kept clean and free from collected mud to ensure that all beating is carried out with a flat, level instrument.

It is often necessary to turf into irregular shaped areas. Whenever possible achieve this by laying the whole turf and cutting back to the required line. Never lay less than half a turf to the edges of the work area or they will too easily break and crumble away.

Any thin, broken or weedy turf should be discarded and remember also to allow for some wastage either from rejected turves or from wastage due to cutting when you are ordering from your supplier.

It is often recommended that newly turfed areas should be top-dressed to fill in cracks between the joints. I am generally not in favour of this as you invariably bury a proportion of the grass and can cause considerable damage to the very fine grass.

Never top dress lawns with grit or sand. This can have a very abrasive effect on new grass, particularly where there is likely to be a lot of wear and tear by foot or machine traffic. If you have to top dress then wait until the turf beings to grow and use a top dressing mixture of peat, sand and soil to fill in any cracks or hollows that occur.

Once the turf has begun to root it may be lightly rolled and as the grass stands up after this rolling so cutting can commence.

Seed

Seed sowing is the cheapest method of producing a lawn. In addition you have the advantage of being able to choose the most suitable type of grass from the many seed mixtures available to suit the soil conditions and the type of lawn that you hope to produce. It is relatively free from weeds, particularly if a quality mixture is purchased and can be stored for weeks or even months without deteriorating. It can also be bought well in advance of sowing and held until conditions are suitable for sowing.

However, it does have its disadvantages.

It takes 9–12 months from sowing to produce a true turf. Two years or more must elapse before that turf could be cut and lifted for re-use elsewhere.

Grass seedlings are easily damaged and subject to various damping off diseases, and fungi in wet weather.

The preparation of the soil must be very thorough, the sowing dates are critical and more extensive management and after care is required while the grass is in a young state. Lawns from spring sowings are more likely to require watering than turf lawns or autumn sown lawns.

Turf

Turf produces a lawn very quickly and could even be used and looking well after just a few weeks. Provided the turf is adequately laid and well-watered there are usually no problems in establishment through such things as damping off or bird damage.

The preparation of the ground need not be as thorough as for seed bed preparation, and it can be laid over a very long period — from October to April provided that the ground is not frosted. One of the biggest disadvantages of turf is that much of that offered for sale is of a poor or variable quality. It can contain a high proportion of coarse, or otherwise unsuitable grass species, weeds and even weed grass such as couch.

Good quality turf is very expensive and it has the further disadvantage that the best time for laying it is often the worst time for lifting it as the growing field may be water-logged or frosted.

Early care

When newly seeded grass is about 1½in (4cm) high, gently brush or wire rake the surface to remove worm casts, leaves and other debris. This must be done when the surface is dry to prevent soil disturbance or damage to the young seedlings.

Follow this by lightly rolling the lawn surface. The back roller of a mowing machine is often sufficiently heavy for this purpose, and will encourage the seedlings to "tiller" at ground level and produce additional blades of grass. "Tillering" is just like pinching out the top of any plant in that it encourages side-shoots to grow from the base of the plant, thus thickening the lawn. The roller also helps to firm back the soil, lifted or loosened as the seeds germinate.

When the grass is about 2in (5cm) high, it is ready for its first cut. Set the mower high so that only the tips of the grass are removed. You must leave a minimum of 1in (2.5cm) of grass or even more on rough grass areas. The mower blades are lowered a little at a time at each successive cut until the required mowing height is reached.

Two basic types of mower, rotary . . .

. . . and cylinder.

Lawns from seed and turf

Colour guide on page 34

Lawn weeds, Greater Plantain.

Dandelion

Daisy

Weed control should commence immediately after the germination of the grass seed. This can be done by hand weeding areas, removing perennial weeds and weed grasses. On larger areas or where there is a heavy infestation of weeds suitable chemicals may be used, but don't use normal strength lawn weedkiller. There are special low-strength formulations available.

Do not worry if there is a light cover of annual weeds such as *Shepherd's Purse, Groundsel* or *Chickweed*. Annual weeds will not stand mowing and it is unlikely that more than a handful of the more persistent types will survive the first three cuts.

This is not true, however of the more persistent lawn weeds particularly those that are low growing such as the *Speedwell, Clover* or *Daisy* or those that form rosettes of leaves at ground level such as *Dandelion*, some *thistles* and *Cat's-Ear*.

Watering is essential if a dry spell occurs soon after sowing or after the grass has germinated. Pay particular attention to the watering of turf or seeded areas in the spring. The treatment of turfed areas is basically similar except that one begins cutting earlier and heavier rollers can be used.

The brushing and raking operations described for seeding also apply to turfed lawns. Where grass has germinated unevenly and patchiness occurs rake over the poor areas with a wire rake taking care not to disturb any grass that has survived or to upset the soil levels. Mix one part of seed with ten parts of dry sifted soil. Spread this evenly and thinly over the bare patches at about $\frac{1}{2}-\frac{3}{4}$lb per sq yd (240–360gm per sq m). Rake in and lightly firm and do not allow the patches to dry out excessively particularly when the second sowing of grass seed has germinated.

There are a number of soil conditions which can cause patchiness on newly sown grass areas. They are as follows:

1. The seeding rate was too low or unevenly distributed. Incorrect raking in of the seed can bury a proportion of it so deeply that it fails to germinate.
2. Poor site preparation. This includes uneven depth of cultivation often caused by grading after cultivation has taken place. Uneven depth of top soil, failure to remove buried obstacles such as builders' rubble, old paths or bad drainage caused by panning. This generally occurs where the site has been subject to heavy foot traffic, wheelbarrow traffic during site preparation or a deeper pan caused by builders' vehicles.
3. Unsatisfactory weather conditions. Dry spells after sowing on light land, particularly damaging once the seed has germinated, or prolonged wet spells which cause water-logging on heavy land and wash away available plant foods on lighter soils.

Hawkbit

Lawn care

Colour guide on page 36

A FINE lawn is the result of good husbandry. No matter how good the original seed mixture, or how fine the turf, without good management, it will soon revert to pasture. Conversely, a patch of cow-pasture, with constant care, can be transformed into the finest bowling green. It all depends on you.

Most of us, of course, don't want a bowling green. That sort of lawn is time-consuming and expensive and in any case, much too tender for the hard wear a garden lawn has to take. But it is an example of what hard work can achieve.

Of course, if you're starting a new lawn, it's best to start right and make it easy on yourself. If the drainage is good, the site properly levelled and the seed or turf of a good quality, you are halfway there already. But even then, you'll need to look after it to keep it that way.

Imagine what would happen if you sowed a fine lawn and then simply left it to its own devices. Very soon, coarse rough grasses would start to colonise the area and fight the finer grasses for food, water and space. And, left alone, the coarser grasses always win. These would be followed by broad-leaved weeds and eventually by shrubby plants and even trees. Left alone, your lawn would soon become a forest.

Fortunately, this unwelcome invasion can easily be controlled. The coarse grasses cannot stand having their heads cut off at regular intervals while the fine grasses thrive on it. So, just by regular mowing, the rough grass and the broad-leaved weeds will disappear. Then, if you can give the fine grasses a bit of encouragement, they'll grow strong and healthy. Then just let those unwelcome foreigners try to poke their noses in!

Spring cleaning

Your grass has had a good rest during the winter and now it's chafing at the bit to get growing again. It is probably being hampered a little by the debris of last year's efforts, so the first job is to give it a good clean-up to let in light and air.

Start by going over the whole area with a stiff brush. A "besom" or witches' broom is ideal, but if you haven't got one, a stiff yard-broom will do. This brushing will clear away most of the fallen leaves and rubbish left from last autumn. It will also spread worm-casts, and that is most important.

The soil digested by our old friend the earthworm, is fine and fertile. Flattened by the mower, it makes an ideal seed-bed for any weed seeds that may blow in. So, spread them about and let them do some good.

The next job is to clean out all the old, dead grass to give the young buds a chance to breathe.

Each year, a certain amount of older grass dies off and the dead leaves settle to form a sometimes quite dense mat on the surface of the soil. This is all to the good during the winter when it protects the younger growths from the ravages of hard weather.

But when spring arrives, it has served its purpose and should be removed. Otherwise it will prevent light and air circulating round the young growth buds and will also prevent water penetrating the soil.

The ideal tool for the job is a spring-tine rake. Don't try to do it with an ordinary garden rake. You'll pull out as much young healthy grass as dead.

If your lawn has a moss problem, delay the raking operation until the moss has been killed. Raking out living moss will simply spread millions of tiny spores which will flourish in any bare spaces and choke out the grass.

Drainage

Raking the lawn will go a long way towards draining the surface area, but most lawns need a little extra. Bear in mind that most grass areas receive much more traffic than any other part of the garden. Even the weekly mowing must consolidate the soil considerably.

On most soils, it will be sufficient to simply spike the area with a garden fork. Push the fork into the soil to its full depth, wiggle it around a bit and pull it out. This should be repeated at about 6in (15cm) intervals. It's a time consuming job, but it will enable the life-giving water and nutrients to reach the lower levels where the roots live, as well as draining away surface water.

If the soil is heavy, it is likely to become over-compacted. And then sterner measures are required.

The answer is to use a hollow-tine fork to remove a core of soil. The soil can then be laid on the surface and later brushed loosely into the holes. Alternatively, if the problem is acute, remove the soil entirely and fill the holes with lawn peat.

Feeding

The best and easiest way to feed a lawn is with a lawn food made specifically for the job. Of course, you can mix your own, and many of the older gardeners always did. But mixing must be very thorough and the cost is only marginally lower.

Solid lawn fertilisers are easiest to apply, but are rather more expensive than liquids and many need watering in.

If you intend to apply the fertiliser by hand, it is essential to mark out the area with a garden line. Mark out a 3ft (1m) strip and then use a 3ft (1m) cane to measure along the line. Thus, you will accurately measure 1sq yd (1sq m).

Weigh out a handful of fertiliser so that you know pretty accurately how much you are putting on, and make sure that you keep the fertiliser within the limit of the line.

Alternatively, use a specially calibrated lawn-spreader. If your lawn is big, it may be well worth your while investing in an adjustable spreader, but they can often be borrowed from a shop or garden centre when you buy the fertiliser. These will spread the lawn-food accurately and automatically and save an awful lot of messing about.

Put the feed on, and if it hasn't rained within 24 hours, water the lawn with a sprinkler. Failure to do this could result in scorch.

If you decide to feed with the cheaper soluble fertiliser, put it on through a watering-can fitted with a special sprinkler bar. These are really nothing more than a perforated plastic tube and are readily available from most garden shops. The same rules of accurate measurement apply.

Weeds

The best way to have a weed-free lawn is to avoid weeds.

In other words, keep the grass growing vigorously, so that weeds don't have a chance to get established. If you make your lawn well in the first place and then maintain it properly, you won't have a lot of trouble from weeds anyway.

But most lawns are not that Utopian and weeds are generally a problem. If your lawn is brand new, you are almost certain to get a healthy growth of annual weeds before it is ready for its first cut. Generally, you won't need to lose any sleep over those. All but the "rosetted" types (those that grow close to the ground) will be cut off with the mower and will soon die.

If you don't have many "ground-huggers" that the mower blades won't reach, the best way is to simply cut them out with a knife.

But if your lawn is dotted with daisies and dandelions, they must be attacked with a week-killer. There are several on the market, most containing 2,4D and MCPA which will kill most common lawn weeds. Apply them at the rates shown on the back of the bottle, through a watering-can or a sprayer.

Broad-leaved weeds will suffer most

Lawn care

Colour guide on page 36

when they are growing strongly, so an application a week or so after feeding is ideal. Don't cut the grass just before applying the weed-killer or it may suffer too.

Alternatively, to save time, use a "weed-and-feed" preparation containing both fertiliser and weed-killer.

Moss-killers should be applied in the same way and, once the moss has died and turned black, it should be raked out.

Don't use a weed-killer too soon after sowing a new lawn. There are one or two preparations on the market that are, in fact half-strength weed-killers, especially formulated for new lawns. But even these should be used with care.

Edging

Neat, clean, well trimmed edges add the finishing touch to a good lawn. After mowing, they should be trimmed with a pair of long handled edging shears. But edges do tend to get broken down, especially during the winter when the soil is wet and soft, and this makes trimming difficult.

Generally, the edges can be cut back just a little at this time of year to give a good, cuttable border.

Always work off a board. This way you will avoid further damage to the edge and you will make sure of straight lines.

Use a half-moon edging iron to ensure a straight, clean cut — the blade of a spade is slightly curved making it difficult to cut dead-straight lines.

Throw the soil up away from the edge of the lawn to make a little gulley so that the edging shears can be freely used. Pick up any bits of turf that have been cut off and put them on the compost heap.

Obviously, every time you cut the edges back, the lawn gets a little smaller. So, you can't go on doing it forever. Where edges are badly broken and in order to get a straight line or regular curve you would need to cut back too far, you will have to re-turf.

Sticking a small bit of turf on the edge of a lawn is doomed to failure. The first time it is trodden on, it will simply fall off. So, it is necessary to cut out a large area of turf.

Cut back to about 2ft (60cm), carefully lift the turf and move it towards the edge. The space left further in from the edge can then be filled with soil to make it level, compacted by treading, and re-seeded.

If you have the time, trim the edges with lawn shears after every mowing. Nothing spoils the look of a well cut lawn as much as scruffy, unkempt edges.

If you have a lot of edges to cut, it may be worth investing in an edge trimmer.

Basically, there are two types. Some makes are man-powered — you simply push them round the edges — while others are mains-electric or battery powered. They'll save you a lot of time and they do a good job.

Mowing

A good, well set up, sharp mower, regularly used will make more difference to the quality of your grass than any other single factor. Regular mowing discourages the coarse-leaved grasses and weeds and helps create a closer turf.

Every time the top is cut off the grass, and the leaves are bruised by the mower's roller, the young buds at the base of the plants are encouraged to grow out.

Close, thick turf then, is the result of *regular* mowing. The closeness of the cut has little to do with it.

Two things should be avoided. First, never allow the grass to grow very long and then cut it close. If, for some reason it has overgrown, set the blades high and cut off only a little. The cut can then be successively lowered at each mowing.

Secondly, never "shave" the grass. All this does is to create bare patches that will be quickly colonised by moss and weeds.

When mowing for the first time after the winter rest, set the blades as high as they will go, taking off only the top ¼in (6mm) or so. Next time and with each successive cut, lower it a little until it is cutting to within about ¾in (2cm) of the soil. There is no need to cut any closer than this.

Ideally, each successive mowing should be in the opposite direction to the last. For obvious reasons, this is difficult to achieve if you cut straight up and down the lawn. You won't remember from week to week in which direction you cut.

It's easier if you start in one corner and cut diagonally across the lawn. Put a short cane in the corner you started from as a reminder, and next time start in the opposite corner and cut at right angles to the previous cut.

But these points are niceties. The main things to remember are to keep your mower sharp and to mow regularly. If you cut it once a week you'll have a very good, general purpose lawn. If you cut twice a week you'll be able to puff out your chest with pride.

Whether or not to leave the grass cuttings on the lawn has long been a bone of contention amongst gardeners. There are, of course some advantages and some disadvantages. Leaving them on returns a certain amount of goodness to the soil

and provides a mulch in dry weather. On the other hand, it can spread weed seeds, it can encourage fungus diseases and it looks pretty messy. It's best to remove the grass cuttings at all times except when the weather is very dry and for the last cut of the season.

Finally, choose your time for mowing carefully. Don't cut the lawn when the weather is very dry, when the grass is wet or when a sharp frost is expected. And *never, never* even walk on the lawn, let alone mow it when it is actually frozen.

Choice of mower

Lawn mower manufacturers seem to have a great number of variable theories about the best mower for the job. They vary mainly according to the type of mower each one produces.

If you want a really good lawn, cut it with a cylinder mower and bear in mind that the more blades there are on the cutting cylinder, the finer the cut will be. If you have rough grass that you only cut perhaps once a month, a rotary mower is the tool for the job.

Motive power varies between petrol engines, mains-electric, battery and sheer hard work.

Petrol engines are perhaps the most versatile in that the power unit is entirely self-contained, so the machine can be used anywhere in the garden. And these days, starting troubles have been cut to a minimum.

Mains-electric mowers are cheap, light and easy to use. They have the disadvantage that they need to trail that enormous length of cable around, but with a little thought, there is no reason why this should be a nuisance. They are generally cheap and ideal for a small garden.

Battery machines need no cable, but they do have to be recharged every so often. Apart from that though, they are perhaps the most convenient. There is no problem with starting — simply lift a lever and away they go. They can be used miles from an electric supply and are very quiet to run.

Push mowers are ideal for small gardens. Certainly they take a bit more effort, but a bit of exercise never did anyone any harm. Side-wheel mowers seem to be going out of fashion now. And a good thing too. They have the great disadvantage that they will not cut close to edges, so choose a roller model.

A fairly new introduction is the machine that cuts with a couple of lengths of rapidly revolving fishing line. These are absolutely ideal for cutting those awkward corners and around trees and other obstacles.

Paving

Colour guide on page 38

WITH an attractive area of paving, a few comfortable garden chairs and a couple of big glass doors, you'll add an "outside room" to your house that is ideal for summer relaxation after a day's work in the garden.

On fine summer days you can eat outside, entertain your friends, catch up with that reading you've been promising yourself or simply lie in the sun and get your legs brown before you go on holiday.

But, if you're going to embark on what is not after all a cheap project, it's worth taking a bit of trouble to ensure that it's there for keeps.

Throw a few slabs down on a bit of sand and they'll sink all over the place within a couple of months. They look unattractive and can be downright dangerous.

It's a false economy to try to cut corners and invariably fails.

Choice of slabs

This must, to some extent, be a personal choice. Modern houses may look fine with a highly coloured patio, while the same slabs would look quite out of place around an old cottage. But, whichever colours you choose, it's worth buying good quality.

Remember first that, if you need to cut slabs around manhole covers or drainpipes, you will be better off with a slab you can cut with a chisel. Concrete slabs do not cut well this way, and for a neat job you'll need to hire a stone saw. Better choose those made with reconstituted stone.

Bear in mind too, that big, 2in (5cm) thick slabs are heavy, so you'll need help to lift them.

Ideally, go for 1½in (4cm) hydraulically pressed slabs made from reconstituted stone. They are strong, light and cut easily with a chisel.

If a patio or path is to be in permanent shade, it is likely to develop a film of algae on the surface, making the slabs slippery and very dangerous. There are several slabs with a rough, non-slip surface, ideal for this situation.

Ordering materials

Before ordering paving, it will be necessary to decide on a pattern. The simplest way, of course is to use square slabs, laid down in "tramlines". Simple to lay, but not too attractive. Far better than this "municipal" looking finish, is rectangular paving in random sizes.

There are two ways of laying random paving. Either work out a pattern first or simply lay the paving entirely at random

as it comes to hand. If you decide on a pattern, work it out to scale on a piece of paper first. This way, you will know exactly how many slabs of each size to order.

If you prefer an entirely random, less formal design, measure the total area of paving and ask for your order to be split up into equal *areas* of each sized slab. Note the emphasis on equal *areas*, rather than equal *numbers*. If you order equal numbers, you'll find yourself with far too many big slabs, and fitting them together will then become a headache. Working out the amount of ballast and cement needed is not as difficult as it seems at first.

Unless your base is very firm, you'll need to put down 3in (7.5cm) of concrete. All-in ballast is generally sold by the cubic yard or, if your builder's merchant has "gone metric", he will be able to work out the equivalent.

One cubic yard of ballast will cover 12 sq yds of ground and will require 5 bags of cement. For each cubic yard of ballast, you will also need ⅛th of a cubic yard of builder's sand — or sharp sand for a really strong job — and an extra bag of cement to make the mortar. As an example, if you have 24 sq yds of paving to lay, you'll need 2 cu yds of all-in ballast, ¼cu yd of sand and 12 bags of cement.

Preparing the base

Under certain circumstances, it is quite possible to lay paving on sand with no concrete base. If the ground underneath is really well compacted and there is no possibility of sinkage, you can dispense with concrete. But those situations are few and far between.

Only if you are to put the paving on a piece of land that has been undisturbed for years — an existing path for example — is it wise to dispense with concrete. Even then, if you intend to run a car over it, concrete is essential.

If you are paving near to a new house, you can be sure that a certain amount of sinkage will occur however much the soil is compacted.

And if sinkage does occur, the paving will move unevenly, resulting in a highly dangerous shambles. Do the job properly and lay your paving on a good firm base.

The first step is to decide upon the level at which you want the paving to finish. You should allow two courses of bricks below the damp-proof course (DPC) if you are to pave against the house. This will ensure that water does not splash up above the DPC even in the heaviest rain. You can recognise it quite easily. Normally the thickness of mortar between

There are many materials from which paths can be made; these are wood blocks.

Planting of creeping Thymes and other low growing plants in a natural stone pavement.

Paving

Colour guide on page 38

bricks is ½in (13mm), but there is generally about twice that where the DPC has been inserted. If you have outside doors, the DPC will generally be immediately below the bottom of the door.

If you have a large amount of soil to dig out before paving you will have to dig it out roughly first in order to set level pegs. Once you have a rough level, it is essential to level accurately.

Cut enough pegs to be able to put them at about 6ft (2m) intervals over the whole area. Measure from the top of the peg to allow for the thickness of the paving plus 1in (2.5cm) of mortar and mark a line. The line indicates the finished level of the concrete base.

Set the first peg near to the house with the top at a level with the DPC. Now set more pegs at 6ft (2m) intervals in a line parallel to the house, and exactly level with the first peg.

The next row should be 6ft (2m) away from the first row. The tops of these should slope very slightly away from the house.

Once the whole area is adequately pegged and carefully checked with straight-edge and spirit level, remove any excess soil that does not allow 3in (7.5cm) of concrete to be laid.

Now you are ready to lay the base.

Concreting

Using ¾in (2cm) all-in ballast and cement, make up a 6 to 1 mix. On patios which will not be expected to take heavy traffic, an 8 to 1 mix will suffice.

Don't overdo the water. The drier the concrete is, the stronger it will be, and remember that there is no need to achieve a fine finish.

Cart the mixed concrete on to the site and spread it so that it comes to a fraction above the line on the pegs. Compaction either by treading or beating it down with the back of a shovel will bring it to the required level line.

After compacting it, go over the whole area carefully checking that there are no high spots. It is better to be a fraction too low than too high, since you can always make up the extra with mortar. Allow the concrete to set for a few days and you are ready to start paving. Remember though, that frost will seriously weaken the concrete, so in very cold weather it should be covered with sacking or straw while it hardens.

Laying the paving

The first slab is always the most important. Get that one right, and the rest will follow. Get it out of level or out of line, and you'll be in all sorts of trouble.

The mortar mix for the paving should be made with a 3 to 1 mix of builder's sand and cement. If you want a really strong job, use sharp sand instead. Mix the mortar fairly dry as well, or it won't take the weight of the slabs.

Decide on the size of the first slab and put down five piles of mortar — one at each corner and one in the middle of where the slab is to be laid. Set the slab carefully on the piles and tap it down with the handle of a club hammer.

Now it is imperative that the first slab — which sets the pattern for all the rest — is exactly in line with the edge of the house and exactly level. If it deviates slightly from the line it will be several inches out by the time you get to the other end.

Set the slab 1in (2.5cm) away from the house (just to allow a little margin for error), and stretch a tight line along the inside edge of the slab and to the other end of the house wall. This way you should be able to get it exactly in line.

When you are quite sure it is straight, put the spirit level on the top of the slab and rest the other end on the top of the nearest peg. Then tap it down level. Check that it slopes slightly away from the house by putting the straight-edge from the slab to the top of a peg further away from the house.

The remainder of the slabs are simple. Set them all on five points of mortar butting one tightly against the other to obviate pointing. Check every slab against the pegs using the straight-edge. You simply can't do this too often — it's amazing how easy it is to start to go wrong so constant checking is essential.

If you are laying to a pre-determined pattern, keep the plan by your side and you won't have any trouble. If you are laying the slabs entirely at random, the art is to avoid long straight lines. So you will have to think a couple of slabs ahead to make sure that you "break" the lines at intervals.

When you come to a peg, it will have to be either knocked out of the ground or banged down into the concrete.

If you need more than one day to finish the job, don't forget to cut away any excess mortar around the slabs before you finish work for the day. The following morning it will be hard and you'll have a lot of trouble removing it before you can lay the next slab.

When the paving is finished, it only remains to point in with the 3 to 1 mortar along the house wall — and to keep the children off the paving for at least a week.

The essence of good paving is firstly to make sure your levels are right. Check constantly with the straight-edge and you won't go far wrong. And make sure you don't trip over the pegs while you're working. They can cause nasty accidents, but worse still, you may knock them out of level.

Secondly always work clean. As you lay an area of paving, brush it down with a soft broom to remove any blobs of mortar that may be stuck to it. Left for too long, it will cause nasty stains on the paving.

Finally, when you finish for the day, clean your tools thoroughly. There is nothing worse than trying to work next time with a shovel or trowel covered in half a hundredweight of hard mortar.

Planting into a path gives a charming 'cottage-garden' effect but can be a problem if it is much used.

Here, where there is space planting in a paved area is particularly striking.

Pebbles can be set into spaces left between slabs for variety and economy.

Walls and steps

Colour guide on page 40

MAKE sure first of all that you choose a stone that will fit in with your paving and will blend with the house.

If you settle for artificial stone you *must* ensure that it is in fact stone and not concrete. Though concrete blocks are fine for a formal wall, you will not be able to trim them to give the attractive "rock-face" possible with natural or reconstituted stone walling.

"Facing" the walling

The natural effect on the face-side of the stones is made by trimming the edges of each block.

If you have a lot to do, it's worth making yourself a bench of roughly the right height. It will save you an awful lot of backache. A 40 gallon drum with a paving slab on top is ideal. Alternatively, a Black and Decker "Workmate" bench, again with a slab on the top will fit the bill very well.

Start by marking a straight line about ½in (13mm) from the front edge of the block. Then, using a brick bolster (the heavier stone-bolster is better but difficult to come by) chip off the top edge of the stone along the line.

Now turn the stone on end and repeat the process. Make sure when you do this, that the cut is exactly at right-angles to the first cut. This will ensure that your wall goes up straight and doesn't lean. Now mark a line on the bottom side of the stone and chip away that edge. It all sounds rather long-winded, but in fact it is not such a long job once you get the hang of it and it will make all the difference to the finished look of your wall.

Footings

If your wall is to be built alongside paving, you will already have the main part of the job done. All that remains is to fill in behind the paving with a mixture of 6 to 1 ballast and cement to bring the concrete level to a fraction below the paving.

If you have no paving base already laid, you will need to dig out a trench and make a concrete foundation. The depth of the concrete will vary according to the height of the wall, and the soil beneath it. Generally, a 3ft (1m) wall on firm soil will need a footing 6in (15cm) deep and twice as wide as the width of the wall. For every extra 1ft (30cm) add 2in (5cm) to the footing.

Once the foundation has set hard, the walling can be laid.

Mortar

Mortar for walling is made by mixing together 3 parts of building sand with 1

Walls and steps

Colour guide on page 40

part cement and, of course, a little water. Bricklayers use mortar that's about as sloppy as hot custard. That's fine for an experienced man laying bricks, but a disaster for an amateur working with stone. While it is quite easy to remove excess mortar from the face of a smooth brick, it will stick to a rough stone face like glue and your wall will be ruined. So make the mortar just wet enough to work and no wetter.

Another thing to bear in mind is the finished colour of the mortar. This will vary according to the amount of cement added to the sand. Unless your wall is very small, you will need more than one mix to complete the job, so in order to get a uniform colour throughout, it's worth using a bucket to measure the materials accurately.

You'll also need a spot-board to put the mortar on while you are working and it should be big enough to avoid mortar falling on to the paving to cause nasty white stains. It's quite easy at this stage to spoil the paving by staining it with mortar, so make sure, after mixing, that your boots are clean. And, if you use a wheelbarrow to cart the mortar to the site, wash the wheel before running on the paving.

Laying the stones

As with paving, the first few stones are the important ones and it's worth taking a bit of care to get them just right.

Start by setting the first two stones at either end of the run. Lay down about $\frac{3}{4}$in (2cm) of mortar and gently tap the stone on to it with the handle of a club-hammer. Check that it is exactly level with a spirit level. This check should be both along and across the stone. If the stones are tilted backwards or forwards, the wall will lean like the Tower of Pisa.

Repeat the process with the stone at the other end of the run, and then stretch a tight line between the two. Anchor the line by wrapping it round a spare stone at each end. The line is then placed accurately along the cut upper edge of the stone, and held in place by resting a loose stone on top of it. Now check to ensure that the two end stones are exactly in line, adjusting them if necessary.

It is now a simple matter to lay the remainder of the course, using the line as a guide, making sure that it runs always along the cut upper edge of the stone.

Bear in mind that it will be necessary to leave "weep-holes" at intervals along the first course of walling. If your wall is being used, to retain soil, they will allow water to seep through. Without them, there is a danger of the pressure of water

PROPORTIONS OF CEMENT, SAND AND AGGREGATE				
TYPE OF FOUNDATION	**PARTS BY VOLUME**			
	CEMENT	**SAND**	**AGGREGATE**	**WATER**
Rough concrete foundation	1	4	6	$\frac{3}{4}$
Better class foundation	1	$3\frac{1}{4}$	5	$\frac{1}{2}-\frac{3}{4}$
Normal above ground purposes — walls, floors and reinforced concrete.	1	$2\frac{1}{2}$	4	$\frac{1}{2}-\frac{3}{4}$
Strong concrete for watertight walls, steps, paths, tanks, etc.	1	2	3	$\frac{1}{2}-\frac{3}{4}$
Fine pre-cast work — fence posts, etc.	1	$1\frac{1}{4}$	2	$\frac{1}{2}$

Foundation Sizes

Wall height	Depth of foundation below ground	Width of concrete foundation	Minimum thickness of concrete foundation
Up to 2' 9" thick	1 brick	15"	3"
2'–4' 9" thick	2 bricks	15"	4"
4'–6' 9"thick	3–4 bricks	18"	4"–6"
Over 6' 9" thick	Take expert advice		

For $4\frac{1}{2}$" walls up to $4\frac{1}{2}$' high — use the same as above but reduce the width of the foundation by half.

pushing the wall over. If the wall encloses the paving completely, the weep holes will also serve to take away excess water from the paving.

The holes can simply be made by leaving a gap about 2in (5cm) wide between stones. Alternatively, a land drainage pipe set in the space looks very attractive.

If you are using larger blocks to create a "random" effect, you will need to leave a space (or remove one of the standard sized stones) and lay the bigger block when you set the second course. Otherwise it will interfere with your line and put it out of true.

When the first course has been laid, point in between the stones with mortar. Don't worry about making a neat job of it at this stage. That comes later when the mortar is almost dry.

The second and subsequent courses are laid in exactly the same way, but now you must make sure that the stones are "bonded". All this mysterious word means is that the centre of each stone should be in line with the joint between the two stones below it. Just like normal brickwork. So, if you are building a single run of walling, you will have to start every alternative course with half a stone. If you have corners, you simply use the end stone crossways on.

Coping

The width of the walling stones doesn't matter because they won't be seen from the back. But the coping will finish above soil level, so it must be uniform in width.

Coping stones must be rock-faced in exactly the same way as the blocks, but here you must ensure that they are of a uniform width. For a single wall, this would normally be about 5in (12.5cm).

Since coping stones are longer and thinner than walling, they need extra care when facing them to guard against breakages.

The most common cause of breakage is an uneven working surface. It only takes a small bit of broken stone under the coping to break it when it is being faced.

So, make sure that the paving slab you are using as a bench is brushed clean each time you finish work on a coping and before you start the next. Never let one end of the coping overlap the slab when you are working on it, and make sure that your bolster is ground sharp before you start.

The copings are laid in the same way as the walling, except that they should overlap the front of the wall by about 1in (2.5cm).

Raking out

There is no need to "point" stone walls in the same way as brickwork. In fact, they will look much better if the mortar is "raked out" to about $\frac{1}{2}$in (13mm) deep.

Wait until the mortar is nearly hard — generally at the end of the day's work — and then rake it out using a piece of wood cut to approximate size.

Cleaning up

There is nothing worse than a wall or an area of paving stained by mortar. It looks messy and may take years to wear off.

The easiest way to clean it is not to get it dirty in the first place.

Keep your boots and your tools clean, and keep the broom going all the time, and you'll save yourself a lot of work in the end.

But, however careful you are, you are bound to finish with a little excess mortar sticking to the walling somewhere. The best way of removing it is with a wire brush. Obviously you must wait to do this until the mortar is quite hard or you'll be brushing out the mortar you have so carefully put in.

Rock gardens

Colour guide on page 42

ORIGINALLY the term "alpines" referred to plants that had their natural homes either in the Swiss Alps or in terrain closely resembling that mountainous region. With the passage of time "alpines" has taken on a wider meaning. Nowadays it is a term applied to a group of plants that have a great deal in common.

By and large they are small, carpeting plants that grow laterally rather than vertically. Most are spring and early summer flowering and without exception they all have a pet hate — they detest being wet around the collar and having their feet in soggy soil. In other words they grow and flourish in well drained soil, but they rot and die off in poorly drained ground.

The important thing to remember is that in their chosen habitat they grow either on steep slopes, in desert sand, or in the open, usually sandy soils, of the foothills. Some species even find their way right up to the snowline and a few are known to survive in the bitter cold of the arctic regions. So provided their abhorrence of wet conditions is respected, these little beauties are tough enough to withstand the rigours of the deepest snows and the hardest frosts.

The obvious place for alpines is the rock garden. There they have good drainage and, provided the slope faces any direction other than north, they will have the sun that most of them enjoy. They are also ideal for planting on top of walls and the majority revel in soil pockets on patios and terraces. To be absolutely sure of success, put a handful or two of coarse grit or gravel around the plants to keep their basal leaves and stems clear of the soil.

Hundreds of types

There are of course hundreds and thousands of different kinds of alpine plants. One of the most popular is the alpine *dianthus* that, given the right conditions, grows and flowers easily and freely. Its light, grey-green leaves that grow in neat hummocks and perfumed flowers appear in abundance in summer.

For planting in dry stone walls the *lewisias* are unbeatable with their dark green rosettes of leaves and long spikes of flowers of pink and red, each petal having a darker coloured stripe running from tip to nectary.

The alpine species of *polygonum* are not only pretty in flower but they are also great ground cover plants. *P. vaccinifolium* hails from the Himalayan foothills and although only 6in (15cm) tall, it spreads to 3 to 4ft (0.9–1.2m). Flowers come in August and September.

Dianthus subcaulis

Polygonum vaccinifolium

Then there are the alpine primulas the best known being *P. auricula*, now called by most gardeners simply *auricula*. The species has the characteristic "Dusty Miller" grey-green leaves with yellow or purple flowers from March to May. Modern varieties of auriculas come in a very wide range of colours, many flowers having a differently coloured central "eye".

Primula allionii is another alpine beauty from the maritime alps. Only 2in (5cm) tall, it spreads to 6in (15cm) or more and in March and April the leaves are completely hidden by purple and rosy-red flowers.

Last but far from least come the ground-hugging perennial phloxes. There is always room for *P. subulata* and its various cultivated, named varieties. This is a closely knit carpeting alpine with very dark green leaves and starry flowers in shades of pink, lavender, mauve and lilac. The variety *Temiscaming* is the most eye-catching with flowers of a brilliant magenta-red colour.

Finally, there is strawberry. It does not produce runners ` but it does bear a generous and repetitive crop of small, delicious berries that make a first rate jam. Alpine strawberries are easily grown from seed and look attractive when the light green leaves are topped with white blossoms. This is an alpine that can be eaten as well as admired.

A great deal of thought must be given prior to building a rockery, otherwise the end result will cause nothing but disappointment. Ideally, an open site facing south, to obtain full sunlight, should be used. However, there should also be scope to build planting pockets at the base of northerly or westerly facing rocks, for those plants which resent full sun all day. Sites beneath, or in the shade of, trees should be avoided, for not many plants will thrive with constant shade and dryness during the growing season. Also, a low lying site or one that is overhung by a building without guttering and downspout will be unsuitable due to waterlogging during the winter months.

The stone

The most important factor to consider, when building your rockery, is the stone, and not enough gardeners know enough to even start selecting. It is fair to say that stone from a local quarry will be cheaper than that transported from other counties, and will blend in far better, particularly in rural areas. On the other hand, some stones, such as **Somerset limestone**, are useless as they break down very quickly. Quarried stone, too must be

Primula allionii

Auricula

Rock gardens

Colour guide on page 42

used with care, if possible setting the natural face outwards, and always making the grain run horizontally or slanting slightly backwards. This is because, this is how the stone is laid down, and nothing looks more unnatural than stone which is set in the opposite direction to that which nature intended.

Another point to watch closely is the weight of the rock, which also makes a great deal of difference if you are thinking of manhandling the stones into place yourself. As an example, a limestone such as **Bath limestone** will weigh 130lb per cu ft, **Wealdon sandstone** will weigh 150lb per cu ft and **Leicester granite** will weigh 165lb per cu ft. Try to visualise the size of a cubic foot of stone, and compare this with the sort of weights we are talking about, before deciding.

This will also help you to determine how much stone you will require for a given area, as stones are usually ordered by weight.

When placing stone, at least a quarter of it will be below soil level, and up to a half of the area should be covered by stone. When placing the rocks, butt them closely together, in tiers or terraces, leaving small or no gaps in the row. The planting pockets should be broad and in some cases deep, between the tiers of stone, to leave plenty of room for different plants to develop.

Soil

The soil in a rockery is often a disgrace for many people have the idea that alpines will grow on rubbish. This is far from the truth, many alpines being lost through being planted either in impoverished dry soil, or solid clay that becomes waterlogged during the winter months.

For the general, run of the mill plant, three parts friable loam, one part old compost or peat, and one part grit will be ideal. As well, special pockets must be prepared to take ericaceous plants such as *dwarf Rhododendrons, Gaultherias* and *heathers*. Here it is necessary to use a mix of one part loam to one part peat. Most alpines, whilst requiring a good growing medium, resent surface wetting during the winter months. *Lewisias, Calceolarias, Erinus* and some *Saxifragas* will often succumb, if they are planted in a wet soil. Such plants are best grown in vertical cracks between the rocks, or in pockets topped with an inch or so of gravel to assist in the dispersal of surface water. Always ensure that the pockets of soil are almost level for severe slopes will result in overdraining during the summer months and much of the compost being washed to the bottom of the slope during heavy rainfall.

Planting

The first consideration when planting a rockery should be the focal points that will lift the flatness like trees in a landscape. Without doubt the finest plants for use as focal points are dwarf conifers for here we can have slim grey spires of *Juniperus communis Compressa*, the neat oval golden outline of *Thuya orientalis Aurea Nana* or the rounded, blue-green ball of *Chamaecyparis Lawsoniana Minima Glauca*. Never place an upright plant on top of a rockery, but rather a little way down, and to one side, otherwise it will appear as a pimple on a mountain.

If uncertain about what to plant in the rockery, go along to a nurseryman who has the right knowledge and ask for a collection of easy but good plants that will give a flowering period from April to October.

The use of bulbs is always advisable to supplement the flowering period, for snowdrops will give colour very early in the year, and the dwarf species of crocus always provide a bold display, some even being autumn flowering. One favourite for the rockery is *Iris reticulata*, for its narrow grass-like foliage will not interfere with the growth of plants around it and its lovely purple flowers which are produced on six inch stems seem bird proof.

Propagation from seed

The majority of plants grown on the rockery will produce seed, but it is fair to say that varieties and plants with coloured foliage will not come true to type from seed, and such plants should be grown from cuttings or division.

Seed is best sown as soon as it is gathered for when it is fresh it will germinate very quickly. However, the seed of certain families is often erratic in germination, often germinating over a period of twelve months or more, so do not be too eager to throw away the pan of seeds that does not appear to be giving results. If the seed cannot be sown immediately, it should be stored dry in paper bags, in a cool place, for if kept warm, the seed dehydrates and loses its viability.

Sow the seed thinly over a suitable, open compost that is just moist. The seed pan should then be lightly watered with a fine rose and a piece of glass or polythene placed over it. Certain families eg *Campanula* and *Saxifraga* are difficult to germinate if covered, as they need intense light. In this case care should be taken to ensure that the pans are kept moist.

Once germination has taken place, remove the cover and place the pan in a shady spot in the greenhouse or frame for if the seedlings are subject to direct sunlight, scorch may result in the death of many.

Seedlings should be pricked off as soon as they are of a manageable size for if left in the seed pan for too long they will, especially if sown too thickly, become drawn and weak. The resulting plants are best planted out in the rockery when they are large enough to survive. Do not, however, put young seedlings out at the advent of winter, rather, overwinter in a cold frame or cold greenhouse, and plant out in early spring.

Cuttings

Cuttings can be taken of most plants,

during the growing season, as soon as the current year's growth is firm enough to handle. The cuttings need not be large, 1½–2in being ideal. In the case of subjects like heathers, even less will suffice. With large leaved plants such as *Ajuga*, all that is required are pieces with two nodes (leaf joints), the leaves from the bottom node being removed. Cuttings of small leaved plants such as *Thymus* will need to have the leaves removed from the bottom two thirds of their length from the base. This is done by stripping with your thumb and forefinger. With a very sharp knife, trim the base of the cutting to just below a node, and also remove any excessively soft growth from the tip. Dip the bases of the cuttings into a hormone rooting powder before inserting them, to aid root formation. The strength of the powder will depend on how hard the cuttings are. However, as a general guide, the medium strength will be suitable for most subjects. Insert the cuttings in a very open mixture of 2 parts sharp sand to 1 part peat. The compost should be firmed and just moist. After the cuttings are pushed in, a light watering will firm them into place. A piece of polythene over them will help create a moist atmosphere. This should not be placed directly on to the cuttings, but held a few inches above them on wire hoops.

Many cuttings will root within two to three weeks, after which the polythene should be removed. As soon as the root system is large enough, the plants should be potted on for later planting out. Often, if the cuttings are not taken until late in the season, it may be necessary to leave the rooted cuttings in their trays until early spring.

Division of strong growing species is often advisable as a method of propagation. Campanula, Ajuga, Sedum and Sempervivum can be lifted and teased apart into smaller pieces. This operation is best carried out in early spring just as the plants are beginning to awaken after a winter's rest.

One of the hardest things to create in a rock garden is a sense of naturalness. Here it has only partly been achieved.

Pools

Colour guide on page 44

MOST gardeners have at least a secret yearning for a pool in their garden! There is something about the combination of water and plants that has a very special appeal, to almost everybody. Whether it is the way the sky and plants are reflected, the range and colour of water plants, whether they grow in the water or round the margins, or whether it is the deep, cool softness, is a matter of pure conjecture, but the appeal is definitely there.

Unfortunately, most people seem to think that a pool is the domain only of the rich man. However, with the advent of synthetic liners, it is not only relatively cheap to construct your own pool in the garden, but it is also quite possible to do so, for the first time!

Prefabricated pools

For quite a number of years now, there have been, on the market, small, prefabricated pools constructed in plastic or glass-fibre. Whilst these may seem ideal to the small garden owner, they have two very big problems. The first of these is, as ever, cost. They are extremely expensive, for what you get.

The other main problem is that they are too small, both in surface area and in depth. Whilst there is no need for a pool to be more than 18in to 2ft (45–61cm) deep at any point, some of these prefabricated pools do not even reach this depth.

Two other less important points are the colours that these pools are constructed in. Very bright blue or grey, usually, which never blend in, or look in any way natural. Finally, the shapes are usually too fussy. Whilst it is usually recommended that a pool be irregularly shaped, the curves should be gentle, and simple. Too many twists and turns, not only make the pool look unnatural, but also make maintenance more difficult.

All these factors added together mean that instead of a cool, clear pond, with lilies and goldfish, and perhaps the gentle splashing of a small fountain, you will get a slimy, green, smelly pond, which doesn't look at all attractive, and will only grow midge larvae and mosquitoes.

What are the advantages of this sort of pool? The answer is convenience! Being rigid to start with, these pools can be brought home from the garden centre in one piece. They can then be installed very quickly and easily. All that is required is a hole of roughly the right size and shape, which can take as little as $\frac{1}{2}$ hour to dig out. The main necessities being a flat base to provide support for the pool, and a level base and surround, so that the level of the water is parallel with the top of the pool, which in turn should be parallel with the surrounding soil.

Obviously, if the pool is a part of a rockery, this last point is not as relevant.

Flexible liners

What then are the alternatives, apart from very costly concrete? For a number of years, now, manufacturers have been producing flexible, waterproof pool liners that will mould to fit any shape and size of pool. These are made from a number of materials, the cheapest of which is polythene. These come in various grades, some more expensive than others, but all suffer from the same weakness. Polythene degrades, ie breaks up, in the presence of sunlight. This means that a polythene liner will have a limited life, possibly five years at best, probably two years being more likely.

The better liners, in terms of longevity, are made from a material known as Butyl. This has all the waterproofing characteristics of polythene or rubber, along with the stretching qualities of rubber, but being a man-made fibre, it will not degrade, under normal conditions, for many years. Some of the original pools made from this material, twenty years or so ago, are still going strong.

After painting such a glowing picture, what are the disadvantages of pool liners?

Punctures

Being flexible, they are very easily punctured, either by a stray fork, a big boot, or if you are lucky enough to live in an area where herons may visit your garden, by the beak of one of these fishermen. Unfortunately, certain water plants produce roots which are quite adequate to the task of growing right through a liner. However, with judicious planting this can be easily averted.

Installation

With any pool, the site is probably the key factor. It should be easily accessible from at least one side. It should be open and sunny (this being particularly important). Never place a pool under trees, as the leaves can cause enormous pollution problems. Finally, it is possibly best to place the pool at the lowest point in the garden. Whilst this is not essential, rockeries again being the exception, we expect to find water lying at the lowest point, and it is surprising how this can affect the overall appearance.

Digging out

When digging out the pool, it is important to remember a number of points. The pool should first of all be marked out, on the ground, using a flexible line, a hose pipe is ideal. This will show you exactly the size and shape you will require, in scale with the surroundings. This should then be marked with stakes, set at about 18in (45cm) apart, which can be levelled round the pool, and across it, with a spirit level, to ensure that the whole thing is absolutely horizontal.

The sides should slope inwards to a degree of about 20°. This, too, is vital, particularly in areas where the pond may become frozen over in winter. As the ice expands, on freezing, it will rise up the sides, instead of causing damage to them. Once you have dug out to about 9in or 1ft (23–30cm), leave a continuous planting shelf, 9in (23cm) or so wide, all round the edge.

This is not essential, and planting shelves can be half way or even oddly spaced at intervals, round the edge, according to what you are thinking of planting. Whatever, this is, excavate a further 9–12in (23–30cm) for the main depth, again slanting the sides in to about 20°. Any less, and a proper balance will not be able to establish itself, which will result in the pool overheating in summer, and freezing solid in winter. Even worse, however, algae will build up, turning the water green, never to clear. Keep the lines simple, and whatever the contortions within the pool, the liner will stretch to fit.

Choosing the liner

When buying the liner, you will want to know exactly what size you will require. This may seem difficult where the pool is irregularly shaped, but fortunately there is a formula. Measure the maximum length of the pool and add this to twice the maximum depth. Similarly, add the maximum width to twice the maximum depth. For example, if the pool is 18in (45cm) deep, 6ft (1.8m) long and 4ft (1.2m) wide, the liner will want to be 6+3½ft which equals 9½ft (2.9m) long, and 4+3½ft which equals 7½ft (2.2m) wide.

Colours range from that virulent blue, again, through a range of greys, even a pebble dash effect, to black, which is the best choice. Whilst all the colours will mellow, under water, with algae and sediment etc, between the water line and the edging stones there is always about 2in (5cm) or so which will never mellow. Black shows up a lot less than any of the other colours, and is, therefore, much less obtrusive. The other point in favour of a black liner is that it tends to give a greater appearance of depth to the pool.

Line the hole

When it comes to actually putting in the liner, it pays to line the hole first. However even and smooth the soil may appear, there may be sharp projections which can tear the liner. Covering all the surfaces with damp sand is one solution. If you do not want to run to that expense,

and have some old carpeting handy, that will serve just as well. Synthetic fibres are better than wool, as they will not rot down, but this is not very important. Even several layers of damp newspaper can be used to good effect, if nothing else is to hand.

Filling

With the liner in position, all that is now needed is to turn on the hose, and fill the pool very slowly. If it fills too quickly, the liner will not stretch evenly, and will probably break free from the weights collapsing into the bottom of the hole. When it is filled to about 2in (5cm) from the top, switch off the hose. All that is needed now is to finish off the top.

Finishing

Any surplus material can be trimmed away, leaving a 6–9in (15–23cm) lip all round. This will then be bedded in, in one of several ways. Probably the most successful is to lay mortar on top, and set paving stones all round. This provides a good solid edge to the pool, and anchors the liner firmly. Alternatively, the edges of the liner can be buried in the surrounding soil, which means that marginal plants, and those which are often associated with water, can be planted right up to the water's edge. If you do decide on this, it is better to place either paving stones or turf up to one side, at least, to provide access to the pool itself.

This problem of finishing off the pool-

side, can be a bit of a puzzle. Many people wish to turf right up to the edge, but are not quite sure what is the best way to do it. If you want grass to the edge of the pool, then, obviously there has got to be sufficient soil in which to grow it. If you leave the lip of the liner only 9in (23cm) below the surface, you may well end up with a ring of parched turf, round a pool of water, during warm weather, which may look a bit odd. The way round this, is to take out a further trench, right round the pool, when digging it out. This can be up to a foot deep, and should be far enough away from the edge of the pool, so as not to interfere with its stability. The edge of the liner is then tucked into this, and the trench filled in.

Perhaps the most satisfactory way of securing both the edge of the liner and the edge of the pool is to lay it in concrete. This again involves some work at the initial excavation stage. Once the main levels have been set, take out a further 4in (10cm) of soil, right round the pool to about 9in (23cm) wide. Fill the pool up to this level, and the edge of the liner will then stand upright, sufficiently to use as a former for the concrete. The shallow depression is then filled with wet concrete. The liner is then pulled tight over the wet concrete and weighted down with the coping stones. Once the concrete edge has set hard, the coping stones can be laid on top. This makes a very secure edge which will neither subside nor allow the liner to pull away.

Stocking a pool

Colour guide on page 46

THE best time to stock a garden pool is during May, June and July. Aquatic plants for this purpose can be divided into several distinct groups, each requiring a different set of conditions.

Without doubt the most popular plants are water-lilies. These can be planted in any depth of water from 6 to 8in (15–20cm) over the soil in which they are grown, depending on variety. There are a number of miniature water-lilies which require as little as 3in (7cm) of water over the soil.

It is important to include a number of submerged oxygenating plants. Several of these can be planted in one container and they will grow in any depth of water. Most of them are rapid growing and should not therefore be over-planted.

A number of species grow on the edge of the water and are referred to as "marginal" plants. These fall into two distinct groups. There are those which will grow in 6 to 18in (15–45cm) of water, such as *reeds* and *rushes*, and those which grow in wet soil not necessarily covered by water, such as *arums, loose-strife* and some *iris*.

Finally there are the group of plants which actually float on the surface of the water. Again many of these can be rather invasive and should be used sparingly.

Planting

It is important to allow a pool to settle before introducing plants, that is unless clean rain water can be obtained. Newly planted containers should initially be set on a stone or bricks so they are just covered by water. Then remove the bricks gradually to increase the depth during the first growing season. This allows the

leaves to reach sunlight quickly and will encourage rapid growth and establishment.

Unless you have a natural pond always plant in a suitable container. Ordinary plant pots will do but it is better to use the plastic containers specially designed for this purpose.

First of all line the container with turf or hessian and fill with good soil. Ordinary garden soil is satisfactory but a good, stiff clay loam is better. Do not add artificial fertiliser or large quantities of organic material.

Place the plant in a partly filled container and top up with a suitable soil. Firm lightly. Many aquatics are very soft and easily crushed; over-firming will cause the plants to rot.

Finally cover the top of the container with a layer of small stones about 1in (2.5cm) deep. This helps to keep the soil in place and prevents it clouding the water unnecessarily.

The smallest of the plant containers is only suitable for two or three submerged oxygenating plants. It is probably better to buy the medium or large size container. A medium container will hold one small lily, two or three deep marginal plants or 12 to 15 submerged oxygenating plants.

Algae

After planting, the water in the pond will turn green. This is part of the natural sequence of events. This green pea-soup effect is produced by millions of tiny algae which flourish on the mineral salts dissolved in the water, especially in bright sunlight.

Since the plants require an open, sunny situation, it is inevitable that the various species of algae that are naturally present will also flourish.

Under no circumstances should the pool be emptied and filled with clean water in an attempt to reduce the algae growth. By doing this you will simply re-introduce more of the plant foods on which the algae thrive and so repeat the process. When the pool is finally settled it will maintain its own balance.

The floating plants and the lilies will cast shade on the water and so reduce the sunlight that is available for algae growth. The fish that you will introduce as the pool settles will also help in its control, and the submerged oxygenating plants will use up surplus carbon dioxide and re-oxygenate the water.

There is another form of algae growth which produces a tangled web of thin green strands. This is known as "blanket weed". Where it is possible blanket weed should be removed by hand or with a

small rake. If it is left unchecked it can become so prolific that it will literally smother and kill all other plants in the pond.

Regular hand-raking will allow the required plants to establish and so cast the shade that is necessary to control the blanket weed and at the same time use up the mineral salts that are absorbed in the water.

If raking fails to control the weed there is a product on the market under the name of "Algimycin PLL". This material is harmless to plants and fish *if it is used as directed*. The application rate is quite critical and you must be able to measure accurately the water content of your pond in order to calculate how much material to apply.

Keep it clean

Another situation that often occurs with new ponds is a black discolouration of the water producing an inky effect. This is caused by decomposing organic matter from fallen leaves and other debris collecting at the bottom of the pond.

The removal of such organic matter will help to prevent this condition arising, and although an annual emptying of the pond is unnecessary, it is worth while clearing out the more obvious and accessible debris in the autumn when the leaves have fallen off the trees, and again in the spring.

Where the inkiness caused by this condition persists, it can have a detrimental effect on plants and fish. A short term control would be to remove half the water from the pond and top up with clean water.

A fountain or waterfall helps to agitate the water and by so doing re-oxygenates it, helping to eradicate any build up of carbon dioxide.

It is possible to stretch a net over the pool during the autumn when maximum leaf fall from surrounding trees and shrubs can be expected and so prevent them getting into the pool. You can buy nets specially for this purpose or, alternatively, make up a suitable frame in lightweight timber and cover it with a fine mesh wire-netting.

This apparatus is particularly useful where there are small children, since it can be put in position quickly and easily when they are playing in the vicinity of the pool. Please remember pools are potentially dangerous and 18in (45cm) of water is more than sufficient to drown a young child.

Never let them play round the pool unless it is protected or they are adequately supervised.

Garden design

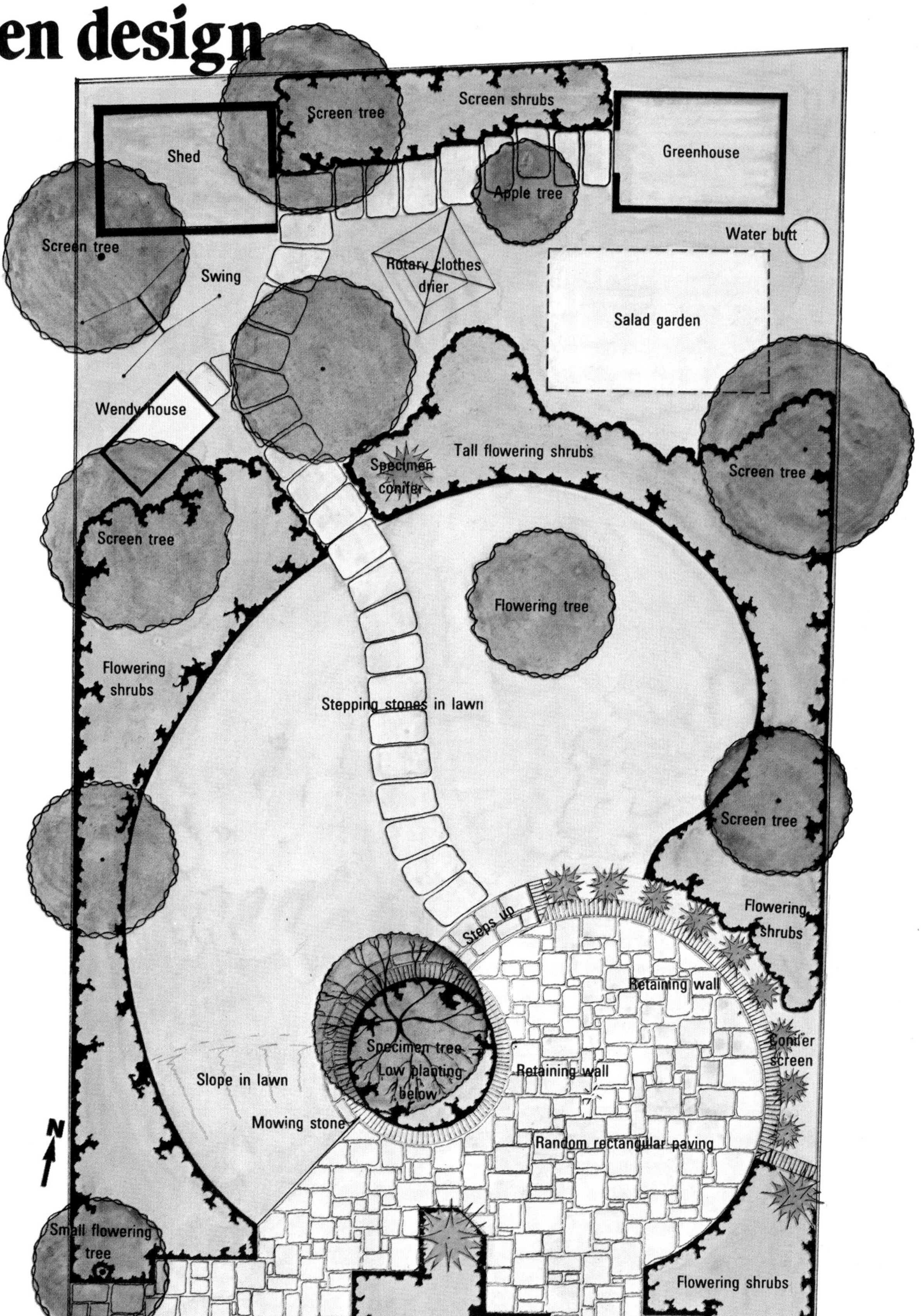

Shed

Screen tree

Screen shrubs

Greenhouse

Screen tree

Apple tree

Water butt

Swing

Rotary clothes drier

Salad garden

Wendy house

Specimen conifer

Tall flowering shrubs

Screen tree

Screen tree

Flowering tree

Flowering shrubs

Stepping stones in lawn

Screen tree

Steps up

Flowering shrubs

Retaining wall

Conifer screen

Specimen tree

Low planting below

Retaining wall

N

Slope in lawn

Mowing stone

Random rectangular paving

Small flowering tree

Low planting

Flowering shrubs

Lawn sowing

1 First cultivate, removing all perennial weeds and burying annuals. Allow time for settling.

2 A much easier method of cultivation is to hire a rotavator. First remove perennial weeds.

3 After cultivating, go over the whole area, levelling roughly with the back of a fork.

4 To avoid local sinkage, the soil must be well consolidated. The best method is to tread over it.

5 Now apply a general fertiliser. Use an autumn lawn food low in nitrogen to avoid soft, lush growth.

6 Rake the area to a level, fine tilth, removing any large stones that may damage the mower.

7 Seed is sown at 2oz. per sq. yd. Start by setting two lines exactly 1yd. (1m.) apart.

8 Using a 3ft. (1m.) cane, mark lines in the soil to divide the area into sq. yds. (sq. m.).

9 Finally rake the seed into the surface, aiming to cover about half. Protect against birds.

Lawn turfing

1 Lay out the first row of turf, preferably starting with a straight side.

4 Standing on the boards, lay out the second row of turves. There is no need to 'bond' them like bricks.

7 Then, when you reach the end of the row, overlap the edging turf and cut off the excess.

2 Tamp the turf down with the back of the rake. There should be no need to be 'heavy-handed'.

5 Using the back of the rake, pull the second row of turves into the first. Then tamp down.

8 Some turves will have pieces missing. Keep a few oddments of turf by you to patch these in.

3 Never tread on the turf you have laid or on the soil. Rather work off boards to avoid making heel marks.

6 If the borders are to be curved, lay out the edge turf as you go, setting it to the correct curve.

9 When you reach the end, lay the edging turf first and then fill in the remaining space.

Lawn care

1 First of all, brush off fallen leaves, worm casts etc. A besom or stiff yard brush are ideal.

4 The first cut of the season should be done with the blades as high as possible.

7 A wormkiller containing Chlordane will kill the worms underground, saving the job of picking them up.

2 Rake all over, very vigorously, with a spring tine rake, to remove dead grass, and open up the surface.

5 Trim the edges, with shears. Where they have grown out, cut back with a half moon or spade.

8 If moss is a problem, a proprietary moss killer can be watered on. For weeds use a selective weedkiller.

3 Spike the entire area with a fork or spiking tool, to improve aeration and drainage.

6 It is also a good idea to apply a wormkiller too. Mix up the concentrate with water in a can.

9 It is best to have a special can for use with weedkillers. The dribble bar ensures even application.

Borders

10 Deep rooted weeds can be grubbed out with a knife, or spot treated with weedkiller.

13 A thin layer of screened compost will help the turf to root quickly, when it is put back into place.

1 After marking the shape of the border, take out a trench one spit deep, placing the soil in a barrow.

11 An application of fertiliser will help the grass to grow strongly. Mark out to get an even spread.

14 Low spots can be treated the same way. Build up by using compost or good loam.

2 This soil is then taken to the other end. Turn the soil over with a fork, making a second trench behind.

12 If you have any high spots which get scalped by the mower, roll back the turf and remove some earth.

15 This area can now be re-seeded, using a seed mixture compatible with the rest of the lawn.

3 At this stage, incorporate any peat or other organic matter, and a good base dressing or fertiliser.

4 Finally, fill the final trench with the soil from the first. Mark where each subject will be, using canes.

7 Some subjects, such as these Iris pumila must not be planted too deeply.

1 Roughly dig out and set level pegs. Ensure that the tops are two courses below the damp course.

5 The planning should be done on paper, beforehand. It pays to plant specimen plants first.

8 Some moisture loving subjects may require 'puddling in', after planting if the soil is dry.

2 Put in and level more pegs at about 6ft (2m) intervals. Slope them slightly away from the house.

6 Smaller subjects can then be planted. Plant in groups of three to five, depending on the scale.

9 Container grown material can be planted at any time of year, and they will often be bigger plants.

3 Now you will see any high spots. Dig out soil that does not allow for the full depth of concrete.

4 Make a fairly dry mix of ballast and cement using six to eight parts of ballast to one of cement.

7 Finally level out the concrete to the mark on the pegs. It is better to be too low than too high.

10 Set a line on the top edge of the slab to check that it is exactly in line with the wall.

5 Cart the mixed concrete onto the site, carefully avoiding the pegs, and spread it out evenly.

8 Once the base has set, mix up some mortar — again keeping the mixture fairly dry.

11 Tap the slab down so that the top is exactly level with the top of the nearest peg and the slab is level.

6 Tread over the area to compact the concrete. If compaction causes low spots, make up with more concrete.

9 Set the slab on the heaps of mortar, leaving a space between the edge of the slab and the wall.

12 Check the level with the straight-edge making sure there is no light between it and the top of the slab.

Walling

13 The remainder of the slabs can now be laid in the same way, butting them against each other.

14 Check the levels regularly and, as the pegs get in the way of the next slab, knock them out.

15 If you don't finish the job in one day, remember to cut away excess mortar before it hardens.

1 Fill in behind the paving with a 6-1 ballast/cement mix. Bring it very slightly below the paving level.

2 The mortar for walling should not vary in colour between mixes, so use a bucket to measure it out.

3 Set the first stone in line with the paving and check with a spirit level that it is level both ways.

4 Repeat the process at the other end and stretch a tight line along the face of the stones.

5 The row can now be easily and quickly laid using the line as a guide for both level and line.

6 At intervals along the bottom row, leave a joint wider than the normal ½in (13mm) for drainage.

7 If you are using large blocks, remove one stone and replace it with a large one.

8 Check at intervals to ensure that the stones are level across the row.

9 Once the row is completed and before laying the next, fill in between the joints with mortar.

10 The copings must all be exactly the same width, so before facing, measure carefully at each end.

11 Set the coping in the same way as the walling except that it should protrude a little over the wall.

12 When the mortar is dry but before it sets hard, rake out the joints to about ½in (13mm) deep.

Peat blocks

1 If soil is not too alkaline, mix in 50/50 moss peat. If very alkaline, use pure peat.

2 Peat blocks are possibly the most natural looking material and can be planted into.

3 Plants such as heathers can be planted directly into the wall.

4 Choose the plants for both vertical planting and the edges. They must spread naturally.

5 After planting, a good dressing of a fertiliser containing magnesium helps. Rose fertiliser has been found to be ideal. Water in well.

Rock gardens

1 A crowbar and a heavy stake can conveniently be used to position smaller stones.

4 Dig out the bank to form a series of earth steps, firm platforms on which to place the stones.

7 Set the plants out in their final positions. Then work systematically, planting as you go.

2 Larger stones can be rolled up planks using stakes as rollers. You may need a neighbour's help.

5 If stones fail to butt together, insert a trailing plant in the crevice and pack it with earth.

8 Knock the plants out of their pots either on stone or on a trowel handle. Don't damage the roots.

3 Set the stones on a firm bed and ram them well with a billet of wood to stabilise them.

6 Individual planting pockets can be prepared, forking in peat, bone-meal and coarse grit.

9 Many alpines benefit from a top dressing of grit, gravel or some chippings applied after planting.

Propagation

1 First fill the boxes for your cuttings, with a mixture of two parts sharp sand to one part peat.

2 This should be lightly firmed, and a board is always useful for this purpose.

3 Take the cuttings from current year's growth, as soon as it becomes firm enough to handle.

4 The cuttings should be about 1½-2in. (4-5cm.) long. Remove the bottom leaves.

5 Dip the cuttings in hormone rooting powder. Harder cuttings need stronger hormone.

6 Either insert the cuttings using a dibber to firm them in, or push them directly into the compost.

7 Once inserted, a light watering will help settle them in and also reduce immediate moisture loss.

8 Once seedlings have germinated, they should be kept shaded until they are large enough to transplant.

9 They should be pricked out as soon as possible, and grown on until large enough to survive outdoors.

Planting alpines

Pools

1 Whilst this looks an ideal planting pocket, it is too open, causing water to run off taking the soil also.

2 Remove the top soil and then build up the front of the pocket by placing another stone in.

1 Mark out the shape of the pool with stout pegs, set at about 18in-2ft (45-60cm) apart.

3 Lever it into exact position, so that it not only builds up the front, but also fits in with the other stones.

4 Once it is exactly in the right position, pack the earth under and around it, so it is absolutely firm.

2 Ensure that you work to a level, so that the top of the pool and water surface are parallel.

5 The plants can now be planted, either as individual subjects, or in this case, as small groups.

6 It is good idea to mulch after planting, using stone chippings or peat.

3 Excavate the first 9in-1ft (23-30.5cm) of soil, sloping the sides in at about 20 degrees.

4 Excavate the second level to about the same depth again, leaving a 9in (23cm) planting shelf.

7 Place the liner over the hole, and roughly cut it to shape, leaving about 18in (45cm) all round.

10 By easing the stones one at a time as the pool fills, it is possible to get a precise fit.

5 If there is a danger of sharp stones etc. line the hole with sand, old carpet or newspaper.

8 Place stones evenly around the edge, to weigh down the liner, all round the pool.

11 Once full, secure the edges of the liner with mortar, and lay paving slabs on this.

6 Ensure that the pool surround is perfectly level to the top of the pegs. Fill depressions with sand.

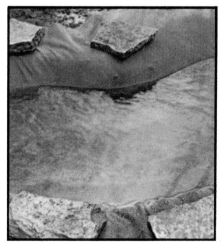

9 Fill the pool slowly, using a hose. The liner will stretch into the shape of the pool.

12 Make sure that these are flush with the surrounding soil, and point the slabs in.

Pool planting

1 Before planting remove old brown roots and cut off dead leaves, rinse the roots in water.

4 For Lilies a large container should be used, make sure the crown is not buried below the soil level.

7 Lower the container into the pool by threading fine rope through the mesh of the basket.

2 Plant in a basket container and if a light soil is to be used, line with clean sacking, never use polythene.

5 Firm the soil with your fingers, but avoid packing it too tight and take care not to damage the roots.

8 To keep the water clear, oxygenating plants are a must, plant 6 bunches into a container.

3 Partly fill the container with soil, the best type being a clay loam, and trim away the excess liner.

6 Top-dress with a layer of pea-sized pebbles, to prevent fish from stirring up the soil and plants.

9 Plants for marginal shelves can be lowered in by hand and supported on bricks.

Bedding plants-sowing

1 Before sowing seeds, ensure that the compost is evenly moist. Wet it and rub it through your hands.

4 Again using the board, lightly press the surface of the compost. Soil-less media need little firming.

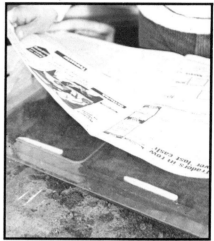

7 Cover the boxes with glass and newspaper or opaque polythene and place in a warm spot.

2 Fill the tray and lightly firm with your fingers, paying particular attention to the sides and corners.

5 Sow the seed thinly, a pinch at a time. Start with the edges and corners and then sow the middle.

8 Larger seeds like these sweet peas are best sown individually to give more space and save pricking out.

3 Using a flat board, scrape the excess compost from the tray to leave a flat, level surface

6 Cover the seed with a little compost. It is better that the seeds are too shallow than too deep.

9 Alternatively, seeds can be sown individually in peat pots ensuring that there is no root disturbance.

Bedding plants-planting

10 Look at the boxes every day. As soon as the first seedlings show, remove the glass and paper.

1 Remove spring bedding and fork over the border soil. And if it is very dry, water well the day before.

4 Remove the plants from their containers by knocking them out carefully as a complete block.

11 When the seedlings are large enough to handle, they should be transplanted or "pricked out".

2 Mark out the planting areas for each variety with either a stick or some garden lime.

5 Separate the individual plants, cutting them apart with either an old knife or a trowel.

12 Handling the seedlings only by their leaves, transfer them to another box at wider spacings.

3 Give 'hardened off' boxes of half-hardy annuals a good watering before planting out.

6 Lay the plants in their proposed positions on the soil. Making sure the design looks well balanced.

Trees & shrubs-cuttings

7 Using a trowel dig planting holes sufficiently deep for the roots, and place the plants upright in them.

1 The first stage is to prepare the soil. Dig in a mixture of sphagnum peat and washed sand, and rake well.

4 Once they are collected, they should be prepared immediately. Trim them to about 4in. (10cm.).

8 Firm the plants in gently with your fingers, being careful not to damage the roots.

2 Erect the tunnel a few weeks before taking the cuttings to warm the soil slightly.

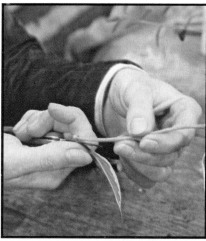

5 Using a very sharp knife, remove all the leaves apart from the top 2in. (5cm.). These would only rot.

9 Water them in thoroughly using a watering can or hose pipe. And in warm weather water regularly.

3 Take the cuttings from plants which are healthy and true to type, removing them with a sharp knife.

6 The cut ends should be dipped in hormone rooting powder, such as Seradix 1, to speed rooting.

Chrysanthemums

7 Insert the cuttings under the tunnel, to about half their length. Spaced 2in. (5cm.) square.

8 Once a batch has been inserted, water them in well, with a solution of captain fungicide.

9 Replace the tunnel, making sure it is well dug in at the sides and gathered at the ends.

1 Chrysanthemum cuttings are best snapped cleanly from the stools to avoid spreading virus diseases.

2 Remove the lower leaves. They can then be inserted as they are, or they can be trimmed.

3 Trimming should be done with a razorblade that has been sterilised in a flame. Cut below a leaf joint.

4 Hormone rooting powder will help speed up rooting, but is not considered absolutely necessary.

5 The cuttings should now be set round the edge of a pot of soil-less or John Innes compost.

6 Alternatively, if there are a lot of cuttings, they can be rooted in seed boxes. Set them 2in (5cm) apart.

7 After placing the cuttings, give them a good watering. They should need no more until they are rooted.

10 Put a little compost in the pot and place the plant so that the lower leaves are at the surface.

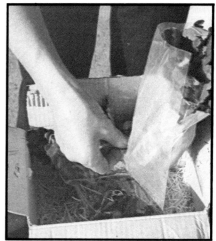

13 If you have ordered new plants, deal with them as soon as they arrive. Unpack them carefully.

8 When rooted, they will begin to "perk-up". When they have made good roots they are ready.

11 Now fill round with compost. A tap on the bench and a good watering in is all that is needed to settle it.

14 The rooted cuttings will be packed in bundles. Gently separate the individual plants and soak in water.

9 Pot them up into small pots first using a soil-less or John Innes compost and "crocking" the pot.

12 Avoid further watering for a few days, but protect them from strong sunshine, with newspaper.

15 They can now be potted as before or, alternatively, set out in deep boxes prior to final potting.

Dahlias

Shrubs-planting

1 Cut shoots and trim them to 3-4in (7.5-10cm) just below a leaf joint. Remove the lower leaves.

4 Prepare the ground and put 5ft. (1.53m.) canes 1ft. (30.5cm.) into it, at 2½ft.-3ft. (76-91cm.) intervals.

1 If planting in grass, remove the turf and then dig out a hole at least twice as big as the root-ball.

2 Dip them in a hormone rooting powder, put them into a pot, about 1in. (2.5cm.) deep.

5 Plant out during May-June when the danger of frost is past. Cover the root-ball and plant up.

2 Improve the soil at the bottom by adding a liberal quantity of peat and a handful of bonemeal.

3 Warmth and moisture are necessary to root them. When rooted they will 'perk-up'.

6 Firm the plants in, leaving a depression for watering. Tie them loosely to the stake with raffia.

3 Fork these into the bottom of the hole at the same time breaking up the soil to the full depth of the fork.

Evergreens

4 The soil you have dug out should also be improved by the addition of peat and bonemeal.

7 Refill around the root-ball with the best top-soil. The peat and bonemeal will mix in.

1 Pieris formosa forrestii is a medium-sized shrub with bright scarlet young growths in the spring.

5 Before planting, drive in a good stout stake. It should be at least twice the diameter of the stem.

8 Firm planting is essential so, as the hole is refilled, tread down the soil two or three times with your heel.

2 Hedera colchica 'Dentata Variegata' is probably the most ornamental of the ivies.

6 Lay your spade across the top of the hole and set the tree so that the root-ball is a bit below the surface.

9 When filling is completed, tie the tree to the stake with special plastic tree-ties.

3 Hypericum calycinum, the Rose of Sharon, or St John's Wort is excellent for ground cover.

4 Chamaecyparis pisifera 'Aurea' is just one of the many colour forms of conifers.

7 Calluna vulgaris, 'Sir John Charrington' is one of the many forms of the ling or heather.

10 Skimmia japonica is a small, dome shaped bush, bearing white flowers and bright red berries.

5 Fatsia japonica is one of the plants which are often known as 'architectural'.

8 Kalmia latifolia, the Calico Bush, is one of the more exotic looking shrubs but quite easy to grow.

11 Garrya eliptica bears these magnificent long tassels of catkins during January and February.

6 Cytisus x kewensis is good in rockeries or where it can cascade over a wall.

9 Rhododendron 'Goldsworth Crimson', one of very many rhododendron hybrids.

12 Camellia japonica produces these magnificent exotic flowers in the early spring, and is perfectly hardy.

Conifers-planting

1 Before planting, set the plants out in their correct positions according to the plan prepared previously.

2 Plant the larger specimen plants first, and fill in afterwards with the lower-growing conifers and the heathers.

3 Hedges are planted in a previously prepared trench to which generous quantities of organic matter have been added.

4 In the early years especially, the plants will need some aftercare but later, work will be reduced to the bare minimum.

Conifers-varieties

Cupressus leucodermis sempervirens.

Juniperus chinensis stricta.

Cryptomeria japonica 'Elegans Nana'.

Thuja occidentalis 'Wansdyke Silver'.

Chamaecyparis lawsoniana 'Pygmea Aurecens'.

Taxus baccata 'Fastigiata Aureomarginata'.

Climbers-planting

1 Plant climbers about 1ft (30 cm) away from the wall. Dig the hole at least twice the size of the pot.

4 Set the plant in the hole. Make sure that the top of the root-ball is just below the surface.

7 Clematis need a different treatment. Remember that they are lime lovers.

2 Spread a liberal quantity of peat or well rotted manure or compost in the bottom of the hole and dig it in.

5 Refill the hole with the soil/peat mixture, firming well with your foot at intervals.

8 It is essential to keep the roots moist so sink a pot near the plant to facilitate watering.

3 Mix some more peat in with the soil you have dug out and sprinkle a good handful of bonemeal.

6 Firm the soil around the plant making sure not to tread on the root-ball.

9 They can be trained up wires fixed to the wall, but a neater job can be made with wood or metal trellis.

Hedges-planting

10 Set the plant in right direction by slanting cane to trellis and tying it on with wire or nylon string.

1 Dig a trench one spade deep and about 18in. (45cm.) wide and apply a liberal dressing of peat or compost.

4 Spread some peat and a handful of bonemeal per plant on the soil you have dug out and refill the trench.

11 Clematis like to keep their feet cool. This can be done either by mulching or with a couple of slabs.

2 Fork over the bottom of the trench, breaking it up to the full fork's depth working in organic matter.

5 Firm the soil well as the trench is refilled, making sure not to tread on the rootball.

12 After planting, the stems should be cut down hard to promote strong growth from the base of the plant.

3 Set the plants up against individual canes about 3ft (1m) apart and surround the roots with moist peat.

6 When the trench has been refilled, tie each conifer to the canes for support.

Windbreaks

1 Use wooden posts at least 2in x 2in (5cm x 5cm) and 5ft (1.5m) long. Soak the bottoms in a copper preservative.

2 Set the posts not less than 8ft (2.5m) apart with 18in (45cm) in the ground. For higher screens set the posts deeper.

3 Fix the netting on the windward side of the posts, using 1½in x ¼in (4cm x 6mm) battens nailed to the post.

4 The screen is now stretched to the next post and fixed in the same way. A helping hand here will make for a neater job.

5 If you need to fix more than one roll of windscreen, place one piece on top of the other before nailing on the batten.

6 Temporary windscreen can be put on lighter posts and need not be set so deeply if guy ropes are provided.

Bulbs-planting

1 Once the bed has been cleared, break the soil down to a fine tilth. And dress with bonemeal.

4 Throw the bulbs so that they land at random over the area in which they are to grow and plant them.

7 Ensure that the bulb fibre or compost is just moist by watering if necessary. It should not be too wet.

2 Lay out the bulbs evenly about 3–6in. (7.5–15cm.) apart. Tulips need to be about 5in. (13cm.) apart.

5 Bulbs planted in grass should be deeper. Plant them so that the nose is about 6in (15cm) deep.

8 Space the bulbs evenly round the bowl. With hyacinths, three or four per bowl will probably suffice.

3 Make a hole with a trowel, so that the nose of the bulb is about 2in. (5cm.) below the soil level.

6 If the soil is at all heavy, place a little coarse sand in the planting hole. Backfill on top of the bulb.

9 Cover with a little more fibre and put somewhere cool and dark until the shoots are 1in. (2.5cm.) long.

Bulbs-spring

Tulip fosteriana 'Dance'.

Fritillaria meleagris.

Mixed Spring bulbs

Mixed daffodils and narcissi.

Muscari 'Early Giant'.

Naturalised crocuses.

Bulbs-autumn

1 'Autumn crocus', Colchicum speciosum. The leaves appear in spring. The flowers in September.

2 Another crocus-like flower is Sternbergia lutea, the biblical 'Lily of the Field', flowering in Autumn.

3 Colchicum hybrid Water Lily is probably the most spectacular, like a rose-lilac water lily.

4 Amaryllis belladonna is the true amaryllis. A delicate, free flowering, hardy garden bulb.

5 Crinum x Powellii will thrive quite happily in a sheltered position. There is also a pure white form.

Sweet peas

1 Old fashioned mixed

2 Sally Unwin

3 Blue mantle

1 Seeds will do well in soil-less composts, or J.I. seed compost. Ensure that it is uniformly wet first.

2 Make a flat surface by pressing with a board. Do not firm too well, or it will be hard to wet.

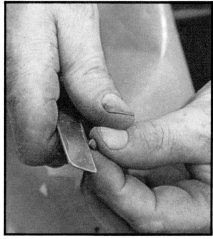

3 To ensure even germination, a small piece of skin should be removed from dark coloured seeds.

4 Set the seeds about ½in. (13mm.) deep and about 2in. (5cm.) apart, spacing them evenly.

5 After sowing, make sure that there is sufficient water for good germination by watering well.

6 Seed trays, pots or tubes should then be placed in a cold frame to overwinter.

Containers

1 It is essential to crock any container to ensure good drainage. Use broken pots or brick.

4 With hanging baskets, first line them, using moss, if you can get it, but polythene will do.

7 You will possibly only need one taller growing plant in the middle, as these will fill out.

2 As with growing in any container, it pays to use a good compost rather than garden soil.

5 Put a couple of handfuls of compost in the bottom, and then cut drainage holes in the polythene.

8 Smaller subjects and more trailing plants are then planted round the edges, to fill in.

3 Always use well shaped plants, carefully knocking them out of their pots first.

6 Plant a few trailing plants through holes cut in the polythene, to hide it as they grow.

9 Finally, trim the edges of the polythene, and water in all the plants, well.

Bedding plants

Colour guide on page 47

ALTHOUGH still popular with municipal parks in some areas, the art of bedding out is becoming less attractive to many gardeners. The reasons for this are twofold, one being the time and effort involved in producing this sort of display, the other being more to do with fashion.

A much less formal style of gardening has become popular again in recent years, and bedding schemes are nothing if not formal. Or are they? In fact, very informal effects can be obtained using the sort of plants which can only be planted out safely when all danger of frost is gone.

Nothing gives such a wealth of colour as these subjects, many of them coming from tropical climes. Nor is it necessarily a laborious or difficult task to produce such a display, provided you choose the right subjects, the right situation, and prepare the ground well, before planting.

Certainly, for earlier displays, some sort of protection is needed if you are to raise your own bedding plants from seed. However, there are ways of overcoming this problem: by buying in plants from a nursery; by sowing later in an unheated coldframe; or by starting off the plants on a warm windowsill indoors. Whichever way you choose, the results will more than justify the little extra effort.

Mention bedding plants to most people, and a picture of neat rows of Alyssum alternating with blue Lobelia, backed by bright red Geraniums immediately flashes in to their minds. Attractive though this sort of display may be, it is by no means the only form of bedding.

Even if you live in a flat, you can brighten up your window or balcony simply and effectively by planting pots and tubs, window boxes and hanging baskets, with the sort of plants that will thrive in our summers, but which need that bit of protection during harder weather. Antirrhinums, Begonias, dwarf Dahlias, fuchsias, Lobelia, Petunias and Pelargoniums can all be grown easily and cheaply in this manner, providing a blaze of colour all summer long.

The majority of bedding plants do have one thing in common. As most of them are from warmer parts, they do appreciate the sun, and an open, well drained situation is to be recommended. However, it is little appreciated that there are several subjects which can be grown even in quite heavy shade. *Begonia semperflorens* has become increasingly popular in recent years, as its usefulness as a bedding plant has become as well known as its capabilities as a pot plant. What is not as well appreciated is the fact that it probably flowers better in shade than it does in the sun. Similarly, plants such as the very well known Busy Lizzie (Impatiens), make admirable bedding subjects for shady areas.

In point of fact, there are plants which come into the half-hardy category to suit just about every need. If you are interested in flower arranging, what better or more spectacular subjects can be found then African Daisies (Arctotis), Strawflower or everlasting flower (Helichrysum), or Zinnias. Or what more subtle than Bells of Ireland (Molucella)?

For scent and old world charm, many well known plants provide the basis of the "cottage garden". Antirrhinums, annual Carnations, Heliotrope, bachelor's buttons (Mattricaria), Stocks and Verbena, are all frost tender, needing to be planted out when all danger is past.

One feature of bedding that many people enquire about is carpet bedding. This is the art of producing a recognisable picture emblem or design, in plant material. In some places, this has been taken to the extreme of producing three dimensional designs. However, this is really outside the scope of the home gardener, requiring as it does, specialist plants in very great numbers, and it is almost a full-time job producing these, showing up the designs, planting and sustaining the display.

However, this is not to say that very attractive pattern effects cannot be obtained very easily, using commonly grown material. Ageratum and Lobelia provide blues, yellows can be produced by using many different plants such as Antirrhinums, Begonias, Calceolaria, Gazanias, and most important — the Marigolds. Reds are available in every hue and shade you can think of, using Begonias again, Celosia (coxcomb) Sweet William, Phlox and Salvias; all these produce neat, shortish plants that can be controlled to give a carpet effect of colour.

Probably the most colourful carpet of all can be produced simply by planting up the bed with mixed colours of one subject, the one that immediately springs to mind being Mesembryanthemum (Livingstone daisy).

Mention has already been made of tropical, or semi-tropical bedding. This is the art of producing an effect which looks as if it would be at home in a hot climate,

Annual border of Tagetes

Bedding plants

Colour guide on page 47

the area is not in use at this time. It is often the case that the ground will be occupied by spring bedding, and of course, this will not be ready for removal until about May. However, after its removal, the same principles of cultivation apply.

The seeds can be sown in March–April in trays, pots, boxes, or indeed, any container which best suits your own requirements. As soon as the seedlings are large enough to handle without damage (normally when they have about two true leaves), they can be pricked off or transplanted into more trays.

The purpose of this is to give them more room to develop. If the seeds were large enough to sow individually, in the first place, then they can be sown far enough apart not to require transplanting. Larger subjects such as Cannas will need to be grown individually in pots. Always use a good seed compost, either of the John Innes type, or a soilless.

Higher temperatures are required to germinate certain subjects, but by far the majority will be perfectly happy without having any extra heat applied, if kept in a cold frame, bedroom windowsill, or indeed anywhere else that is kept frost free. Full details will be on all seed packets. If you find that you have inadvertently purchased a variety which does require some heat and you are not the proud owner of a greenhouse or propagator, don't worry. It is remarkable what you can do by placing the seed tray inside a polythene bag, and putting it on the central heating boiler, over a radiator or over the fire. Watch them carefully, and as soon as the seedlings begin to appear, remove the bag, and if possible move the tray to a lighter position.

As the plants grow, they may become leggy, if they are kept too warm, so it is a good idea to grow them as cool as possible, and harden them off as soon as possible.

Again, this is not difficult, even without a garden frame. All you have to do is place the trays outside, whenever the weather is suitable, bringing them in at night. Do this for a week or two, until all danger of frost is past, and they are ready to plant up. Within a week or two of planting, you should begin to receive the full benefits.

Many plants can be sown direct in their beds outside in late May or June. These include Asters, annual Pinks, Straw Flower, Marigolds and Stocks.

and thus produce an illusion of warmth. It is essential with this sort of bedding to use extremely bright colours, both of leaf and flower, and also exotic, often large leaved subjects. Probably the best known plant which comes into this category is Canna (Indian shot plant), with its huge leaves in green or purple, and its fiery coloured flowers in intense shades of red, orange and yellow.

However, many familiar house plants and pot plants can safely be grown outside during the summer months. Chlorophytum (spider plant), Coleus, Iresene, Ricinus (castor oil plant) and Schizanthus (Butterfly flower) all look very exotic, and all are very easy to grow.

For adding the same touch to hanging baskets, it is remarkable what can be done with Thunbergia (Black-eyed Susan).

As far as producing the display, one of the most important items is the plan, drawn up well in advance. Decide the area of the display, draw out a plan to scale, and fill in the details of what is to be planted, where it is to be planted, how many of each subject etc. This will enable you to order only as many seeds as you require. As soon as the weather is satisfactory in March or April, prepare the ground as if for seed sowing. This means breaking it down to a fine tilth, usually by raking and treading. This is assuming that

Annuals

Colour guide on page 47

IN GARDENING terms an annual is defined as a plant that completes its full life cycle in the course of one year. It comes to life from a seed in spring, grows to maturity, flowers and finally produces seed. Once the seeds are ripe, the plant considers that its useful life is over and quietly dies, leaving the seeds to start a new generation the following year.

A hardy annual is a plant, that besides being an annual, has the added distinction that its ancestors were natives of Britain, or of countries whose climates approximate to ours. They are therefore at home in our temperate weather and their seeds do not need the additional warmth of a greenhouse or propagator to spur them into growth. In short, they can be sown straight into the open ground where they are required to flower.

Their hardiness is our good fortune. It means that, as a group, the hardy annuals represent convenience and economy. These days the average price of a packet of hardy annual seeds is minimal. A mere six packets of such seeds sown judiciously will be sufficient to provide the average garden with a wealth of colour from summer's beginning to its end.

We can have a garden full of glorious bloom for a modest outlay.

Soil and preparation

Their sheer simplicity, however, should not be taken to mean that hardy annuals do not appreciate care and attention.

They are not hungry plants like dahlias and vegetables, and in fact it is a mistake to sow them in highly fertile soil. When hardy annuals find their roots in ground that is very rich in plant food, they respond by concentrating their energies on growing into large, leafy plants, to the detriment of their flowering potential.

They need feeding of course, but theirs should be a modest diet that provides just enough nitrogen, phosphate and potash to keep them healthy and to urge them into flowering.

About two weeks before sowing, fork the ground over to a depth of from 6–9in (15–23cm) and remove weeds, stones and foreign bodies as they appear. Leave it for a day or two and then, provided the soil is reasonably dry, tread it over to firm it.

After treading, rake it level and in gardeners' jargon — reduce it to a "fine tilth". The term "tilth" describes a soil of which the top couple of inches is made up of fine granules, with no large, uneven lumps.

Lastly, spread about 1–1½oz per sq yd (30–45gm per sq metre) of general fertiliser over the area and leave it until you are ready to sow, in about a week's time.

General fertiliser means any inorganic, or organic feed that contains fairly equal amounts of the three essential plant foods. You could use the organic "fish, blood and bone", which releases its goodness gradually into the soil during the growing season. You could also use "Growmore" or any of the compound proprietary organics such as "Organic 100" or "FYM".

The all important question is — when to sow to be sure of good germination? It is no good trying to go by the calendar. Our climate is so variable that whereas the last week in March may have been ideal for sowing last year, this year the ground may be frozen stiff or covered with snow on the same date.

The answer lies in waiting until you see the annual weeds pushing up through the soil. This is a sure sign that Nature is telling you to get on with outdoor sowings.

It pays to sow thinly. The thinner you sow, the further the seeds will go and the less thinning you will have to do later on.

Planning

What are the criteria that govern our seed selection? In order to achieve a colourful border that is totally pleasing we should give thought to colour blending, to the varying heights of the different plants and to their diversity of form and shape.

Short, compact plants are the obvious choice for the front of the border. Their beauty would be lost if they were tucked away behind taller subjects.

Behind the front rankers we want 1½–3 footers (45–91cm) as the main design of our floral carpet and at the back we need

Lavatera trimestris rosea

Calendula officinalis (Marigold)

Salvia horminum (Clary)

Annuals

Colour guide on page 47

the tall stately sorts to give height and balance.

In a circular or oblong bed, the tall varieties would of course occupy the centre position with the shorter subjects sloping downwards from them.

Before buying your seeds therefore, draw a rough plan of the border on a piece of paper and outline the position of each annual variety on it. If you colour each area with its appropriate hue, you end up with a map with the coloured areas representing plant "counties".

Sowing

The next step is to transfer the map from paper to plot. Give the bed a final raking, then with the blunt end of the rake handle mark out the "county" boundaries. Within the boundaries sow the seeds thinly and after each "county" has received its quota of seeds rake the soil lightly to tease the seeds in just below the surface and finish off by firming the soil using the back of the rake head.

Thinning

When the spring weather is warm and the soil moist you can expect seedlings to appear in from 10 to 20 days' time. The germination time can vary from variety to variety, so don't expect all the seedlings to appear at the same time.

Let them grow until they have formed from four to six leaves, then thin them to the distances apart recommended on their respective packets. As a rough guide the spacing you leave between plants should correspond to their heights at maturity.

It may be that due to the vagaries of the weather or the soil you will find a few bare patches in some of the plant "counties". To achieve an even population of plants lift a few of the overcrowded seedlings very carefully, taking care not to break their roots, and use them to fill the vacant spaces. Whilst you are thinning you can also yank out any weed seedlings that are present and add them to the compost heap.

Until the hardy annuals are well established regular, once-a-week weeding is important. Left unchecked the weeds will tend to smother and weaken the growth of your chosen hardy annuals.

After care

During the growing and flowering season hardy annuals need very little attention other than weeding and dead-heading.

Dead-heading merely involves nipping off the flowers as soon as they have faded

Limnanthes douglasii (Poached egg flower)

to prevent them setting seed. This is done to encourage the plants to produce still more flowers in a valiant effort to ensure a supply of seeds and the survival of the species. The plants will consequently continue to give a good show of colour right through the summer until the first autumn mists and frosts put an end to their display.

Even at this late stage the plants still have value. Don't throw them away, put them on the compost heap to rot down into next year's natural fertiliser. Remember, the good gardener wastes nothing; not even a dead hardy annual.

Pelleted seed

That is all there is to sowing and growing annuals, it is as simple as buying a packet of seeds. The job can be made even simpler by using pelleted seeds in place of ordinary ones. A "pellet" is a seed coated with an inert, clay-type material that increases its overall size and makes it big enough to be handled individually and easily.

This means that pellets can be sown at the correct distances apart and there is no need for tedious thinning later on.

As a precaution against uneven germination sow the pellets twice as thickly.

Alyssum 'Tiny Tim'

Lavatera 'Silver Cup'

In other words if the final thinning distance is 6in (15cm) sow the pellets 3in (7.5cm) apart. This allows for failures and gives plenty of spare seedlings for gap filling and for planting in odd empty corners elsewhere.

The only added precaution if you are using pelleted seeds is to keep the soil moist from the moment they are sown until the seedlings appear.

Choice of varieties

To the uninitiated the choice of hardy annuals may seem bewildering. To help you select the right and best ones for your garden and your requirements, here is a list of very lovely and varied kinds.

Front rank

Sweet Alyssum *(Alyssum maritimum)*. Height 3–6in (7.5–15cm). The old sweet-scented alyssum *Little Dorrit* grows into a rather loose plant with small white flowers. Some of the newer varieties are far more ground-hugging and come in a variety of colours:— *Carpet of Snow* — 4in (10cm), *Royal Carpet* — 4in (10cm) — purple flowers, *Violet Queen* — 6in (15cm) — violet blue, *Wonderland* — 3in (7.5cm) — cerise.

Poached Egg Flower *(Limnanthes douglasii)*. Height 6 in (15cm). Bees are attracted to the butter-yellow flowers that are edged with white. The dwarf spreading plants seed themselves freely and once grown, limnanthes will keep popping up year after year.

Virginian Stock *(Malcomia maritima)*. Height 9in (23cm). This is a dainty, upright annual with small flowers in shades of red and blue with some yellow and whites.

Middle-men

Butterfly Flower *(Schizanthus pin-*

Annuals

Colour guide on page 47

Delphiniums

natus). Height 12–18in (30.5–45cm). Schizanthus is usually thought of as a pot plant, yet this variety may be sown outdoors in late April and early May. It likes a sunny, sheltered spot to reveal its multicoloured flowers marked and spotted in a variety of soft shades.

Pot Marigold *(Calendula officinalis)*. Height 1–2ft (30.5–61cm). History has it that hopeful maidens used a dye extracted from calendulas to colour their hair. The variety *Champion* is 2ft (61cm) tall whereas *Baby Gold* and *Baby Orange* are more compact 1–1½ft (30.5–45cm) plants.

Clary *(Salvia horminum)*. Height 1½ft (45cm). Although popular with flower arrangers, clary is not seen often enough in our gardens. It is grown for its colourful violet-blue, pink and white bracts that are attractively veined. In vases the bracts keep their colour for several months without fading.

Farewell-to-Spring *(Godetia whitneyi)*. Height 9in–2ft (23–61m). This is a favourite hardy annual. Godetias grow into rounded bushes and in flower they resemble the beautiful azaleas. One of the best for a mixed colour effect is *Dwarf Bedding* 12in (30.5cm) and the 1½ft (45cm) tall *Azalea Flowered* mixture is also superb.

Back-row

Larkspur *(Delphinium consolida)*. Height 4ft (1.2m). The tall stately spikes look like smaller versions of the delphinium and have just as varied a colour range of blues, pinks and white.

Annual Mallow *(Lavatera rosea)*. Height 3–4ft (91cm–1.2m). When fully grown the lavateras may be mistaken for permanent shrubs with woody stems. They make first class, if temporary, hedges or screens of light green leaves dotted with rose-pink veined flowers as much as 4in (10cm) in diameter.

These nine hardy annuals should be enough to satisfy any gardener's desire for beauty of form and flower. In addition he could also choose from candytuft, cornflower, clarkia, Californian poppy, gypsophila, linum, nasturtium, nemophila, nigella, sunflower, sweet pea and many more.

Trees and shrubs

Colour guide on page 49

A MONKEY puzzle tree stuck in the middle of the front garden must surely be everybody's idea of a Victorian gardening cliché. When the Victorians started planting these fashionable oddities for effect they had no idea that in sixty years' time they would grow to twice the height of the house. And what's more suddenly take it upon themselves to drop complete branches for no apparent reason.

But at least they had the right idea, which was to plant something with a particularly striking shape and appearance as a focal point. It was just unfortunate that they didn't have the wide range of plants available to us.

You don't have to consider these only as specimen plants either. You can place them strategically to screen off the local car dump. Or use them to "frame" the view from your picture window. You can even use prostrate forms to conceal manhole covers in the lawn.

The most popular are probably the "weeping" trees. In fact the weeping willow is fast becoming a sort of latter day monkey puzzle. Which is an equally unfortunate choice, as it quickly makes a very large specimen. In any case, willows really only look right if you plant them so that they overhang water. If you don't they will seek out their own water supply. Which will probably be your, or your neighbours drains.

There are plenty of other weeping trees that you could plant, that are far more at home in a small garden. There is the willow leaved pear, *Pyrus salicifolia pendula*. Or Young's weeping birch, *Betula pendula* "Youngii". Cheal's Weeping Cherry, otherwise known as *Prunus* "Shidare Sakura" is also very popular. If you fancy something a little out of the ordinary and don't mind hunting around for it, you can get a weeping version of both the beech and copper beech (*Fagus sylvatica pendula* and *F. sylvatica purpurea pendula*).

Upright growing, or fastigiate shrubs, are another popular and useful shape. Starting with one of the largest, *Libocedrus decurrens* the Incense Cedar, is often seen in the gardens of stately homes. Fully grown specimens of course, take a long time to mature. Coming down a bit in scale, the popular Japanese flowering Cherry "Amanogawa" grows bolt upright, and best of all stays small. Anyone wanting a tree in even the smallest garden could find space for this one. Another good upright one, is *Prunus Hilleri* "Spire".

There are several upright growing species of poplars of course, such as the Lombardy Poplar, *Populus nigra italica*.

Fagus sylvatica purpurea pendula

Trees and shrubs

Colour guide on page 49

Catalpa bignonioides aurea

Like the weeping willow though, they have the distinct disadvantage of quickly outgrowing most gardens and taking all the available moisture out of your garden soil, not to mention the foundations of your house. Amongst the conifers there are several upright forms well worth growing. *Cupressus arizonica* or *glabra glauca* as it is sometimes sold as, is a very attractive blue grey. A much smaller growing one suitable for the rock garden is Juniperus "Sky Rocket".

The great thing about architectural plants, is that when they lose their leaves in winter you are still left with a shape.

In fact, if you choose one of the corkscrew trees, the effect is even more pronounced after the leaves have fallen. There is the corkscrew willow, *Salix matsudana tortuosa*. Or as an alternative, the Corkscrew Hazel, *Corylus avallana contorta*. If you are a flower arranger you can make some very expensive looking "accessories" by stripping the bark from "corkscrew" branches and varnishing them.

Also popular with flower arrangers are the "Spiky" types of plants, such as Phormiums and Yuccas. They look rather artificial, and over severe, but there is no doubt that in the right place they can set the scene perfectly. Bamboos could be included in this category. Like weeping willows, they look best planted alongside water, as half their beauty is in the reflections they cast.

There are a few species of trees and shrubs that are particularly striking because of their large leaves. *Vitis coignetiae*, a climber has large heart shaped leaves that turn bright red in the autumn. *Fatsia japonica* is an evergreen shrub with large "fig" leaves, which looks good grown as a climber on an old brick wall. Rather less well known is *Catalpa bignonioides*, the Indian Bean Tree, with its enormous heart shaped leaves. Its variety aurea, with bright golden yellow leaves is not often seen, but deserves to be much better known. It makes a small tree, whose new growth is faintly purple tinged, altogether a very outstanding plant. *Aralia elata* "Variegata" is another small tree, this time with large compound leaves splashed white, almost as if someone had been careless with a bucket of whitewash.

If you want to hide a manhole cover, or need a plant to cascade over stones on a rockery, or even just to smother weeds in a ground cover scheme, one of the creeping or prostrate species would fit the bill.

The Herringbone Cotoneaster, *C. horizontalis* is evergreen and also has berries. Some of the very prostrate

Salix matsudana

conifers such as *Juniperus horizontalis*, are rather disappointing, when they are so very flat to the ground they get splashed with mud every time it rains. Try, instead, *Juniperus x media* "Pfitzerana Aurea" which is low and spreading without being entirely flat.

The only plant that will always grow in a perfect cone is *Picea albertiana* "Conica". It is also one of the slowest growing plants, and perfect for miniature gardens and rockeries.

Genista "Lydia" is another small neat growing shrub for a dry stone wall or rockery. It makes a compact rounded shape that never seems to get straggly and untidy like the larger members of the broom family.

Not perhaps strictly architectural in shape, but certainly striking in winter are a group of plants grown for their bark. The so-called snake bark maples such as *Acer pensylvanicum* have bark striped, as the name suggests, like snakeskin.

Even more dramatic are a few trees whose bark peels away to reveal the bright coloured young wood beneath. *Acer griseum* is very well known.

The paper bark birch, *Betula papyrifera* is not often seen though it deserves to be more popular. *Eucalyptus gunnii* on the other hand is now a very popular tree in gardens. Besides looking "sculptured" in its own right it also has bark that peels very attractively, once it has reached a reasonable size. To keep it producing the attractive round juvenile leaves though, it needs cutting back from time to time.

Planting trees and shrubs

Colour guide on page 52

OCTOBER to March is the time for planting trees and shrubs. As these are generally regarded as permanent features of a garden, it is always worthwhile taking extra care when preparing sites and planting. Once a tree or shrub is in position and growing, there will never again be an opportunity of carrying out thorough ground preparation or deep cultivations without risk of damaging the roots. Ensure, therefore, that the ground is adequately dug and prepared, that any necessary soil improvements have been carefully carried out, and that there are adequate reserves of organic matter and plant food available.

Preparing the site

Sites for shrub planting should be prepared by hand-digging, preferably trenching. Dig out a trench one spit deep and about 1ft (30cm) wide, spread manure or compost into the base and fork this into the full depth of a fork. Remove the topsoil from the next spit, place over the prepared ground and repeat the operation. If the soil is in particularly poor condition, either wet and heavy, or light and sandy and lacking in nourishment, peat can be spread on the surface and forked in during the planting operation.

Where individual specimens are to be planted, and this particularly applies to trees, specimen shrubs or conifers on lawns, planting positions can be prepared by digging out a planting pit about 3ft (90cm) in diameter for trees and 2ft (60cm) in diameter for average sized shrubs.

The pit should be one spit deep, the topsoil carefully set to one side, manure spread into the base of the pit and forked in (to the full depth of the fork to ensure adequate drainage).

Lightly firm the base of the hole after forking, place any turf that has been removed from the lawn into the hole, grass side down, and chop up finely.

Planting

If a tree is to be planted, position the stake in the centre of the hole and drive it in until it is firm. Place the tree against the stake, ensuring that the roots are adequately spread. Cut off cleanly any roots that are broken or badly damaged. Ensure that the tree is set into the ground at exactly the same level at which it was originally grown. This can easily be checked by looking at the soil mark on the stem of the tree.

Begin back-filling around the tree or shrub using the very best of the topsoil to which has been added a little moist peat and bone meal. Shake the tree or shrub

Prepare the planting hole with care, you will not get another chance.

occasionally to ensure that soil filters down between the roots and that there are no air pockets. When the pit is about a third full, firm lightly using your heel; firming with a flat sole will form a surface pan but will leave the soil underneath uncompacted.

Repeat the filling operation, firming again when the pit is two-thirds full, and finally when the pit is completely filled. The soil will settle a little and can be left slightly high. Do not, however, mound the soil up around the stem of the tree or shrub.

Secure well

Trees should be secured to the planting stake with at least two ties. There are very good plastic ties on the market for this purpose. One should be placed at the base of the tree about 1ft (30cm) above ground level, and, ideally, the second tie should be at the top of the stake immediately under the branch system of the tree. The ties should be well secured, allowing a little room for the tree to grow, and will need to be checked each year to ensure that they are not too tight.

Always position the tree so that prevailing winds tend to blow it away from the planting stake. This will minimise any chafing of the bark that could occur if the tree is continually blown towards the planting stake. Keep the ground around the tree or shrub free of weeds and, if necessary, mulch with peat, well-rotted compost or manure, to keep down weeds and conserve moisture.

Remember that the plant may need watering in the first summer.

Container-grown plants

A word about container grown shrubs, which are now readily available at most garden centres. Generally speaking these represent very good value since the risk of failure is very much reduced. They can also be planted at any time of the year.

Shrubs should be container grown and not containerised. Container grown shrubs have spent their entire life in a pot or container of some description. The root ball is firm and well established. Containerised shrubs are often lifted from the bare ground where they were originally grown and placed into a pot ready for sale.

Very often, containerised plants have an inadequate root ball which may fall apart when the plant is removed from the container. Most container grown plants are now offered for sale in flexible plastic pots or polythene bags, and the best method of planting these is described below.

Prepare the ground in the manner described for trees and shrubs; set the plant in its container in the prepared site, and at the correct depth. When the plant is in position, slit around the base of the plastic container with a sharp knife and slide the plastic base out from under the plant with minimum disturbance. Then slit up the side of the plastic container, removing it in one piece.

In this way the root ball will be left intact and undisturbed and you can back-fill and firm in the way described for trees and shrubs. Do not attempt to break open the root ball or spread the roots in any way as this will defeat the object of the exercise.

Planting trees and shrubs

Colour guide on page 52

After-care

One word of caution regarding container grown plants. Invariably they are grown in conjunction with some form of irrigation system and it is important to continue watering after planting until they are established.

If the ground is moist and the plants appear to wilt or wither in cold winds or hot sunlight, try overhead syringing either with a hand-held hosepipe or with a fine-rose watering can. Apply just sufficient water to moisten all the foliage and only water the roots as the soil begins to dry.

This syringing down operation is best carried out in the evening, particularly after a warm day. Gradually reduce the amount of water applied, as the plants become harder and more able to fend for themselves.

Planting which is carried out in the winter months when the trees or shrubs are dormant will need re-checking in the spring and often re-firming. Winter winds have a habit of loosening plants which are not firmly rooted and frost causes the disturbed moist soil to expand as it freezes and can leave it very loose and uncompacted as the frost thaws. Always check newly planted material after a severe frost and re-firm with your heel.

Your trees and shrubs should be with you for a very long time, and the thorough preparation and planting recommended will allow them to establish quickly and make good specimens which will handsomely repay the time and effort you have invested, for many years to come.

Plan for perfection

How do you begin to prepare a planting plan? Well, obviously it is an advantage if you use only plants that you know, failing this use a good reference book that will give detailed and accurate descriptions of the plants. Prepare a list of species that are suitable for the site and then grade them into heights, selecting plants that are suitable for the back of the border, the middle and front rows.

Next group the plants according to their colour and flowering season. Many people experience difficulty in calculating the distance apart that plants should be placed. A simple rule of thumb is to add together the known spread of each shrub and its neighbour and then divide by two. This will give the distance that the two plants should be placed apart. For example, say we have a shrub with a spread of 4ft (1.2m) next to a shrub with a spread of 6ft (1.8m). Add the two

together to give 10ft (3m), therefore plant the shrubs 5ft (1.5m) apart.

Some allowance should be made for slow growing or quick growing species. Early maturing plants can be given a little more space and prominence, and those which are slow to mature can be given less space. Remember that often the slower plants can be the longest lived and could ultimately be the main feature of any planting.

Do not attempt to fill a border with all of your favourite plants. It is better to show off a favourite plant by planting a suitable background or contrasting plant with it so as to form interesting colour groups and shapes.

Remember also that the foliage of plants in its many contrasting forms can be attractive long after the shrub has ceased to flower, and make use of this in your plan.

This particularly applies to some of the variegated shrubs, those with purple, yellow or grey foliage, and plants with an interesting leaf shape.

It is better to have a selection of plants that are easy to grow and suit your site so that they thrive and look healthy, rather than a collection of more exotic species which struggle and never look wholly at their best.

Water container grown plants before planting ...

... so the root ball stays intact.

Evergreen trees and shrubs

Colour guide on page 53

NO garden is complete without a selection of evergreen shrubs. Nevertheless, people still throw up their arms in horror at the mention of evergreens. The image still persists of rather dull, Victorian gardens flanked with laurel, euonymus and privet, growing under the dense shade of surrounding trees. This type of planting is about as dull and uninteresting as you can get. However, there are very many evergreen plants worthy of garden space.

Silver-leafed shrubs

Amongst the most useful in small gardens are the evergreen, or evergrey, plants. This list includes *Lavender, Artemisia, Senecio, Convolvulus cneorum, Cistus, Hebe pagei, Helichrysum lanatum* and *Santolinas.*

They all have one thing in common; they enjoy plenty of sunlight and good drainage. They prefer light, sandy soils and will often grow in the hottest situations where other plants fail.

Many of them can be grown on stiffer land, provided it is well-drained and never waterlogged. A number of these plants have either scented flowers or foliage and associate well with roses, particularly the old-fashioned shrub roses, and are generally considered to be useful, summer-flowering, species.

Foliage colour

Some evergreens are worth growing for their foliage alone, often having no conspicuous flower to speak of. One of the finest examples would be *Elaeagnus pungens Maculata* with its robust evergreen foliage evenly splashed with gold. It makes an attractive plant even in the depths of winter. It is also useful for cutting and flower arrangements.

Other plants which fall into the same category and require ordinary garden soil would include the *Photinia* (The Chinese Hawthorn), particularly some of the newest varieties such as *fraseri Red Robin*, which has coloured foliage similar to a *Pieris*, but is much easier to grow and somewhat hardier.

There are many good varieties of the spotted laurel, *Aucuba japonica*. These appear under several different names and it is important to select carefully to get a good form.

Fatsia japonica, often found in Victorian gardens, has an enormous leaf rather like a fig, and although it does flower, it is worth growing for its foliage effect alone.

There are numerous members of the privet family, including ordinary golden privet, which can be very useful and are

Cotoneaster horizontalis.

good for cutting, and finally in this group there is the vast majority of conifers in the many shades, colours and forms that are available.

Ground cover

Evergreens make splendid ground cover plants. These are plants which, when introduced into clean soil and allowed to ramble and scramble amongst other planting, help to keep down weeds.

Any of the low-growing *Cotoneasters* are suitable. There are numerous evergreen *Berberis*, several *Euonymus* such as *Silver Queen* and *Emerald 'n Gold*, which are first-class plants.

Include here also prostrate conifers and heathers for sunnier situations, and in shade any of the Ivies, particularly *Hedera hibernica* and its varieties, or the variegated *Hedera colchica Dentata Aurea*.

Also useful in shade are the *Vincas* or "Perrywinkles". There are two distinct types; *Vinca major* with a large leaf form, and the more rampant shrub, *Vinca minor* with a smaller leaf which forms a much more compact plant. Both are available with flowers in various shades of blue or white and with either green or silver and goldmarked leaves.

Do not forget to include in your ground

cover list *Hypericum calycinum*. It is completely evergreen, has yellow flowers for much of the summer, is one of the most persistent weed suppressants and grows almost anywhere.

Wall cover

No list of evergreens would be complete without a selection of plants which will clothe walls. Amongst the most useful in difficult, shady situations are the many varieties of *Hedera*, already mentioned. *Pyracantha* and *Cotoneaster lacteus* are also useful in similar situations. In full sun try training an *Escallonia* or a *Caenothus* on to a wall to see them at their best, and on a shady wall find space for *Clematis balearica* which is really semi-evergreen. It flowers in the winter with a tiny, creamy flower set against feathery foliage that is tinted bronze in the colder weather.

If you have a good west wall try the evergreen *Clematis armandii*; difficult to grow but a very spectacular plant when successful.

This is obviously only a short list of the many splendid evergreen plants that are available to you.

Flowering evergreens

Evergreens for flower include some of

Evergreen trees and shrubs

Colour guide on page 53

the most spectacular plants we can grow. Perhaps the most widely known would be the *Rhododendron,* but as everyone knows you need quite specialised conditions in order to grow these and other ericaceous plants. Basically what is required is an acid soil with a high organic matter content, that is moist and at least semi-shaded so as to create a humid atmosphere.

Remember that the majority of Rhododendrons are natives of high, mountainous regions where the soil is thin and free draining. Soggy, heavy soils will not suit them at all.

Camellias require similar conditions but will take more sunlight. For many gardens these are best grown in tubs or containers so that they can be placed in the sun during the summer to ripen the wood and produce flower-buds, and then moved into a shady position for flowering in the winter. The important thing to remember is that the morning sun must be kept away from any blooms for if the blooms are frozen the sun will cause them to shrivel and drop. But if the frozen blooms are allowed to thaw slowly without direct sunlight, they will survive even the hardest winters.

Other plants that require similar conditions would include *Arbutus unedo,* the "Strawberry Tree", (although it will take a drier site than most), *Mahonias, Skimmias,* which are grown for their berries, and *Pieris forrestii,* not forgetting *Kalmia latifolia* the "Calico Bush", one of the choicest of evergreen flowering plants when grown in suitable conditions.

There are many flowering evergreens which will take a sunny situation. These include the Blooms, the evergreen *Caenothus, Escallonias* and *Hebes.*

Garrya elliptica is another easy shrub to grow in partial shade, with enormous silver-yellow catkins in February, making a splendid show at a difficult time of the year.

Similar conditions would be ideal for *Choisya ternata,* the "Mexican Mock-orange". This one has a light-green leaf which is aromatic when crushed, and white-scented flowers in May and periodically throughout the year.

Amongst the flowering evergreens there are a number with good, scented flowers; such as *Viburnum burkwoodii, Daphne odora Variegata,* which would be worth growing for their scent even if they did not also produce beautiful flowers.

We have already mentioned *Skimmias* as being useful berrying shrubs. There are a whole group of easily grown evergreen shrubs that provide splendid winter interest with their fruits and berries. Some of the best would be found in the *Cotoneasters* and many of these are semi-evergreen. The *Pyracantha,* or "Firethorn", is a berrying shrub worth a place in any garden, and is particularly useful when trained on to a north-facing wall.

Finally, in this group remember to include the Hollies. Apart from the many variegated types there is a particularly good Holly with dark-green, leathery leaves that are almost spineless, that regularly produces crops of brilliant red berries, *Ilex altaclarensis* (J. C. van Tol).

Choisya ternata

Kalmia latifolia

Planting evergreens

Colour guide on page 55

FROM the beginning of April to early May is a good time to plant evergreens. Amongst the most useful of these are the conifers. We refer to them as "evergreens" but in fact they are available in many different colours, from every conceivable shade of green, through yellow and gold, various blues and greys, to bronze bordering on red. Conifers are extremely versatile, varying in size from the Giant Redwoods of North America to the dwarf alpine forms suitable for pot culture, or growing in stone troughs or rock gardens. In addition to providing a useful range of hedging plants, screens against noise or unsightly views, and shelter against cold winds, they also make attractive backgrounds for other planting. The more shapely forms create attractive focal points for prominent positions in the garden, either as upright growing types, short bushy forms or prostrate species which provide splendid ground cover. They can be grown in association with heathers, most low-growing shrubs, and a wide variety of herbaceous ground cover material.

Most conifers will grow on ordinary garden soil. With a few exceptions, they resent water-logging and in the main are drought tolerant when established. Very few conifers will tolerate a cold, draughty corner. This may seem unusual when you think how often we use conifers to provide wind shelter, but it is a fact that a plant may succeed out in the open where it is buffeted regularly by strong winds, but can fail when it is planted in a position that is constantly subject to cold, draughty winds, blowing and eddying around the corners of buildings.

To get the best out of any conifer planting it is worthwhile preparing thoroughly. Pick an open site, if possible in full sun. (There are a few exceptions to this as some of the more exotic kinds prefer shade.) Ensure that there is adequate drainage by breaking up the subsoil and adding plenty of organic matter, preferably peat, but alternatively well-rotted farmyard manure and compost will suffice.

Conifers are usually sold with their roots wrapped in hessian, a synthetic fibre, or they are container grown. It is always best to remove the root covering. If the root ball is at all loose, stand the conifer in the prepared hole at the correct planting depth, untie the wrap from around the neck of the plant, and tuck the corners neatly under the root ball. This will cause minimum disturbance to soil adhering to the roots, and even with synthetic materials the roots will grow over and around it. Plant and thoroughly

Break up the subsoil at the bottom of the planting hole.

Hessian is commonly used to wrap the roots of conifers.

Planting evergreens

Colour guide on page 55

firm in the usual way, adding a mulch of peat.

The best time for planting conifers is late autumn or in April. Preferably always plant before the turn of the year and try to avoid the times when severe gales or cold, frosty weather are likely. Most evergreens, including conifers, grow away quickly if they are planted in soil that is warm and have an opportunity to make a little root before they are subject to extreme weather conditions.

Tall growing types that are used for screening benefit from staking. An ordinary garden cane is quite suitable for this purpose and the conifer can be secured to it with raffia or soft string. Avoid tying with synthetic materials as these can chafe or cut into the bark and cause serious damage.

Prostrate conifers tend to be rather one-sided when young and careful positioning is required to show the plant to best advantage. Do not assume, because the branches are growing in one direction when the plant is small, that it will continue to grow in the same direction as it matures.

In the first summer after planting, conifers can suffer from drought, particularly if the root-ball is damaged. Heavy watering under these conditions is not the answer. A damaged root system cannot take up the water and heavy watering will only exacerbate the situation, leading to water-logging and the eventual death of the plant. It is far better to ensure that the ground is adequately moist and is maintained in this condition by periodic watering and mulching, and then to lightly syringe over the plant, particularly in the evenings after warm, still days. You can begin the syringing in April as soon as the spring sun begins to gain a little strength, and continue right through until early June, gradually reducing the amount of water that is applied and increasing the intervals between applications.

This syringing technique can be applied to most new plantings. What in fact happens is that the plant takes up moisture through the foliage to compensate for loss that has occurred during the day, without placing undue strain on its root system. Once new roots have formed they will search out and take up sufficient water to support the plant.

Remove the wrapping with care.

Protect from the wind at first.

Roses

AS one flowering season draws towards its close, we should look towards the preparations for next year. Whilst most of the rose bushes will still be producing intermittent flowers at this time, it is not too early to start thinking about replacing those that are coming to the end of their useful life. It is at this stage that you may have doubts. You may have a rose bush in your garden that is at least 20 to 40 years old, and it still flowers well. Whilst this may be the case, with some of the older varieties, now rarely available, we are assured by growers that plants only give of their best for the first five years or so after planting, and should be replaced after this time. Who are we to argue? But even if we do want to argue over this particular point, there are plenty of other reasons for wanting to buy new rose plants.

One very good reason is that new varieties are being produced all the time, improving on all sorts of characteristics, from colour to disease resistance to tidier habit of growth, but never, never, alas for scent. However, this too may be a good reason for wanting some new plants to replace some of the newer ''improved'' varieties with older, more fragrant ones. It is in this area that it really does pay to go to some of the big flower shows and have a good look at the new varieties as they are unveiled (have a sniff at them too, if you can get close enough). Make a note of any that particularly catch your eye, so that when the catalogues start to come out, you will be able to get your orders in, as early as possible, and so avoid any disappointment.

Having established that you want to buy some new roses, the next question is what sort. There are hybrid T's, multifloras, floribundas, shrub roses, modern shrub roses, species roses, tender roses, and crosses between many of these, not to mention climbers and ramblers, making the whole choice available somewhat extravagant. Fortunately, some of the categories will suit certain requirements better than others, making choice a little bit simpler.

Hybrid Teas

This is the one group that surely everybody knows. The flowers are large and elegantly shaped, and are usually produced singly on long stems. Occasionally, they are cluster flowered, but where this occurs, it is often best to thin to one bud per stem, for absolutely perfect flowers. Many are beautifully fragrant, and the colour range includes everything from pure white through cream and buff to yellow, and through

Rambling rose, Chaplin's Pink Companion.

Roses

apricot and orange to scarlet and crimson, as well as bicolours between any of these. In fact the only colour still to elude us is the true blue, and even this is being worked on. So far, the nearest that breeders have been able to get is a soft lilac sometimes verging on grey, which can be very effective for cut flower work, and under artificial lighting, but is not really a true blue yet. Foliage too, can be quite striking, in form and colour. Ranging from a pale pea green through to a rich, velvety green often with a bronze tint, particularly in the new foliage, it can often make the difference between a variety that is worth growing or not.

What more is there to say about this the most spectacular of garden plants? Perhaps only one thing! As they are so spectacular, they are probably best grown in a bed on their own. Unlike most other flowers, the colours of many modern varieties do not blend quite naturally with other flowers, and indeed may clash horribly.

Floribundas

Many gardeners would recommend planting these rather than H.T.s. The flowers are borne in large clusters, rather than singly, so that even though the individual flowers may be small, single flowered or semi-double, they make up for it by sheer numbers. Where a mass of colour from late June to the end of September at least, with minimum maintenance, is required then you can do no better than to plant a bed of floribundas. As a single bush in a mixed border, they can probably provide more colour than any other single plant, and at the same time require less attention than any other plant in the garden.

Included within this group are the so-called multifloras, which seem to be very popular these days. These are basically floribundas with big double flowers like an H.T. This would seem to be the ideal, having the best of both worlds, but, in fact, they can be over fussy and therefore not as attractive as they should be. Again, though, one, in the middle of a mixed border can look very effective indeed.

Shrub Roses

This is by far the most varied group, the biggest group, and probably one of the most difficult to place in anything but a very large garden. However, if you can find room for even one large shrub rose, you will be admirably rewarded. What exactly are shrub roses? Many of them are old fashioned roses, which have been superseded by the modern hybrids, which will often produce

Rosa Moyesii

Miniature rose, 'Darling Flame'.

flowers over a much longer season, be neater in habit, and are often more weather resistant. Why bother growing the older roses at all, then? The reason is in the old fashioned charm of many of these plants, and more often than not, the fragrance that is lacking in so many modern hybrids.

Most people have heard of the old fashioned Damask roses, Moss roses, China roses and Bourbons, though few people, even quite keen gardeners would be able to tell which was which. As well as these, there are the Albas, Musk roses, Noisettes, Burnets and many more. Most will only flower once in the year, though when they do, the branches are often weighted down with bloom. Often the shrubs will grow up to twelve or fifteen feet and as much across, with long straggly branches that are quite often cruelly barbed, so that they can be very difficult to place. They really are worth it though, if you want to sacrifice that Forsythia, or lilac, in the corner.

However, as well as these old fashioned roses there are many 20th C. roses which come into the same category. Often these will have the same habit as the older roses, but as well, they have many of the attributes of the modern H.T.s. An excellent example of this sort of rose is "Nevada", raised in 1927. The bush will grow to about 8–12ft (2.4–3.6m) in either direction, and is covered in large (up to 5in (12.5cm) across) semi-double, creamy–yellow flowers, from the beginning of June. The long arching stems are covered from one end to the other. The main point about this, however, is that it is slightly recurrent. That is, it will flower again, once the main flush is over.

In addition to these very useful roses are an entirely new breed of shrubs which have the charm of the old fashioned roses, flowering throughout the summer in the same way as a floribunda, on bushes that are small, neat and tidy, so that they will fit into any garden.

Species Roses

This is a group that is not as well known as it should be. These are the true wild roses, and in some cases, near hybrids, and they come from many different parts of the world, so that their requirements are often quite different.

On the whole they are single flowered, usually with quite small blooms, and they flower only once during the season. However, they make up for this with dainty foliage, in many colours, and usually also with bright hips in the autumn. In addition, it is only amongst this group that a true canary yellow will be found. True, these days, the colour has been bred into many H.T.s and floribundas, but there is always a creaminess or blush pink in the colour as well. Amongst the species, however, there are quite a few pure yellows.

Climbers and Ramblers

This is in fact, two distinct groups. In reality the habit of a true climber is very different from that of a rambler, but they are always classed together. In fact, the true climbers are relatively stiff stemmed, and the flowers tend to be large and showy. They are ideal for growing against walls, where they will come into flower early in the season, and depending on variety, continue to flower throughout the season. They are also ideal for growing up pillars, over pergolas or against a trellis. Included amongst these are climbing sports of many of the best H.T.s, but on a climbing plant.

Ramblers, on the other hand, tend to be very vigorous in growth, reaching anything up to 25ft (7.6m) or even more for some of the species. The flowers tend to be quite small, but borne in enormous clusters, and so they depend for their effect upon mass display.

Cultivation

Before planting, it is always a good idea to prepare the ground well, as it will not be treated again for many years, perhaps. This entails digging over thoroughly, to at least one spit depth, and incorporating as much well rotted manure, compost or other organic material as possible. If the soil below is not of a very good standard, e.g. very heavy clay, it is usually better to leave it where it is, and concentrate on enriching the top soil. As well as organic matter, it is always useful to enrich the soil further by the use of fertilisers, particularly nitrogen and phosphates. A slow release fertiliser such as Hoof and Horn, applied at a rate of anything up to 2oz/sq yd (60gm/sq m) will be available for at least the first season, so that little or no further feeding will be required.

When planting, make sure that you obtain good plants, with moist roots. For H.T.s there should be at least three good strong stems coming from the base, floribundas, shrubs and climbers even more.

Take out a hole large enough to accommodate the entire root system, without having to bend or fold any of the roots, and then spead these out well. Backfill a little of the soil, and firm it well with the heel of your boot, taking care not to stamp on the roots, causing damage. Continue backfilling and then firm the plant in well. If the plant has not been pruned already, then prune quite hard, especially in the case of H.T.s and floribundas. Take back the growths to about 2–3 buds each.

During the first season, little will be required, except, perhaps occasional dead heading, to keep the plants looking reasonably tidy. Even this is not essential, however. The two main jobs that will be required subsequently are annual feeding, and pruning.

There are probably as many different formulas for the feeding of roses as there are people growing them. However, to be honest, for the average home grower, it is difficult to beat a proprietary rose fertiliser applied as frequently as the instructions on the packet advise. This, together with an annual mulch of well rotted compost or manure will be perfectly adequate.

Pruning and Training

The initial pruning, immediately following planting is to ensure that the plant establishes a good root system, without having to spend too much of its energy on unwanted top growth. This is why it is best to prune to about 2–3 buds per shoot, and remove any weak growth, leaving just the strongest shoots. This can apply to climbers and shrubs, just as much as bush roses. For the next two seasons, you will then be building up a framework. The shape of this will depend on the type of plant.

Hybrid Teas

These can either be pruned in autumn or in spring, or both, and it really is a matter of personal choice, based on knowledge of the sort of conditions likely to be encountered in your area, through the winter. If you are on a particularly exposed site, it may pay to prune in autumn, which will then reduce wind-rock, which can cause serious loosening of the plants.

On the other hand, if you know that your garden is a frost pocket, it may well be as well to leave pruning until the spring, so that any frosted wood can be cut out. In addition, the extra wood can help keep the frost off the crown of the plant to a slight extent. Or, you may decide to remove say ⅓rd of the wood in the autumn, and then prune later.

Two systems are used, one much more severe than the other. This entails cutting out all weak and diseased growth, together with any crossing or inward growing branches. This will then leave a number of thick, vigorous shoots which

Hybrid tea rose, 'Peer Gynt'.

Rosa spinosissima, 'Burnet Rose'.

81

Roses

can be cut back to about three buds. This will concentrate all the growth into those new shoots, so that the flowers, produced slightly later in the season will be of very large size and good quality, though slightly fewer in number.

The other system is similar except that instead of pruning hard back each year, the shoots are only reduced by about ⅓rd of the current season's growth. Every few years they can be cut back, to maintain vigour. This system will produce more flowers of slightly lower quality and size.

Floribundas

These can be treated like H.T.s except that after the initial hardpruning they are light pruned every year, removing a percentage of older wood each year also, to keep the bush open.

Standards

The building up of the stem, and of the head should have been completed by the nurseryman before you buy these plants. Afterwards, pruning is the same as for bush roses, the majority being well known hybrid teas grafted or budded onto a long stem.

Shrubs

In general, the pruning of shrub roses causes little or no problem. None is necessary. As the plants are being grown to produce large shrubs, all that is needed is to keep the shape, by removing unwanted growths, and a little light pruning after flowering, removing the shoots back to a sound young shoot. Any old, exhausted wood can be removed at the same time. During the winter, the tips of over vigorous shoots can be removed by about one third.

Climbers

These tend to flower on the lateral shoots, so pruning is geared to the production of these. However, to start with, you need to build up the framework. This is achieved by allowing the main shoots to extend as far as they will grow. These are then tied down, as horizontally as possible, to the wall. Any side shoots from these main stems can be reduced to about two buds. The following season these will tend to grow upwards and they can be allowed to do so. Again, at the end of the season, they are tied horizontally, and the side shoots pruned back again. This is repeated each year until the available space is taken up. From here on, the side shoots are pruned back to 2–3 eyes each season. They should also be thinned out, leaving only the strongest ones on each main stem.

There are several reasons for pruning. The exhibitor who wishes to force his roses to have a few big flowers rather than a lot of little ones reduces the number of sources which can bear flowers.

Then there is the gardener who wants to keep his bushes trim. Maybe he has a certain height in mind, or wants his beds and borders to remain nice and even. So he tends to prune his roses to a level height.

But what does the rose want? Does it want to be pruned at all? Back in its ancestral instincts, the rose is in business to produce seed. It can't be too pleased with the exhibitor, who not only reduces its sources of seed, but then cuts off what is left and takes them to a rose show.

It can't be all that pleased with the gardener, because you only have to look at wild roses to see that they are no more level than the waves of the sea. They believe in free expression.

But they do prune themselves. They need to be pruned for two reasons, age and frost.

Old wood

When you go pruning, look for the old wood first. You can recognise it as being gnarled and black. Probably stout shoots have broken out low down on it, or below it. Those are the new channels for the sap. If the old wood has nothing young and strong breaking from it, cut it out, just above a strong off shoot if there is one. And if there isn't, cut it out at the base of the plant.

What a clearance that can make! You see the bush in a new light. Whip out any nasty stubs at the base of the plant while you are at it.

The next way to help the rose is to remove its frozen wood. But how do you know which is frozen?

None we hope, after a mild winter; but the mildness of the winter is not the point. It is the ripeness in October that matters. To see what damage has been done, snip more ends off some of the remaining shoots, and look at the pith. If it is white, all is well. If it is brown, it is frozen. And you can then snip off the frozen shoots, until you arrive at white pith, which may not be until you are down at the base of the plant.

It can be a sad business. But when it is done, you should have removed all the wood which sap cannot run through. And you should have left all that is eager to grow.

Disease and damage

And grow it will. Unless, of course, you have murdered any of it with your fork, spade, hoe or boot, or unless such things as rabbits or canker have attacked it. So take a look at the remainder of the plant for damage. And if there is any, cut it off.

As far as the rose is concerned, you can stop there. It is satisfied. It has all the wood it needs to grow seeds on. But you didn't buy the bush and give it board and lodging for the sake of its seed. You were thinking of flowers, like the catalogue or the carton showed you. Now you have to imitate the exhibitor a little.

A fair guide is to imagine yourself going into the garden in the summer and cutting a bunch of roses. You will have a fair idea of what kind of a stem will stand in the vase. Not a miserable twig, that is certain.

Remember that a shoot does not normally bear a subsidiary thicker than itself, but one thinner. With that in mind, look at the bush, now shorn of its old wood, its frozen wood, its damaged wood.

Shorten what remains to a point where it is a little thicker than the stem you would like to stand in a vase.

Many people worry unnecessarily about cutting buds when pruning.

The first essential is to do the job before there is much growth on the move. If that means doing it quickly and inaccurately, just go ahead, and don't waste time looking for buds.

Correct errors

Sometimes in April or early May, your roses will be shining with their new leaves. And the sun will shine too. And then you can saunter around, in luxury and ease, and you can correct the errors of your hasty pruning.

They will be easy to see, because instead of looking for a bud, you will be looking for a young shoot. And if there is a stub above it, with no bud to grow, you will trim it off, down to the growing shoot, with a neat, sharp cut, on the slant, leaving the shoot on the high side of the slant.

Of course, if you saw the bud in March, you would have cut there anyway. But buds are not always obvious, and time is more important than accuracy. Once the roses grow, precious sap is flowing, and you must not let it flow to the wrong places.

The best time for pruning is undoubtedly in March. If you prune in Autumn you will be throwing away all the flowers you might have had in the winter.

Bulbs

Colour guide on page 60

WHETHER you have a very large garden, or no garden at all, you will have room for some spring flowering bulbs. They can be planted by the thousand in rough grass to naturalise, or you can place a single hyacinth on top of a jam-jar full of water on the kitchen windowsill. Either way, the fresh, bright colours and perfume of these subjects is always more than welcome at the end of the long dreary winter months.

For most gardeners, the first real harbingers of spring are the crocuses, with their vivid oranges, purples and whites. Before even these, there are the snowdrops and aconites outdoors, and a whole host of different subjects which can be grown indoors. In fact, with a little careful planning, bulbs can be giving you pleasure from before Christmas until well into the spring in every section of the garden, and indoors as well.

For the earliest displays, it is necessary to purchase prepared bulbs. These have been treated so that they have already experienced a hard winter (in a refrigerator) by the time you buy them. Once given the relatively mild conditions necessary for growth, they will quickly grow away. Prepared hyacinths should be planted before the end of September, tulips by mid-September and daffodils by early October. They are not suitable for outdoor planting.

Brought into the light by the beginning of December, they will be in flower for Christmas. Untreated bulbs, planted at about the same time, will continue the display, and if planted in fortnightly succession, can produce a show until the garden bulbs can take over.

Outdoors, the uses to which bulbs can be put are numerous: in beds and borders, between trees and shrubs, filling in the herbaceous border, in the rockery, naturalised in lawns, orchards or the wild garden, in neat rows for the production of cut flowers, or even in tubs.

In beds and borders

Bulbs are excellent value in the border, as once planted, they will require little further attention. The bulbs can be left to multiply and divide, so that what is lost in size of individual blooms, is made up for in number. Indeed, the best displays are often produced several years after planting.

In the herbaceous border and between trees and shrubs, bulbs often provide the only colour available early in the year, and then die down as the other subjects grow and take over the space. For this sort of use, almost any of the bulbs available will be suitable. For early spring, use

Bulbs at their best, under trees in drifts.

Bulbs

Colour guide on page 60

galanthus (snowdrops), chionodoxa (glory of the snow), Crocus, scilla (squill), muscari (grape hyacinth), eranthis (winter aconite), and iris such as reticulata, bakeriana and danfordiae. Follow these with narcissus, tulips and hyacinths, together with anemones, fritillaria, leucojum (spring snowflake) and erythronium (dog's tooth violet).

For more normal areas, such as the narrow borders surrounding a patio or terrace, or in the top of a retaining wall, it is better to keep to plantings of single subjects, or at most two subjects together. This is because in restricted areas of this sort, more impact will be gained from a mass of a single colour or form than from variety.

Naturalising bulbs

The most satisfactory way of growing bulbs is to naturalise them. That is to plant them in such a way that they look and react as if they were growing in their natural surroundings. Planted in this way, many subjects will multiply by both seed and by division and offsets. After a number of years, large clumps will build up to provide colour year after year, with little or no further attention.

Scatter the bulbs when planting so that they look as if they have developed in the situation quite naturally. For this type of planting, subjects which have not been too developed by the breeders are best. Those bred especially for showing often have double or highly developed colouring of the flowers, and thus the "natural" effect is lost.

For naturalising in grass, under trees or in similar positions, it is probably better to stick to such subjects as narcissus, crocus and snowdrops. But these are by no means the only ones that can be naturalised. In a woodland or wild garden, there are many species which can be made to grow successfully. Whilst few bulbs will succeed in heavy shade, the exceptions are the hardy cyclamen, anemone, nemerosa and convallaria (lily-of-the-valley).

Many will be quite at home in semi-shade: snowdrops, winter aconites, anemones, crocus, narcissus and muscari can be used, together with such subjects as eremerus (fox-tail lily), endymion (our native bluebell), camassia (an American bluebell), some of the wild hyacinth species, dodecatheon (angel's tears), snowflake, and trillium.

The rockery

The scope for planting bulbs in the rock garden is nearly limitless. As most bulbs come from mountain areas where their natural conditions include poor, sun baked soil in summer and deep snow for most of the winter, they naturally take to this sort of position.

It is on the rockery that tulip species and varieties really come into their own. Many of the shorter varieties such as the Gregeii hybrids, Kaufmanniana hybrids, *T. tarda dasystemon* and *T. praestans* and its varieties will all give a trouble-free, brilliant display for years if left undisturbed.

Crocuses are probably most at home too, in these conditions, the range of species and varieties being exceptional.

Others to try include: *Anemone blanda, Fritillaria meleagris* (snake's head fritillary), many dwarf and bulbous iris species, the dwarfer species and varieties of narcissus (including cyclamineus hybrids) bulbocodium hybrids, and triandrus varieties.

Also suitable are dog's tooth violet, glory-of-the-snow, angel's tears, ipheion (an unusual blue star shaped flower), squill, puschkinia (like a pale squill) and a number of hardy cyclamen.

All of these subjects are best planted in full sun 2–4in (5–10cm) deep, into a well drained soil.

For cut-flowers

Many spring bulbs make excellent cut-flowers. To avoid making holes in the garden display, it is a good idea to set aside an area to grow such things as narcissi, tulips, snowdrops and hyacinths purely for cutting.

Tubs and window boxes

Where room is very limited, or where there is no garden at all, bulbs can still be made to give a cheerful display. All that is required is a container of some description with adequate drainage. Filled with a good compost, this will make an ideal home for bulbs, and can be placed almost anywhere. The bulbs should be planted so that they almost touch. In fact, it is possible to plant bulbs in containers of this sort in several layers, provided the layer above does not hinder the growth of the bulbs planted deeper. In general, the species used will be shorter stemmed as in the rock garden.

Fritillaria meleagris

Anemone blanda

Tulipa tarda

WITH one or two exceptions summer-flowering bulbs tend to be less popular than their spring-flowering counterparts. The reason is simply that they are faced with intense competition from a vast range of flowering annuals and herbaceous perennials, whereas the spring flowering bulbs have the garden stage virtually to themselves. This is a pity because the summer bloomers are just as beautiful and possess an even wider diversity of form and colour.

Furthermore they represent very good value for money. This may not be immediately apparent to a gardener asked to pay around 40–50 pence for a single lily bulb or 30–50 pence for five gladioli.

The value of the bulbs lies in their permanence. Once bought, they will reward their new owner with many years of pleasure.

Bulbs are also a good way of getting children interested in gardening. In the case of spring-planted bulbs there are visible signs of growth quite quickly and by their very nature, the bulbs are possibly the most foolproof of all summer flowering plants.

Bulbs, corms and tubers

The term "bulb" is often used loosely to refer to plants that possess storage organs that are not strictly and botanically bulbs. The true bulb is a plant organ composed of swollen, compressed leaves — the plant's survival mechanism that enables it to assimilate enough food from its leaves in summer to see it through the winter in a totally dormant condition.

The bulb stays at rest until it is re-awakened by the gathering strength of the spring sunshine. When this happens the sugars and starches in the leaves are released and the bulb surges into growth.

Packed tightly within the compressed leaves, the well fed, healthy bulb also has a tiny stem and an even smaller embryonic flower. As the leaves grow and unfold, so too do the stem and flowers until the cycle is complete and the plant dies down in the autumn and prepares for its winter hibernation.

Many other plants however rely on different storage organs for their rest period. Gladioli and montbretias, for instance, have corms that fulfil the same function as bulbs, but they do it in a different way. Instead of using the leaves as food reservoirs, they utilise their stems. A corm is nothing more than a stem base swollen with plant food and possessing minute growth buds on its upper surface.

Yet another kind of storage organ developed by plants, that include dahlias and begonias, is the tuber — a food-packed underground stem. Whilst others such as some irises depend for their survival on rhizomes, that are almost the same as tubers except that they have a permanent root sytem.

Soil and feeding

Whatever type of storage organ the plants possess, the common denominator that unites them all is that they are perennial and that, provided they are well cared for they will bloom for many years.

Most important of all, they must be well fed during their period of summer growth. The feeding will not make much difference to their flowering during the current year. What it does is to provide the raw materials that enable this year's plant to develop a good, fat storage organ ready for an encore next year.

Before planting any kind of bulb, work plenty of well rotted compost or manure into the soil or apply a "complete" fertiliser such as Growmore or fish, blood and bone at 1½–2oz per sq yd (45–60gm per sq metre).

The ideal soil for bulbs needs to be well drained. They want moisture of course, but they hate having their feet standing in water. They also like to have their heads in the sun and they flower better in full sunshine than in shade.

Consider before buying your bulbs, whether you want those you can stick in the ground and forget, or are you prepared to choose those that are not fully hardy if left in the ground all winter, except in the mildest parts of the country? Dahlia tubers and gladioli corms for instance are not completely hardy and need to be lifted and stored indoors.

Dahlias

For sheer display potential the dahlias are unbeatable, but remember they are as demanding as new born babes. They will take all the feeding you are prepared to give them and they must never run short of water at the roots.

Dig in as much organic fertiliser as you can spare, a few weeks before planting and follow this up with a handful of Growmore per plant as soon as growth appears above ground.

Dahlias come in all shapes and sizes. For general garden purposes it is sufficient to classify them firstly according to their height.

In broad terms the flowers can be classified as *single* — like large daisies in assorted colours, *pompom* — round balls of tightly whorled petals, *cactus* — flowers with attractive spiky petals, or

Dahlia, 'Cheerio'.

Bulbs

Colour guide on page 60

Acidanthera

Tigridia (Tiger Lily).

Begonias.

NAME	FLOWERING TIME	HEIGHT	STAKING	COLOUR	HARDY
Acidanthera	August–October	3 ft (91cm)	No	White, maroon blotch	No
Agapanthus	July–August	2–3ft (61–91cm)	No	Blue spot	In sheltered spot
Anemone De Caen St. Brigid	July–September	6–9in (15–23cm)	No	Reds, whites & blues	Yes
Begonia Large flowered Multiflora Maximum Multiflora Pendula	July–October	1–2ft (30.5–61cm)	No	Various	No
Chincherinchee	August–October	1½–2ft (45–61cm)	No	White	No
Crocosmia	July–September	3ft (91cm)	No	Orange-red	Yes, but give shelter
Dahlia	June–October	1–5ft (30.5cm–1.5m)	Yes	Various	No
Gladiolus	August–September	3–4ft (91cm–1.2m)	Yes, except for Coronado	Various	No
Incarvillea	May–July	2ft (61cm)	No	Carmine-yellow centre	Yes
Ismene	July–September	1–1½ft (30.5–45cm)	No	White	No
Lilium	June–August	2–4ft (61cm–1.2m)	Yes	Various	Yes
Montbretia	July–September	2–2½ft (61–76cm)	No	Orange	In sheltered spot
Nerine bowdenii	September–Nov.	2ft (61cm)	No	Soft pink	In sheltered spot
Ranunculus	June–September	1–1½ft (30.5–45cm)	No	Various	Yes
Sparaxis	June–August	9–12in (23–30.5cm)	No	Violet	In the south
Tigridia	July–September	1–1½ft (30.5–45cm)	No	Red-yellow shades	No

Crocosmia masonorum.

Lilium, 'Hearts Desire'.

decorative — flatter blooms with whorled petals. These groups are further sub-divided according to size into *giant — 4–6ft (1.2–1.8m)*, large — *4–5ft (1.2–1.5m)*, medium — *3–4ft (90cm–1.2m)*, small — *2–3ft (61cm–90cm)* miniature — *up to 2ft (61cm)*. When buying therefore, be careful and select the right kind to suit your garden.

If in doubt choose the dwarf bedding varieties — they grow to 2–2½ft (61–76cm) and can be relied upon to give a carefree show of colour.

Gladioli

Gladioli are also deservedly popular.

One unusual way to plant them is 6in (15cm) apart in groups of six or eight in among the other annual or perennial plants of medium height.

Large-flowered gladioli need staking to protect them from wind and so too do the smaller flowered ''butterflies'' varieties. Although quite tall, the ''butterflies'' have smaller individual florets, but what they lack in size they make up

for with vivid and contrasting colours.

A recent introduction is the *Coronado* strain of gladioli, these newcomers grow to only 3ft (90cm) in height and each corm will give at least two, sometimes three, flower spikes.

Begonias

Tuberous-rooted begonias appreciate a good rich soil and ample water — without it they have a tendency to drop their flower buds before they open. The large flowered double begonias are lovely, but in a wet summer they hang their heads and much of their beauty is lost.

Equally colourful are the smaller flowered begonias — *Multiflora maximum*. Their blooms are less than half the size of their big brothers, but they hold them high and proud and you get more flowers per plant, so for bedding their overall colour effect is just as spectacular.

For window boxes select the still smaller-flowered *multiflora* begonias and in particular the clear, clean yellow

variety **Mrs Helen Harmes**. The *multifloras* are dainty, delightful plants and in a good summer may have well over fifty flowers on one plant.

Lilies

Last but not least in terms of beauty and elegance come the gorgeous summer lilies. The trumpet-flowered lilies such as *L. auratum* — The Golden Rayed Lily of Japan — are quite delightful.

There are dozens of other lovely species and varieties, some scented, some not, but all utterly beautiful. The bulbs are very loose-scaled and should be planted on arrival, 6–8in (15–20.5cm) deep in fertile well drained soil.

Lilies like to gaze into the sun from a cool soil, so for the best results plant them in groups of six or more between low-growing shrubs.

Dahlia cuttings

Colour guide on page 52

FOR the gardener bent on filling his garden in summer with a mass of bloom, there is no better way of increasing your stock than by taking cuttings.

Start tubers into growth

As a first step, extract the overwintered dahlia roots from store and examine them carefully for damage. Any that have signs of rot or decay *(Botrytis cinerea)* need not be discarded, but can be cut back to clean, healthy flesh. Any signs of fungus — usually in the form of a grey mould — should be wiped away with a soft cloth impregnated with flowers of sulphur dust.

When it is seen that the stock is one hundred per cent, the roots should be set up in trays containing peat, fine soil or leaf mould and positioned directly above the heat source on the greenhouse bench. It is advisable to moisten the medium beforehand, and if the dahlia tubers are pushed into the mix rather than "planted", they will have a better chance of survival in the early stages of development.

Taking and rooting cuttings

It takes approximately a fortnight for the first buds or growth "eyes" to show. They will appear at the base of the old stem — known as the "crown", and once they show themselves, the trays should be watered regularly to maintain steady growth.

Cuttings are best taken when they are about 3in (7.5cm) long. The fat, hollow type should be discarded, the ideal material for rooting being a cutting that is solid of stem and about as thick as a knitting needle. At the correct length, each cutting should be severed from the parent tuber with a sharp knife or razor blade. Make the cut fractionally above the growth point, so that further cuttings may develop — an insurance against initial failures and, the means whereby many more plants may be produced.

Trays or small pots of a good open compost (peat and potting gravel or sand in a balance of 50:50 is ideal) are needed for the cuttings to grow roots. These should be placed on the staging so that they have the advantage of rising heat — that is a gentle warmth from below. Prepare the cuttings by trimming them just below a leaf node and to hasten the rooting process, dip each one into a rooting powder or liquid. Next the cuttings should be inserted into the pots or trays to a depth of 1in (2.5cm) firming each gently around the base. It is possible to position forty cuttings in a standard seed tray, or six around the edge of a 3½in (9cm) pot.

With the cuttings set up, it may well be necessary to shade them with newspaper or muslin in the early days, as bright sunlight will cause them to flag. A spray, once or twice each day, is also advised, using a fine mist sprayer. This helps to combat excessive transpiration and ensures unhindered rooting.

Treatment after rooting

It takes approximately fourteen days for a dahlia cutting to develop roots of its own. It soon becomes obvious, even to the unaccustomed eye, that a dahlia has rooted, as the foliage will glow and the cutting "perk" up. A gentle tug will confirm that rooting has taken place when the new plant (because that is what it has now become), hangs on grimly in the rooting medium!

At this point in the propagating cycle it is necessary to act quickly. Cuttings taken in a mix of peat and sand have no nutrient on which to feed, and if they are left for any length of time they tend to elongate or "draw out", thus making a thin unsatisfactory plant.

The next step — potting on — should take place as soon as the majority of the cuttings have rooted. Carefully extract each from the rooting medium and install it into its new home — an individual pot or in deeper trays — spaced about 4in (10cm) apart. The potting medium can be any of several used successfully by dahlia growers — John Innes No. 1 potting compost or one of the modern "soilless" mixes like Levington or Arthur Bowers peat based products.

Firm the cuttings into the chosen compost, taking great care that the fresh, new root is not damaged in the process. A further note of caution. If you are using old clay pots or wooden trays, that do not have the advantage of built-in drainage as with the modern plastic containers, then "crocking" (layering the bottom with broken pieces of pot) is necessary to ensure that the plants do not become water-logged.

Freshly potted cuttings should be removed to a cooler part of the staging in your greenhouse, and for the first few days shaded from bright sunlight. Very soon they will take a hold in their new home and the shading can be removed so that they take full advantage of the cosy conditions in which they find themselves.

Next month, the new dahlia plants that you have created can be transferred to a cold frame, where they will grow on steadily, building up strong stems and spreading their leaves in preparation for the time (usually around the end of May) when they can be set out in the open garden to produce a mass of blooms.

'Cactus' Dahlia

'Water lily' Dahlia

'Ball' Dahlia

Shade problems

ALMOST every garden has a difficult corner where nothing seems to grow. Yet even the most unpromising area can be turned into an attractive winter flowering border. As an example take a north facing corner with a blank uninteresting wall.

Most border plants will grow in ordinary garden soil, provided they are not subject to extremes such as waterlogging in winter, drought in summer, or cold winds. They are tolerant of some shade, which, in this situation, they will experience during the winter months, but none of them will object to a little sun during the growing season.

First of all prepare the border by hand-digging, preferably trenching, with compost or well-rotted farmyard manure worked into the second spit, then add a layer of peat and fork this slightly into the surface. Do not bury the peat; aim at producing a mixture of peat and soil in almost equal parts in the top 6in (15cm). A light dressing of bonemeal can also be worked in at the same time, as this always seems to help newly planted subjects to make root quickly.

It will be necessary to erect some form of support for the climbing plants on the walls. The best method is undoubtedly to use wall nails or "vine eyes". Wall nails are wedged shaped and are driven into the mortar between the brick courses; vine eyes are screwed into prepared holes in the brickwork that have been suitably "rawl-plugged". Space the vine eyes to support wires 1ft (30.5cm) apart along the wall. Allow one vine eye for every 6ft (1.8m) run of wire. Thread the wire through the vine eye, attaching at each end only. In this way it will be possible to remove the wire easily for maintenance purposes by cutting with pliers at each end and pulling out the unwanted wire. The plant can then be laid flat on the ground, new wires put in position, and the plant re-tied having first cut away the unwanted wood.

The climbing plants suggested include *Garrya elliptica*, which is a shrub that lends itself easily to wall training. It is completely evergreen and benefits from wall protection in colder areas. Only male plants are grown and these carry yellow catkins, some 6in (15cm) long. They are visible from Christmas until March, and at their best in February.

Clematis balearica is winter flowering and carries small cream coloured bells, and although it is likely to lose some leaf in the winter, the majority will remain and assume a bronzy tint which shows off the flowers to perfection.

Jasmine nudiflorum is the winter-flowering Jasmine, and has bright yellow

Jasminium nudifolium

Shade problems

Erica carnea.

flowers on the almost leafless branches. In suitable weather conditions these will begin to appear in late autumn and continue to flower spasmodically through to April. Cut sprays will open well indoors.

The shrubs include *Chaenomeles simonii* which is a flowering quince. This is low growing and carries dark red flat flowers on the leafless branches from February until, in a suitable year, May.

Euonymus Emerald 'n Gold is a ground cover plant that is completely evergreen and forms a dense mass of foliage which is cream and green, but flecked with pink and bronze in winter.

Daphne mezereum carries purplish flowers on the leafless branches in February and March, and is one of the best scented shrubs.

Cotoneaster conspicuus decorus is a low-growing Cotoneaster rarely making more than about 3ft (91cm) in height. It is evergreen and produces a good display of bright red berries from autumn into the new year.

Elaeagnus pungens Maculata is an evergreen shrub that can be grown in sun or partial shade, and although it can become large it responds well to pruning and the cut branches are useful in flower arranging.

Mahonia aquifolium Purpurea. A purple-leaved form of this well-known Mahonia, completely evergreen, and carrying sweet scented yellow flowers in the early spring, providing a splendid contrast to the coloured leaves.

Aucuba picturata. A new form of the old spotted laurel, common in Victorian gardens. A hardy evergreen with leaves attractively splashed with gold, almost bordering on white. There is much more colour in leaves of the new varieties than in the traditional forms, and they are well worth growing.

Berberis wallichiana Purpurea. A small upright growing Berberis with mid-green leaves that are blue on the under side. The foliage assumes an attractive bronzy, purplish tinge in the winter.

Mahonia Charity. An upright growing evergreen with Lily of the Valley scented spikes of bright lemon yellow flowers. (Charity is not the best scented form but has the most handsome foliage.)

You could also use groups of winter-flowering heathers in the front of the border. Heathers will in fact grow well in full sun but do not object to a little shade. The *Erica carnea* types which are winter flowering are often mistakenly described as "lime loving". They are in fact tolerant of some lime and benefit from heavy dressings of peat or leaf-soil to reduce the alkalinity in any soil. They are comparatively trouble free, provide splendid ground cover and an edging to borders. They are best grown in groups, or drifts, amongst other suitable shrubs. The varieties suggested, and there are many others, will give colour from November to April.

Obviously there are many other shrubs which are suitable for the conditions described. The selection offered does provide winter flower, scented shrubs, coloured foliage, berries and cover for uninteresting walls. Quite a lot to cram into a small corner, but the finished effect would be very pleasing in the depths of winter when there is little else to see in the garden.

Windbreaks

Colour guide on page 59

AN exposed garden is inevitably a problem garden. Excess winds can cause physical damage, will reduce temperatures, evaporate water from plants and soil, can cause soil compaction and erosion. They will certainly make gardening downright uncomfortable.

Much research has been carried out recently on the effects of wind in commercial horticulture and on preventative measures that growers and farmers can take. There is much that the home gardener can glean from this research, too.

The work of the Ministry of Agriculture experts shows some quite startling results.

In the Ministry booklet "Windbreaks" compiled by expert Sheila Baxter, it is shown, for example that up to a 70% increase in the yield of strawberries has been achieved simply by protecting them from wind.

Advantages

The reduction of wind speed can have a variety of beneficial effects on plant growth.

On very exposed sites, leaves and stems may actually be physically damaged, and plant growth reduced significantly. Only very hardy, generally native plants will tolerate these sort of conditions, so the provision of a windbreak may enable you to grow a much wider variety.

And growth will be better too. Though different plants react in varying degrees to protection from wind, they will generally grow away better and give earlier and bigger yields because of reduced water loss, higher temperatures and slightly higher humidity.

Add to this the fact that plants will lose less water, that there is less evaporation from the soil and that the soil temperature can be raised by as much as 5°F (3°C) and you'll see that protection from wind will improve your chances of success in the garden considerably. But apart from these major considerations, there are several "bonuses".

By providing shelter, pollinating insects are encouraged to remain for a while, so pollination of fruit is improved. Hedges will also provide a home for pollinating insects and for many of the enemies of insect pests.

Diseases can also be reduced, especially those that are windborne, such as rust diseases, mildews and the arch-enemy *Botrytus*.

And if you live near the sea, a windbreak will protect your more tender plants from the very harmful effects of gales and salt spray.

A windbreak on a vegetable plot can increase yields.

Windbreaks

Colour guide on page 59

Disadvantages

Inevitably, there are some snags. If, for example, the windbreak is too dense, it can cause turbulence and so make the situation even worse.

If you are using a "living screen" the roots of the hedge can compete with other plants in the garden for water and nutrients and they can provide living quarters for a number of pests.

Increased humidity can also bring its share of problems, particularly in the encouragement of diseases such as scab, canker and *Botrytus*.

On balance though, the advantages of reducing windspeed greatly outweigh the disadvantages.

General principles

The first thing to bear in mind is that a windbreak, to be effective, should *reduce* the speed of the wind and *not* stop it altogether.

In fact, a solid screen can have quite the reverse effect to the one desired. It has been shown that, when a strong wind meets a solid object like a fence or wall, it tends to "jump over" the screen and straight down the other side, creating an area of turbulence that can cause more damage than it would if the screen were not there at all.

Even worse is a solid screen with gaps in it. The wind tends to be funnelled through the gaps and its speed can be actually *increased* by as much as 50%. This situation often occurs between two houses creating the all too familiar "draughty corner". The effectiveness of a windbreak also depends upon its height. It has been found that a reduction of windspeed occurs at a distance up to thirty times the height of the screen. But at this distance, the wind will have almost reached its original speed. The maximum benefit occurs at a distance of up to ten times the height of the screen.

Generally then, with a normal sized garden, a windscreen 6ft (2m) high around the edge of the garden will provide adequate protection for low growing plants.

One of the major disadvantages of providing a sheltered area, is that it can prevent the "drainage" of cold air. Air frost is then trapped in the area and so the risk of frost damage is increased. In such situations, the bottoms of plants used as a windbreak should be kept bare or manufactured windscreen materials should be raised off the ground to allow the cold air to filter away.

Living screens

Living windbreaks have the great advantage of looking attractive and providing privacy and a barrier to people and animals, apart from the windscreen effect. But they do take up a fair space.

In small gardens particularly, careful choice of planting is essential because there is no doubt that any hedging plant will compete with other garden plants for water and nutrients as well as excluding a certain amount of light.

Though deciduous plants will still give some benefit during the winter, in the garden it is probably better to stick to evergreens. Not only will they provide all-year-round protection, but they also give privacy during the winter and provide an attractive background for other plants.

But remember that even a hedge can become too dense to be effective as a windbreak. A really close hedge can act in just the same way as a fence or wall, causing wind to leapfrog over it and set up turbulent areas. A little judicial pruning may be needed from time to time to allow the wind to filter through.

Conifers

Probably the most popular hedging plant bought today is *Cupressocyparis leylandii*. It's attractive, fast growing, evergreen and, when established, quite dense. Its only real disadvantage is that it is shallow rooted and therefore needs staking at least for the first few years of its life. Its shallow roots also make it susceptible to drought, so in dry weather, make sure the roots are well mulched and apply water by hand if necessary.

Make sure too, that you buy your plants from a reputable nurseryman, and buy them all at the same time. This is because there are several different parents or "clones" of *C. leylandii* and many of them have quite different growth habits. So, for complete uniformity, try to buy plants that all originate from the same clone.

Not so fast growing as *C. leylandii*, but probably less trouble is *Chamaecyparis lawsoniana* (Lawson's Cypress). It does not need staking and will probably be a little cheaper too.

But surely the most attractive of the hedging conifers is *Thuja plicata*. Again, not quite as fast as *C. leylandii*, but its bright, fresh green foliage makes an ideal backing for other plants.

Shrubs

The main disadvantage with many other evergreen shrubs, is that they are slower growing. Not only does this mean that you will have to wait a bit longer for your windbreak, but they will also cost considerably more. Holly, laurel and the wild rhododendron for example, all make excellent hedges, but they will cost you a lot of money and may try your patience somewhat too.

There are, of course, other plants grown specifically for hedging that will cost a fraction of the price and will establish a quick screen.

Privet is undoubtedly the best known and has all the characteristics needed to make it a really excellent hedging plant. It's hardy, generally evergreen, fast growing and attractive. But it has one big snag. Plant a privet hedge, and you can virtually kiss goodbye to about 6ft (2m) either side of the hedge. So, for small gardens it's best avoided.

Lonicera nitida is not so hungry and will form a good, close evergreen hedge. But, it tends to get a bit floppy after about 4ft (1.2m) high and really needs to be kept down to that height. If you are looking for something taller, you'll be better

off with *L.yunnanensis*.

Informal hedges of such subjects as *Cotoneaster simmondsii* or *Spiraea arguta* make an attractive feature and will serve well as a windbreak, but since they are not trimmed but just allowed to grow naturally, they do take up a fair amount of space.

Remember too, that a border of mixed evergreen shrubs will serve well as a windbreak for other plants and will always look good in any garden.

Planting

It's worth taking a bit of trouble over planting your hedge and its subsequent aftercare. All too often, hedges get forgotten, but they do, of course need as much attention to feeding, watering and pruning as do the other plants in the garden.

Make sure that the ground is well prepared before planting. You'll never be able to get organic matter underneath the plants once they are planted, so be a bit liberal at the planting stage.

There is however one problem with windbreaks. They are planted with the express intention of shielding other plants from the harmful effects of wind. But what protects the windbreak? The answer is that, on exposed sites, the windbreak must itself be protected at least until it has had the chance to establish. And that's one of the functions of manufactured windscreens material.

Man-made windbreaks

One of the most effective man-made windbreaks is Netlon mesh.

This is an extruded plastic mesh that has been so designed to reduce wind speed by about 50%, making it the ideal windbreak.

Though the word "plastic" still sends shivers down the spines of some gardeners, this is an attractive material that will not look out of place in the garden and makes a very good backing for plants.

It can be used on a temporary basis to protect your living windbreak until it gets established and can then be taken down and re-erected round the tomatoes or other sensitive crops to give that extra bit of protection.

Or it can be used to make a permanent screen. It has a life of at least ten years and probably considerably more, and will also serve to mark your boundary and to keep out animals and people.

But do remember that the same rules apply to this material as those for living windbreaks. If you live in a "frost-hollow" or on sloping land that is subject to ground frosts, beware of trapping cold air by lifting the screen a few inches off the ground.

A solid hedge of Cupressus lawsoniana.

Tubs and troughs

Colour guide on page 64

YOU can grow almost any summer bedding plants in a tub.

Paved areas, balconies, open porches, windows and even a concrete back yard can be transformed into a riot of colour with tubs, window-boxes and hanging baskets. This sort of gardening is particularly useful in small town gardens or even where there is no garden at all.

Choose a container

Visit any garden-centre and you will be faced with a vast array of containers varying from a plastic "Grecian urn" to a miniature wheelbarrow. If you can afford it, it's still possible to buy a container in stone or lead. But don't be too scathing about plastic. There are some very good "imitations" in fibreglass now and, where plastic has been used as a material in its own right, the results can be very effective, especially in a modern setting.

But different materials have a different effect on plants and it is often necessary to vary your growing technique to suit the container.

For example, stone, concrete, asbestos and terracotta pots will dry out much faster than plastic. So, if you cannot be sure that you'll be able to give them the attention they require, stick to plastic.

Conversely, plastic containers will need careful attention to drainage. No plants like to be in waterlogged soil, so if you live in a high rainfall area, or are confident that you can supply enough water in dry weather, a stone or concrete pot may be preferable.

The size and depth of the container will affect the types of plants you can grow. Shallow bowls will be satisfactory for shallow rooting subjects such as hardy annuals, but will not do for the more deep rooting plants like fuchsias and geraniums. And obviously, the bigger the tub, the more scope there is for imaginative planting.

If you live in a spot that is subject to high winds, make sure that you buy a pot with a broad base. Tall, narrow based vases may look very attractive, but they are easily blown over.

Personal preference will, of course play a large part in your final decision. But try to fit the container to its surroundings. Ultra-modern designs and materials look fine in a modern house, but in a country cottage they can stand out like a sore thumb.

Finally, and inevitably, your choice must be influenced by hard cash. Genuine lead or stone tubs and troughs look marvellous but are expensive. Concrete, plastic and asbestos are cheap by comparison and in the right setting, look good.

If you get a chance to lay your hands on an old beer barrel, grab it with both hands. Cut in half they'll give you two fine tubs that will fit in almost anywhere. And in a few years time, they are likely to be collector's items.

Compost

A well drained, light, open compost that will not dry out too quickly is essential. While peat based composts are excellent for smaller pots, they can be the very devil in tubs, troughs and window-boxes. With the very best intentions, it's only too easy to forget to water your tubs regularly, and when you go away on holiday it may be impossible. And once you let peat composts dry out, they are very difficult to wet again.

So, all-in-all, it's best to stick to the good old-fashioned John Innes mixes. J.I. potting No. 3 is ideal. But, whatever you do, don't expect to get success from soil you have dug out of the garden. In the unnatural conditions of a tub, plants need that little extra that only a special compost can provide.

Filling

It can't be over-emphasised that good drainage is the first essential of successful container growing. So, before filling your tub with compost, make sure that excess water is going to be able to get away.

Check first that the container has holes in the bottom. Most that are made specifically for outdoor culture do have, but some of the plastic types are made to double as troughs for indoor plants and so have no holes. If they haven't, drill three or four 1in (2.5cm) holes either with an ordinary wood drill or, in plastic tubs, with a red-hot poker.

Set the tub in position (large tubs are heavy to move about when they're full) and start by covering the holes with some large pieces of broken pot or stones. On top of these put some coarse gravel, and then a layer of rough, lumpy soil. Broken-up turves are ideal. Now you can fill up with compost, confident that excess water will drain away.

Planting

Again, personal preference must be the deciding factor in what to plant, but there are one or two basic rules.

Try to get a little height in the planting by including a few taller subjects towards the middle of the container. You could use geraniums, fuchsias or perhaps even a hydrangea at the centre.

Surround this with slightly lower growing subjects like salvias or petunias and plant the edge of the container with low growing plants such as alyssum or lobelia. Finally, soften the lines of the container by planting trailing plants — trailing geraniums, fuchsias, ivies etc, to hang over the sides.

Much the same rules apply to planting hanging baskets, though here you can push a few plants through the lining material underneath the basket to hide it and eventually form a complete ball of colour.

Feeding and watering

Remember that, unless the season is exceptionally wet, the only water and food the container will get is what you supply yourself. So, try to make a habit of regular inspection. Hanging baskets particularly are easy to forget.

Feeding is a matter of striking a balance between producing good healthy plants that are big enough to carry a lot of flower, but not making them so leafy and healthy that they have no urge to make flowers.

Annuals will always make more flower in poor soil, so unless you want lots of leaf and little flower, go easy on the fertiliser. Initially there will be quite enough in the compost itself, and indeed this may be enough for the whole season. Only feed them when the plants are beginning to look as if they have stopped growing. Then, a "tonic" of a general liquid fertiliser will be appreciated.

Fixing

Window boxes and hanging baskets must be fixed firmly. They are pretty heavy when full of wet compost, and it goes without saying that a weak fixing will lead to disaster.

Window boxes can be fixed with four screws set in *Rawlplugs*, but the safest method is to use *Rawlbolts*. These are special bolts with an expanding "collar". They are pushed into a hole drilled into the brickwork (not the mortar) and then the bolt is pushed through the hole in the box. A nut goes on the end and when it's tightened it automatically expands the collar giving a rock-solid fixing.

Try also to slope window boxes very slightly to the front and drill the holes near to the front edge. This way you won't get nasty streaks of dirty water running down your wall.

Moving mature trees

With a mature conifer dig around the root ball to cause as little disturbance as possible.

MANY gardeners are confronted with the problem of moving a mature specimen tree or shrub that is in the wrong position. If it is an easily propagated subject, then it is best to take a cutting, and once rooted, plant it where you wish the new subject to grow. Once it has reached a reasonable size, the old, misplaced specimen can be removed.

Sometimes this isn't always desirable, or possible. Perhaps the plant has sentimental value, or is very slow growing, so that it becomes important to move it intact. However, whilst it is possible to minimise the risk, it is always a big chance, moving a well established specimen tree.

In the case of deciduous species, which shed their leaves and become almost dormant in the autumn, there need not be too much difficulty. At almost any time during the winter (weather conditions permitting) the tree can be dug up, the roots being damaged as little as possible. In the case of very well established specimens, this may entail some preparatory work. The autumn before the move is to take place, it is a good idea to cut some of the longer roots to encourage the plant to produce more fibrous roots close to the trunk.

The best way to carry this out is to draw a circle at about 2–3ft (61–91cm) from the base of the trunk. Divide this into four quarters, and then take out a trench from two opposite quarters. This need only be the width of a spade, but should be about 3ft (91cm) deep, round the circumference of the circle. Cut through all the roots that are encountered. This done, the trench can be refilled, and left until the following autumn. When it will be time to move the tree. The other two quarters of the circle can be cut, the trenches dug out, and then the entire root ball can be undercut.

This work can be carried out in one season, but obviously the tree will have more of its longer roots to be cut, and this will mean that it will be replanted with more damage to its root system. Therefore, greater care will have to be taken during the following season to ensure that it re-establishes.

Once the size of the root ball has been discovered, the new site can be prepared to receive it. Take out a hole that is large enough to take the entire ball, the surface to come just flush with the top of the ball. It is a good idea to work plenty of peat and bonemeal into the bottom of the hole, so that a perfect medium is provided for new roots to grow into.

Staking

Now comes the most difficult part, and this may need help from your friends and neighbours. The entire specimen must be lifted out of its hole, and deposited in its new site. Mature trees, and even what appear to be quite small shrubs, can be remarkably heavy. Therefore, it is better to lever the soil ball out of the ground, than to try to lift it directly. Do take care not to damage the root ball, however.

Once in its new position, all that

Some roots will have to be cut.

Moving evergreens

Prepare the new hole carefully and break up the subsoil below.

Finally firm the tree into its new home.

remains is to stake the tree adequately. This can mean a very big stake as it has to go through the root ball into the ground below. Alternatively, place the stake at an angle, so that it is firmly embedded in the ground to one side of the tree. Backfill round the soil ball, and make sure that this soil is well firmed.

Evergreens

The process for evergreens and conifers is very similar, but does pose one or two additional problems. Obviously, these will not lose their leaves and become dormant in the autumn, and indeed, they will remain active throughout the winter months. Therefore, it is very important that the root ball is disturbed as little as possible, and any unnecessary moisture loss avoided. This means that it is vital to choose the correct time for moving these sort of plants. In the autumn, the soil will be warm from the summer, and the root system will establish that much easier. In addition, the weather will be moist, so that there will be less water loss from the foliage. Wet weather may also occur in the spring, but there is the chance of very cold, drying winds, and the soil will be

colder than at the end of summer. So, on balance, the best time to move this sort of specimen is from about the end of September to the end of November. Fortunately, conifers do tend to have a less extensive root system than broad leaved trees and shrubs. This means that the root ball may be smaller, and it is a relatively straightforward matter to wrap this up so that it does not disintegrate during the move.

Traditionally, a large piece of hessian is used for this purpose, and has the additional advantage that it can be left in place when the tree is replanted to rot away naturally. However, there is no reason why some other material cannot be used, provided it can be removed, or will rot away equally quickly when the specimen is replanted.

Because evergreens and conifers are losing moisture from their foliage all the time, it is a good idea to provide some extra protection at replanting time. Often the worst enemy is wind, which can dehydrate plants far more than the sun, a fact which is not often appreciated.

To avoid this sort of damage, a temporary wind-break is a good idea, particularly if you know that the new site will be

draughty. Again, an old piece of hessian will serve admirably. Place three or four canes around the tree, and wrap the hessian round these, making sure that it is secure. This will give the tree the chance to establish a good root system, and greatly improve the chances of success.

Watering

One modern advance is S600, a plastic compound which is available either as an aerosol or as a liquid dip. This is applied to the foliage, and cuts down the transpiration without stopping the plant from breathing.

Because of the large leaf area of conifers, staking is essential to prevent "rocking". This is best done with three wires arranged in a triangle and pegged firmly into the ground some distance away from the plant. Make sure you protect the stem first by wrapping sacking around it. The wires should remain until the plant is well established.

Finally, it will be necessary to keep a careful eye on it for at least one season after planting. The roots must never be allowed to dry out, and regular watering will be essential.

Soil cultivation

Colour guide on page 129

Double digging

DOUBLE digging will ensure a good, deep root-run, will improve drainage and allow soil-improving organic matter to be placed well below the surface.

Normally of course, you won't have to double-dig the whole plot each year, every three or even five years will do. Start double-digging by dividing the plot in half. At one end, take out a trench one spade deep and about 12in (30cm) wide across half the plot. The soil from this trench is placed just off the edge of the opposite half of the plot.

If you are using manure or compost, put a good layer in the bottom of the trench and then break up the bottom with a fork.

The next step is to mark off the next trench exactly the same width as the first. Dig this one out in the same way, but use the excavated soil to refill the first trench. Then repeat the manuring and breaking up as before, progressing gradually down the plot. When you get to the end of the first half, turn round and work back down the other half.

Single digging

Here the soil is only broken up to the depth of the spade, and is certainly adequate for most crops most years.

Again, divide the plot in half, but this time, it's enough to simply throw the soil from the first trench on to the end of the opposite half of the plot.

If you are using manure, spread it out over the plot first. When you have dug the first trench, simply scrape the manure from where you are to dig the next trench, into the one you have just dug. Then, dig back, throwing the soil forward as you go.

Manure and compost

The good vegetable gardener should manure at least half his plot every year.

Any form of organic matter will improve the soil structure, helping to retain water and plant food, allowing excess water to drain away and providing a home for millions of beneficial bacteria.

Farmyard manure is ideal, but if you can't get hold of it, use spent mushroom manure, peat, spent hops or, well rotted garden compost.

The one great advantage that compost has over all other forms of organic matter is that it is virtually free, so every vegetable gardener worth his salt should have a compost-heap.

Fertilisers

All vegetables will do better for a taste of fertiliser.

One of the cheapest and most con-venient compounds is 'Growmore' and all the fertiliser recommendations in this section are based on this.

Lime

Most vegetables prefer a fairly chalky soil, but there are one or two distinct exceptions.

So, it will pay to test your soil with a lime-test kit before sowing or planting to determine the correct amount of lime to apply. The unit for measuring lime content is pH and the correct levels for each crop are given in the cultural instructions in this section.

One point to remember. Never lime at the same time that manure is applied. This will simply release ammonia and both will be wasted.

Incorporate manure or compost into the bottom.

Fertilisers

Colour guide on page 129

TO understand fully plant feeding, it is necessary to have some idea of the chemical requirements of plants.

All garden plants need regular supplies of three major nutrients — nitrogen, phosphorous and potassium — and minute quantities of the so called "trace elements" — calcium, magnesium, iron, manganese, boron, molybdenum, copper etc.

Generally speaking, they need nitrogen for leaf and stem growth, phosphates for roots and potash (potassium) for flower and fruit formation.

So, it can be seen that certain plants will need more of one particular nutrient than others. Tomatoes, for example, are grown primarily for their fruit so, while it is still necessary to provide the other nutrients for balanced growth, they will need more potash than plants grown for their leaves. Lawn grasses are grown simply for their leaf growth, so nitrogen is the main feeding requirement for a healthy, green lawn.

Fertilisers can be bought in two basic forms — straights and compounds. A "straight" fertiliser is one that contains only one of the major plant nutrients. Some of the organic "straights" also contain small amounts of others. A "compound" fertiliser consists of generally three or more chemicals to produce a balanced plant food.

Straights

These are used either to correct mineral deficiencies, to give plants a boost when they need it, or to mix together to form a compound. Accuracy in their use is rather more critical than in the use of compound fertilisers.

Mixing your own compound fertilisers from straights is undoubtedly cheaper, but it's a risky business. Measurements must be very accurate and mixing very thorough, or you may do more harm than good. On balance, it is probably better to stick to compound fertilisers wherever possible.

It is however sometimes necessary to supply only one of the three major nutrients either to correct a deficiency or to get plants growing well again after a check.

The following list of commonly available straight fertilisers should help you decide which to use.

Bone-meal. An organic fertiliser containing mainly phosphates and a small amount of nitrogen. It is slow acting, releasing its nutrients over a long period. The rate of release of phosphate depends upon the size of the particles — the coarser it is ground, the slower and longer lasting it will be. For some unaccountable reason, bone-meal has gained the reputation of being a "complete" fertiliser. It is not. Most useful to add to soil when planting, and as a constituent of compound fertilisers.

Hoof and Horn meal. A slow release, organic nitrogen fertiliser. Again, the rate of release depends on the size of the particles. It is used particularly in potting composts and where a steady release of nitrogen is required. A relatively expensive fertiliser.

Dried Blood. An excellent, quick acting nitrogen fertiliser, entirely organic but rather expensive. It is often used as a liquid feed to "green up" pot plants and as a boost to overwintered plants in the spring.

Nitrate of Potash. Contains nitrogen and potash in ready available form. Used mainly as a soluble fertiliser for pot plants. It is too expensive for general use outside.

Nitrate of Soda. A quick acting nitrogen fertiliser often used for top-dressing in the summer. It must be used with care as it will damage foliage.

Nitro-Chalk. This is, in fact a compound of ammonium nitrate and chalk. It is used however as a straight fertiliser to apply nitrogen without leaving the soil acid. It is mainly used as a spring and early summer top-dressing on vegetables.

Sulphate of Ammonia. The most commonly used nitrogen fertiliser for home gardeners. It is relatively safe to use as it is not too quick acting or caustic. Used widely in potting composts.

Sulphate of Iron. Used simply to correct iron deficiencies and sometimes as a fungicide to kill toadstools on lawns.

Sulphate of Magnesium. (Epsom Salts.) Used only to correct magnesium deficiencies.

Sulphate of Potash. The most widely used potash fertiliser for home gardeners. Used particularly to encourage flowering and fruiting.

Superphosphate of Lime. A quick acting phosphate fertiliser. Despite its name, it does not affect acidity. It can cause damage to some delicate foliage.

Compound Fertilisers

Most compound fertilisers contain the three major nutrients in varying quantities. Because different types of plants need varying amounts of nitrogen phosphates and potash, some manufacturers offer specific compound fertilisers for particular crops. Tomatoes, roses, lawns, dahlias, chrysanths, carnations etc, all have very specific needs and, if you are specialising in any of these, the easiest way is to use one of the specific fertilisers made especially for the crop.

Most manufacturers also make a so-called "general fertiliser". These vary quite a bit in content and you may well find that one or the other suits your soil and growing conditions better than the other. But there is no such thing as the "miracle plant food". The best a fertiliser can do is to provide as near as possible the plant's requirements, and that is that.

Choose one with roughly the same percentage of the three major nutrients. Growmore, for example contains 7% of each and makes an excellent feed for most plants.

Trace Elements

Most soils contain sufficient trace elements for plant needs. They will also be added in manure or compost dug into the soil, so deficiencies are relatively rare.

If plants do exhibit deficiencies, however, they must be added. There are one or two special trace element fertilisers available, or if you can recognise a specific deficiency, correct it with a "straight" fertiliser. Remember that they are only required in tiny quantities, so don't overdo applications.

Application

Fertilisers can be applied in any one of three ways, and the method of application has a marked effect on the speed of response and the length of time the nutrients remain effective.

Solids. Plants can only take up nutrients in liquid form, so solid fertilisers must combine with the water in the soil to become a solution before being available. They are therefore slower acting and longer lasting.

Liquids. Being already in solution, liquid fertilisers are immediately available to plants and therefore quicker acting. Their effects last for a shorter time than solids, so applications must be regular. Soluble fertilisers are simply solids that are easily dissolved in water to form liquids.

Foliar Feeds. Plants can absorb nutrients both through their roots and their leaves. Foliar feeds are applied through a sprayer or fine-rosed watering can to the leaves of plants. They are very fast acting and so often used to correct deficiencies. Their effect lasts only a short time, however.

Compost

Colour guide on page 130

GOOD, old fashioned manure will improve the structure of the soil, making it lighter and more easily worked and far more conducive to good root growth. It will improve drainage on wet soils and will help retain water and nutrients on light land. It will also add a certain amount of plant food and will increase bacterial activity. In short, your plants will reward you handsomely if you treat

Almost anything that rots composts.

Mineral Deficiencies

Mineral	Symptoms	Cure	Notes
Nitrogen	General yellowing of leaves from base of plant upwards.	Apply 2oz per sq yd sulphate of ammonia and water in.	Aggravated by straw composts.
Phosphorous	Slow growth. Older leaves turn purple in early stages of growth.	Apply 2oz per sq yd (60gm per sq m) superphosphate.	Especially common on peat soils.
Potassium	Older leaves "scorch" round margins. Dead spots on underside of leaves.	Apply 2oz per sq yd (60gm per sq m) sulphate of potash.	Common on sandy soils.
Calcium	Young leaves curl inward. Tip-burn in lettuce. Black heart in celery. Bitter-pit in tomatoes, melons and peppers. Bitter-pit in apples.	Apply lime. Avoid use of potash and acid fertilisers. Spray with calcium nitrate at $\frac{1}{2}$oz per gallon.	
Magnesium	Old leaves yellow between veins.	Apply Epsom Salts at 3oz per gal (20gm per litre) fortnightly.	Common on sandy soils.
Iron	Young leaves turn pale or even white between veins.	Apply sequestered iron.	Acid lovers, i.e. rhododendrons, are very susceptible.
Manganese	Old leaves become faded and may curl inwards. Yellowing between veins.	Spray with manganese sulphate at $\frac{1}{4}$oz per gal per 10 sq yd.	Occurs on peat soils especially if overlimed.
Boron	Very similar to calcium deficiency. Blackening and death of growing points. Die-back in trees. Cracking and corkiness on apples. Cauliflower curds brown. Brown patches in roots of swedes and turnips.	Apply borax at 1oz per 10 sq yd (3gm per sq m).	Common on light soils and after heavy liming. Also in dry summer following wet winter.
Molybdenum	Leaves become whip-like and very narrow. Growing point stunted or blind.	Lime to bring pH to 6.5–7.	
Copper	In peas and beans the young leaves turn grey/green and then yellow. In onions the leaves turn yellow and then white.	Spray at mid-growth with cuprous oxide at 0.1oz per gal per 10 sq yd.	Most common on peat and chalky soils.

Compost

Colour guide on page 130

them to a good load of muck every year.

But that's easier said than done. Farmyard manure is becoming scarce and expensive.

But there is still one good source of soil-improving organic matter. And it's in your own back garden. Compost is freely available to every gardener. It's a fine soil conditioner, a good way of getting rid of garden and kitchen waste, and above all, it's virtually free.

Home-made containers can cost little or nothing. Even if you decide to buy one of the more expensive compost containers it will repay you in the first season.

Perhaps the reason why compost is not so popular as it certainly should be, is the elaborate and exhausting methods of making it which are often recommended. Layers of compost topped by barrow-loads of soil plus lime and fertiliser, constant watering and turning etc etc.

Well, take heart. These days, none of that is necessary. All you need is a container, a packet of compost activator and, of course, something to rot down.

What to compost

There are dozens and dozens of old wives' tales about what to put on the compost heap and what not to. Most of them are nonsense.

Generally, you can say that, if it will rot down reasonably quickly it will compost. There are one or two exceptions.

Don't try to compost diseased material. It is quite possible that the disease will be able to survive in the heap and will be spread about the garden with the compost.

Don't compost weeds that are carrying seeds. It is likely that the seeds will be killed by the heat of the heap, but it's not worth the risk of spreading your problems.

Don't put waste from the kitchen on the heap unless it is protected from rats, and never try to compost meat. A good method of beating the rats, by the way, is to put a strip of very fine wire mesh round the bottom of the container.

Other than these few exceptions, you can use almost anything. Grass cuttings are ideal since they are soft, rot down quickly and so generate a lot of heat. All weeds and vegetable waste from the garden can go on, vegetable scraps from the kitchen, old woollen clothes (not man-made fibres), screwed up and wetted newspaper that old flock mattress, tea-leaves, egg-shells, wood ash — in fact almost anything vegetable.

Waste that won't rot quickly, such as tree prunings are best burnt, and the ash used as a valuable source of potash.

Alternatively, if you have access to a lot of this sort of material, it may be worth your while investing in a "digester" which will pulp even large bits of wood into very good compostable material.

If you have lots of leaves, it may be worth making a special heap just for them. They do tend to rot down rather more slowly than softer material, and in any case they will make fine leaf mould on their own.

Making the heap

Start by putting a layer of fairly coarse material in the bottom of the container. This will help provide a free flow of air.

Then add about 9in (23cm) of weeds or grass cuttings etc. Over this, sprinkle a little compost activator. The proprietary activators work very well and need no additions, but if you have access to some dry chicken manure it will do just as well.

The main purpose of the activator is to provide nitrogen to give the bacteria present in the heap, some fuel for their work of rotting down. So really any material high in nitrogen will do.

Many gardeners use sulphate of ammonia, but if you do, you will need to add lime to alternate layers (never add lime and sulphate of ammonia together), to counteract acidity. The same applies if you are using chicken manure. Sewage sludge or dried seaweed are also suitable.

After adding the activator, make another layer of weeds and so on. There is no need to firm the heap unless the material is very loose, and there is no need to add layers of soil. Soil, in fact provides the bacteria necessary for the rotting process, but since there are several millions in the soil on the roots of one weed, there is no need to add more.

Generally, watering is unnecessary unless the material is very dry.

When building the heap, try to mix the compost a little, putting on a layer of coarse material and then a layer of fine. Again, this will help ensure a free flow of air. Most gardeners have seen stinking heaps of lawn mowings that are no more than a slimy mess and certainly useless for the garden. They go that way because of lack of air, so it is important to avoid putting on soft, fine material too thickly.

Once the container is full, cover it to help it heat up and to keep out excess rain. If you buy a proprietary container, it will come equipped with a lid, but the home-made job must be covered either with a sheet of black polythene or preferably with a bit of old carpet.

Once the container is full, start another one. This way, you should always have one container full of useable compost, one in the rotting down process and one being filled.

Dust with an activator.

Crop rotations

IT is not a good thing to grow the same crop year after year on the same piece of land. If different crops are moved around the plot in successive years, a build-up of pests and diseases can be avoided and also, better use is made of valuable organic matter. Some plants require manuring for best results, while others prefer to grow on ground that was manured for another crop.

The answer then, is to put the gross feeders on freshly manured land, and follow the following year with root crops that dislike fresh manure.

PLAN FOR A SMALL PLOT

PLOT A – MANURE AND FERTILISER

Variety and Space Between Rows	Sow or Plant	Harvest	Follow by	Sow or Plant	Harvest
9in (23cm) Spinach 'Super Green'	Apr.	July	Turnip 'Milan Purple Top'	Aug.	Oct./Nov.
16in (40.5cm) Onion sets 'Sturon'	Mar.	July	Radish 'Scarlet Globe'	July	Sept.
15in (38cm) Shallots 'Dutch Yellow'	Feb.	June	Lettuce 'Avondefiance	July	Oct.
20in (51cm) Leek 'Catalina'	June	Nov./ Dec./ Jan.			
18in (45.5cm) Cabbage 'Derby Day' (from seedbed)	June	Aug.			
20in (51cm) French Bean 'Loch Ness'	May	Aug.	Onion 'White Lisbon'	Aug.	Spring
24in (61cm) Broad Bean 'Express Long Pod'	Feb.	June	Cauliflower 'Armado April'	July	Mar./Apr.
24in (61cm) Onion 'White Lisbon'	Mar.	June	Cauliflower 'Flora Blanca'	June	Oct.
24in (61cm) Brussels Sprout 'King Arthur' (from seedbed)	June	Nov./ Dec.			

PLOT B – FERTILISER ONLY, NO MANURE EXCEPT IN POTATO AND RUNNER BEAN TRENCHES

Variety and Space Between Rows	Sow or Plant	Harvest	Follow by	Sow or Plant	Harvest
8in (20.5cm) Lettuce 'Avoncrisp'	Apr.	July	Onion 'Senshyu'	Aug.	June
24in (61cm) Pea 'Green Shaft'	Mar.	July	Lettuce 'Arctic King'	Sept.	April
24in (61cm) Pea 'Beagle'	Mar.	June	Cabbage 'Avoncrest'	Oct.	Feb. to May
24in (61cm) Beetroot 'Avonearly'	Apr.	Aug.			
15in (38cm) Carrot 'Chantenay Red Cored'	May	Sept.			
24in (61cm) Potato 'Pentland Javelin'	Mar.	June	Cabbage 'January Queen'	July	Dec./Jan.
48in (1.21m) Runner Bean 'Enorma'	May	July to Sept.			

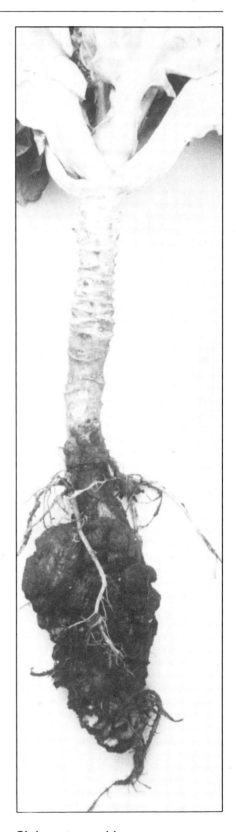

Club root on cabbage.

Crop rotations — large plot

PLAN FOR A LARGE PLOT OR ALLOTMENT

PLOT A – MANURE AND FERTILISER

Variety and Space Between Rows	Sow or Plant	Harvest	Follow by	Sow or Plant	Harvest
9in (23cm) Spinach 'Super Green'	Mar.	June	Tomato 'Gardeners Delight'	June	Aug.-Oct.
18in (45.5cm) Spinach 'Super Green'	Apr.	July	Turnip 'Milan Purple Top'	Aug.	Oct.-Nov.
16in (40.5cm) Onion 'Conquest'	Mar.	Sept.			
15in (38cm) Onion sets 'Sturon'	Mar.	July			
15in (38cm) Shallots 'Dutch Yellow'	Feb.	June	Lettuce 'Avon Defiance'	July	Oct.
48in (1.21m) Cucumber 'Marketeer'	May	July/Aug.			
48in (1.21m) Marrow 'Epicurean'	May	July/Aug.			
36in (91cm) Tomato 'Outdoor Girl'	June	Aug./Sept.			
21in (53.5cm) French bean 'Loch Ness'	May	Aug.			
18in (45.5cm) French bean 'Loch Ness'	June	Sept.			
16in (40.5cm) ½ row Sweet Corn 'Kelvedon Sweetheart' other ½ row	May	Aug./Sept.	Celery 'Avonpearl'	June	Sept.
24in (61cm) ½ row Sweet Corn 'Kelvedon Sweetheart' other ½ row	May	Aug./Sept.	Celery 'Avonpearl'	June	Sept.
18in (45.5cm) French Bean 'Lake Shasta' (wall of celery trench)	May	Aug.			
18in (45.5cm) Celery 'White Ice'	June	Nov.			
18in (45.5cm) Lettuce 'Lobjoits Green' (wall of celery trench)	Mar.	July			
18in (45.5cm) Leek 'Catalina'	June	Nov./Dec./Jan.			
18in (45.5cm) Cabbage 'Derby Day' (plant from greenhouse)	Apr.	May/June	Spinach 'Perpetual'	June	Autumn & Winter
18in (45.5cm) Cabbage 'Derby Day' (from seed bed)	June	Aug.			
21in (53.5cm) Cauliflower 'Nevada'	June	Aug./Sept.			
24in (61cm) Calabrese 'Green Comet'	June	Aug./Sept.			
24in (61cm) Potato 'Pentland Javelin'	Mar.	June	Cabbage 'January Queen'	July	Dec./Jan.
24in (61cm) Broad Bean 'Express Longpod'	Feb.	June	Kale 'Pentland Brig'	July	Winter
24in (61cm) Onion 'White Lisbon' (under cloches)	Feb.	May	Cauliflower 'Flora Blanca'	June	Oct.
24in (61cm) Purple sprouting Broccoli	May	March			
24in (61cm) Brussels sprout 'King Arthur'	May	Sept./Oct.			

PLOT B – FERTILISER ONLY, NO MANURE EXCEPT IN POTATO AND RUNNER BEAN TRENCHES

Variety and Space Between Rows	Sow or Plant	Harvest	Follow by	Sow or Plant	Harvest
24in (61cm) Potato 'Maris Piper'	Mar.	Sept.			
24in (61cm) Potato 'Maris Piper'	Mar.	Sept.			
15in (38cm) Lettuce 'Avoncrisp' (under cloches)	Mar.	June	Onion 'Senshyu'	Aug.	end June
15in (38cm) Lettuce 'Avoncrisp'	early Apr.	early July	Onion 'White Lisbon'	Aug.	Spring
15in (38cm) Lettuce 'Avoncrisp'	late Apr.	Aug.	Onion 'White Lisbon'	Aug.	Spring
15in (38cm) Radish 'Scarlet Globe' ½ row under cloches then fortnightly	Feb. to July	April/Aug.	Lettuce 'Arctic King'	Sept.	April
24in (61cm) Potato 'Pentland Lustre'	Mar.	July	Cabbage 'Avoncrest'	Oct.	Feb. to May
24in (61cm) Pea 'Green Shaft'	Mar.	July	Lettuce 'Arctic King'	Sept.	April
24in (61cm) Pea 'Beagle'	Mar.	June	Cabbage 'Avoncrest'	Oct.	Feb. to May
24in (61cm) Pea 'Beagle'	Mar.	June	Turnip 'Milan Purple Top'	Sept.	Nov./Dec.
24in (61cm) Pea 'Beagle'	Apr.	July	Turnip 'Milan Purple Top'	Sept.	Nov./Dec.
24in (61cm) Beetroot 'Avonearly'	Mar.	June/July			
24in (61cm) Beetroot 'Avonearly'	Apr.	Aug.			
21in (53.5cm) Beetroot 'Avonearly'	May	Sept.			
16in (40.5cm) Carrot 'Amsterdam Forcing' (under cloches)	Mar.	June	Turnip 'Milan Purple Top'	July	Oct.
15in (38cm) Carrot 'Amsterdam Forcing'	Apr.	July			
15in (38cm) Carrot 'Chantenay Red Cored'	June	Oct./Nov.			
15in (38cm) Carrot 'Chantenay Red Cored'	June	Oct./Nov.			
15in (38cm) Radish 'Scarlet Globe'	Apr.	June	Lettuce 'Avon-defiance'	July	Oct.
15in (38cm) Onion 'White Lisbon'	Mar.	June/July			
15in (38cm) Turnip 'Milan Purple Top'	Apr.	July			
16in (40.5cm) Swede 'Best of All'	May	Oct./Nov.			
18in (45.5cm) Swede 'Best of All'	May	Oct./Nov.			
16in (40.5cm) Parsnip 'Avonresister'	Feb.	Oct.			
15in (38cm) Parsnip 'Avonresister'	Feb.	Oct.			
15in (38cm) Parsnip 'Avonresister'	Feb.	Oct.			
48in (1.21m) Runner Bean 'Enorma'	May	July/Sept.			

Tools

MORE than anything, a gardener needs a good strong pair of hands and he must be prepared to get them dirty. Many gardening jobs can be done using the hands alone, but for most, the right tool makes the job considerably easier and quicker. The right tool means the one that has been devised especially for its particular purpose and the one that is, as near as possible, custom made for the user.

Buy the best

For the new gardener, the range and variety of tools is bewildering. If he is lucky he may inherit his father's faithful spade and fork, but usually he is faced with buying his own. This is where his problems begin. Being a new gardener implies that he has recently bought a house and in all probability he also has a young family to provide for. In short his finances are fairly heavily committed.

On top of all this he now has a garden and, not wishing to be surrounded by a waste of weeds, he needs tools to control and cultivate his new found patch of earth. It is naturally tempting to shop around and buy the cheapest tools on the market. If he does, he commits his first cardinal error.

As with most things, cheap means inferior quality, that in turn means inadequacy and a comparatively short tool life. A good tool that costs a bit more will last a lifetime and in the long term is a far better investment.

So, where does the new gardener go from here? How can he best spend his money? First and foremost he must limit his purchases to the bare minimum number of tools to enable him to get started.

Spade and Fork

He needs a spade with a good steel shaft that comes well up the ash or fibreglass handle. Before buying it, he would be advised to get the feel of it. Is it well balanced? Does it feel comfortable? Is he happy with the hand grip which may be T-shaped or D-shaped? He needs a fork that should be of comparable quality to the spade and having similar good points in its favour.

Rake

A rake is of paramount importance and once again there are good ones and not so good ones. The inferior rake has what appear to be 2in (5cm) nails protruding from a metal crosspiece, and it is the very devil to work with. The nails are too thick, making the job harder and soil and stones clog very easily between them. In addition the nails tend to work loose or else they bend and distort.

The good rake is a one piece job with

Tools

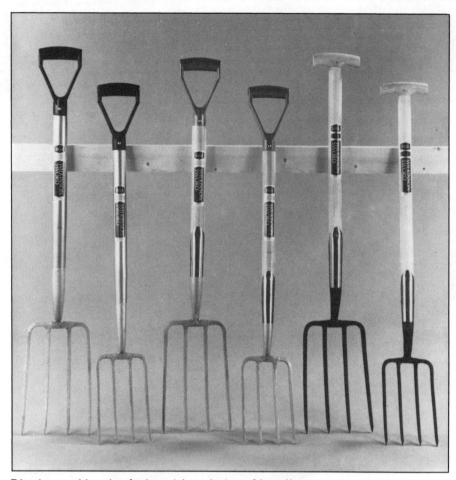

Digging and border forks with a choice of handles.

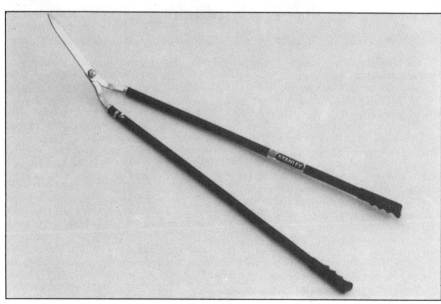

Long handled lawn shears.

teeth that taper to a point. It sings as it rakes and you finish up with a nice fine tilth.

Hoes

There are two kinds of hoe — the draw hoe and the Dutch hoe. Of the two the draw hoe is the first priority, because it is the one that is used to draw out shallow drills for seed sowing. It is also an effective killer of weeds.

The Dutch hoe is a better weed destroyer, because it is used as the user walks backwards. In other words he doesn't walk on the weeds he had dislodged, as he does with the draw hoe which functions as the user walks forwards.

Whether you buy one or both, choose the tool with a good, stout handle and with a head that is not too wide to go easily between your vegetable rows; a 4in (10cm) wide head is about right and very manoeuvrable.

Line, trowel and knife

For seed sowing you want a good garden line and here you need not spend too much money. All you require are two stout pointed pegs about 9in (23cm) long with a hole drilled in each end about an inch (2.5cm) from the top end. A length of strong nylon cord is threaded through the holes and knotted to keep it secure when the line is pulled taut. Finally you will need a good quality trowel for planting such things as bedding plants and cabbage plants and a sharp steel-bladed knife for a hundred and one uses in the house and garden.

The tools listed are the absolute essentials and their cost can vary enormously.

Secateurs

Once you are established and can afford to spend more money on tools, buy a pair of secateurs. Always carry them in your pocket when in the garden. They come in handy for all kinds of jobs in addition to pruning roses and so on. The best secateurs are the "anvil" type where the cutting edge comes down flush on to a metal base. A fairly recent innovation is an anvil secateur with a "ratchet" cutting action, enabling the user to cut through

quite thick wood without straining the secateurs.

Lawn tools

Next in order of priority come the hand tools needed to keep the lawn trim and tidy. An edging-iron to cut neat lawn edges and a pair of edging shears to keep them looking spruce.

A spring tine rake is a useful tool to rake leaves off the lawn and to tease out old, dead, clogging grass before new growth starts in spring. Finally, there is a two-wheeled lawn fertiliser distributor which spreads the plant food evenly and at the correct concentration.

Shears and sprayers

In time the new gardener will have to obtain a pair of hedging shears to control and shape the growth of his living fences. And as the garden matures and plants grow large, he will need a sprayer to apply insecticides and fungicides to protect them. Again it is worth spending the extra pound or two on good quality tools. Cheap shears tend to "chew" rather than cut cleanly and a low-priced sprayer seldom gives a fine mist spray and it usually "conks out" after a season's use.

Useful extras

Other tools that are useful to have around, although not absolutely necessary are a dibber for planting leeks (you can make one from a broken spade handle), a bulb planter, a long-handled tree pruner, a fruit picker, a turfing iron, a hand fork for weeding, and a hollow-tined fork for aerating the lawn.

A most useful tool which may be difficult to obtain, except in certain areas, is the Welsh shovel. It has a heart-shaped "business end" and a 4½–5ft (1.3–1.5m) long, slightly arched handle. It's just the tool for opening trenches for potato planting etc. and it can also be used as a substitute turfing iron. For the gardener who can't or doesn't like bending, it serves as a digging tool.

With the right tool and a good one, every gardening job becomes a pleasant, relaxing operation. With the wrong tool it can be a hard, frustrating slog.

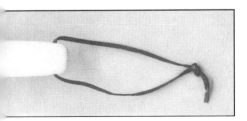

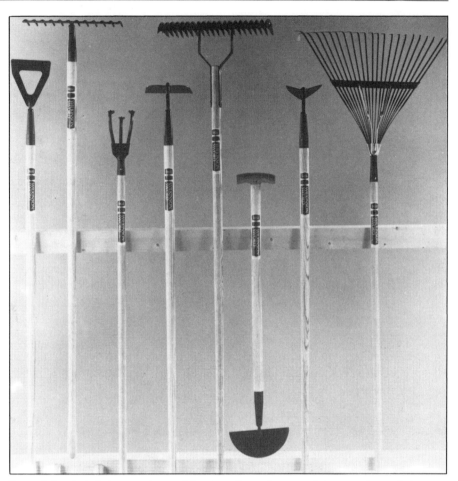

From left, dutch hoe, rake, cultivator, draw hoe, multi-use rake, edging knife, drill hoe and grass rake.

A selection of grass rakes.

105

Weed control

MODERN weedkillers can cut your gardening "graft" in half. But there are dangers, both to the gardener and to his cultivated plants.

Obviously, if you follow the instructions on the package, then all should be well, with no mistakes. The main danger lies in misuse. "Well, I'll just put an extra spoonful in, to make sure" can be very dangerous. Weeds are, after all, only plants which are growing where they are not wanted, so that any chemical which will kill weeds will also kill other plants. So you must discover exactly what your weed problem is, and only use the recommended dose.

Selective weedkillers

In fact, this is a bit of an over-simplification, as certain plants will be affected by some chemicals whilst others will not. This is the principle by which the so-called "selective" weedkillers can be safely applied to lawns, for example, without killing the grass as well. The active ingredients are absorbed by the leaves of the weeds, but the grasses have a thick waxy coating which does not allow the chemical to penetrate.

Total weedkillers

Other non-selective weedkillers such as those containing paraquat and diquat, simply kill any green plant tissue that they touch. This is accomplished by killing off the cells in the plant which contain the green colouring. This is the tissue by which the plants photo-synthesise, that is, manufacture food with the help of the sunlight. So the plant quite simply starves to death. However, some perennial and deep rooted subjects can store up food in the roots so that even with the top burnt off, they will survive and re-grow. These weeds will require repeated treatments to eradicate them. As these chemicals attack the plants through the leaves, they are neutralised when they touch the soil, so that there is no build up.

Unfortunately, these products have attained a certain notoriety, due to the fact that they are poisonous to humans, as well. Whilst they are perfectly safe, used in accordance with the manufacturers' instructions, mistakes, both accidental and intended, unfortunately, have occurred. There is no certain cure!

Residual weedkillers

Finally, there is the group of weedkillers which poison the plants through the root system. These are usually referred to as residual herbicides as they remain in the soil, for varying periods. They can be applied to areas where no plants are wanted, at the beginning of the season, killing all vegetation for that season. Of course, care is needed around ornamental plants, as these are equally vulnerable, but the right chemical in the right place, at the right dosage, can be very useful indeed.

But placing modern weedkillers into a few easily recognisable categories is something of an over simplification. In fact there are a great number of different chemicals, made by different companies, and increasingly, many branded products combine different sorts of chemicals to do a number of jobs at one go. If you know, at least broadly, what the main chemicals do, and what they are called, you will be able to sort out the proprietary brands that much more easily. The table will help, in this respect. It shows some of the major chemicals together with their uses and major brands. As you will appreciate this is not a comprehensive list, but it includes the main brands.

Hormone weedkillers

Another term that may be encountered in connection with weedkillers, is "hormone weedkillers". This is not, in fact, a separate category. A number of chemicals act on plants by interfering with their hormones, and thus the natural pattern of growth. These include many of the so-called selective weedkillers, and also the brushwood killers. Whilst care is always needed, when disposing of surplus material, it is particularly important with these weedkillers, that this surplus is not allowed to find its way into streams or ditches. This interference with plant hormones is carried over to animal life. Fish and other water creatures are particularly susceptible. Do make sure that the surplus is poured down a main drain, and washed down with plenty of water. The apparatus used will need to be well washed out too. In the case of weedkillers containing paraquat, disposal is even simpler. All that is necessary is to pour the surplus into a piece of bare earth. Residues should *never never* be stored for later use.

Safety!

This safety aspect is one that is often overlooked. Whilst, certainly, the chemicals which are used by gardeners are less concentrated than those used by farmers and commercial growers, great care should still be taken. Paraquat is just as fatal in small doses as it is in a large dose. It just takes longer. Always follow the manufacturers' instructions very carefully. Wash out equipment very thoroughly after use, and if possible, use separate sprayers, watering cans etc. for use specifically with weedkillers. Even the smallest residue of one of the hormone weedkillers, for instance can cause widescale distortion and even total loss of a crop such as tomatoes. Always wash your hands after using any chemical sprays, before eating or even smoking a cigarette! If the instructions tell you to wear protective clothing, even rubber gloves, when mixing up concentrates, then it is in your own interest to do it! If the pack recommends using a measured amount of chemical, then it means that more will be just as useless, or even worse, more damaging to surrounding plants and even to you, than less!

TREATMENTS FOR WEEDS

Type of Weed	Situation	Appropriate Chemical	Some Trade Names	Type of Action	Notes and Precautions
Most common, broad-leaved weeds	Lawns	2, 4-D and dicamba	Evergreen Lawn Weedkiller (Fisons) Evergreen Foaming Spot Weedkiller (Fisons)	Absorbed by leaves. Causes distorted growth and death.	Best applied when weeds are growing. Fruit very susceptible so avoid drift. 2,4-D also available in combination with fenoprop and dichlorprop. All are similar.
		2, 4-D and mecoprop	Lawn Plus (ICI) Boots Lawn Weedkiller Supertox (M&B) Verdone (ICI)	''	
Mosses, pearlwort, trefoils and speedwell.	Lawns	Ioxynil and mecoprop	Clovercide Extra (Synchemicals) Iotox (M&B)	''	Mecoprop also available alone (Clovotox M&B) and with MCPA (PBI Lawn Weedkiller)
General weed control	Paths, waste ground, fences, etc.	Sodium chlorate	Boots Sodium chlorate Murphy Sodium chlorate Cookes Chemicals Sodium chlorate	Poisons soil, killing most plant growth.	May encourage moss to form on top of soil, once washed in. Tends to creep sideways through soil.
''	''	Simazine	Gesal Weedex Boots Path Weed Control Murphy Simazine Total Weedkiller	Soil acting.	Apply at beginning of season, as directed.
''	''	Simazine and aminotriazole	Gesal Super Weedex	''	''
		As above, with MCPA	Fisons Path Weedkiller		
''	''	Simazine, paraquat and diquat	Pathclear (ICI)	Attacks through leaves and soil.	As with all compounds containing paraquat, great care is needed when mixing up the spray. Dispose of any surplus material immediately, and very carefully.
Persistent weeds, nettles, underbrush etc.	''	2,4-D	SBK Brushwood Killer Brushwood Killer (PBI) Kilnet	Attacks through leaves and soil.	Best applied when the weeds are growing strongly. Cause distorted growth.
Couch control	Hedges, fence lines, waste ground etc. Also amongst established crops.	Dalapon	Dalapon (Synchemicals)	Attacks through foliage and soil.	May have a slight residual effect.
Mainly annual weeds in established beds but also general weed control.	Established beds, between plants clearing land of weed, etc.	Paraquat and diquat	Weedol (ICI)	Attacks and kills all green plant matter.	Neutralised as soon as it touches the soil. Follow pack directions very carefully.
General weed control	Established crops	Chloroxuron	Gesal weed preventer for flower beds Gesal weed preventer for vegetables	Soil-acting herbicide	Control young weeds between established plants.

Frames and cloches

Colour guide on page 157

THE British growing season is all too short and the weather always unpredictable. So, throughout the ages, gardeners and growers have found ways of lengthening the season and combating the vagaries of the weather.

Cold glass, and these days polythene, will achieve both these ends, increasing productivity and quality and extending the scope of the gardener's activities considerably.

Used properly, your cold glass can be working almost all-the-year-round to extend the season by a couple of months at either end, producing earlier crops, protecting against frost, improving quality and allowing you to grow tender plants that would not do well unprotected.

Frames

If you've got a greenhouse, a cold frame is essential. To bring plants raised in a hot and humid atmosphere, straight out into the cooler, more exposed conditions of the garden will set them back weeks. They must be gradually acclimatised to the harder conditions in a cold frame.

The process, known as "hardening off" involves a gradual increase in ventilation until finally the frame lights can be removed altogether just prior to planting out in their final positions. All plants raised in the greenhouse, or on the windowsill for that matter, will need this toughening-up process to prevent a check to growth.

But this is not the only use for a coldframe. It can be indispensable in the winter for storing stools of chrysanths, for raising sweet-peas, for protecting alpines as well as for raising good quality winter salad crops.

In the spring, it comes into its own to produce early harvests of such crops as lettuce, carrots, radishes and many more, apart from providing earlier plants such as cabbage and cauliflower to set outside in the garden.

When these crops have been cleared, it can be planted up with cucumbers, melons, tomatoes, capsicums or aubergines, to give a quality difficult to achieve outside except in the most favoured situations.

Add a little heat to the frame, and you have a miniature greenhouse that can be used in much the same way as its larger cousin. It has the disadvantages of course, that it cannot be used for tall growing crops, and will not keep you warm while you work. But even so, the low cost of heating a small area will be amply repaid by its extended use.

Month	Sow	Plant/Grow on	Harden-off	Take cuttings
Jan.	Broad bean, Cabbage, Cress, Cauliflower, Lettuce, Radish		Sweet peas	Carnation
Feb.	Onion, Cauliflower, Brussels, Leek, Parsley, Lettuce, Cress, Radish, Celery, Broad bean, Carrot, Dianthus, Pansy, Lupin, Mesembryanthemum	Gladioli		Chrysanthemum
March	Tomatoes, Dwarf runner bean, Beetroot, Carnation, Nemesia, Antirrhinum, Lobelia, French and African marigold	Cauliflower Salad crops	Brassicas Geranium	
April	Tomatoes, French bean, Runner bean, Ridge cucumber, Sweet corn, Turnip, Marrow, Half hardy annuals	Start dahlia tubers into growth	Geranium Fuchsia	Geranium
May	Melon, Frame cucumber	Tomato Melon, cucumber, capsicum, aubergine, and marrow from greenhouse	Half hardy annuals tomato marrow ridge cucumber	Dahlia
June	—	Grow on crops above	—	—
July	Primula malacoides Salpiglossis			Heathers, Semi-ripe cuttings of many shrubs
Aug.	Onion, Hardy annuals for early cutting			As above Coleus
Sept.	Cauliflower, Radish, Lettuce	Freesia Dutch iris Daffodil Narcissus		Hydrangea Hardy Fuchsia Heathers
Oct.	Sweet pea, Lettuce, Radish, Parsley	Tulip		Conifers and some evergreen shrubs
Nov.	Broad bean, Radish	Lettuce Mint in boxes Store chrysanths		As above
Dec.	Broad bean	Cover alpines		

Types of frame

It's a very simple matter to make a good cold frame yourself. Two or three Dutch lights supported on a wooden base (old railway sleepers are ideal), will do the job very well.

Dutch lights consist of a wooden frame which is grooved to take one sheet of glass of a standard size — 56 × 28¾in (140 × 72cm). They are light and easy for one person to handle and let in much more light than the old fashioned multi-paned variety.

For the less practical minded, there are many excellent cold-frames available from most garden shops or centres.

Use a stepped wedge to ventilate frames.

The trend these days is towards aluminium frames with glass right down to the ground. These will let in more light than the wooden-sided models, but tend to be colder at night. Sited in a sheltered position, however, they are ideal.

An added advantage with the small aluminium models, is their portability. They can be set up in a favoured position for the hardening-off process and later moved to the vegetable plot to cover cucumbers or tomatoes.

Cropping

Plan the crop rotation of your frame well, and it will be in use nearly all the year round. The possible permutations are endless and you should be prepared to be flexible, but the table should help make the maximum use of your frame.

Types of cloche

The price of glass seems to have rocketed in the last few years, making a couple of rows of glass cloches quite an expensive proposition. They do have advantages over polythene, however.

Perhaps most important, they are a little warmer. Provided they are placed close together so that cold draughts do not whistle through the spaces, they will warm up the soil more quickly and efficiently than polythene.

Most of the rigid plastic cloches will last a long time, if carefully handled to avoid scratches, but those made with sheet polythene will need to be recovered every couple of years at least.

However, polythene cloches are very convenient to erect, easy to move and to water and above all, they are cheap.

Finally, there are still a few types of the original ''bell'' cloches available and these are invaluable for protecting individual plants in the border from frost and wet, and for forcing some winter flowering plants. Put one of these over a clump of Christmas roses, for example, and you will really get them to flower for Christmas.

Cropping

Careful planning will not only enable

you to use your cloches for most of the season, but it should also cut to a minimum the chore of shifting them about.

First, select a site in a reasonably sheltered situation in full sun if you can. The land should be capable of retaining moisture. If it is too well drained, the watering problem could become acute, so make sure there is plenty of organic matter dug into the land before you start. This way, it is normally possible to apply water over the top of the cloches without moving them. Enough will spread sideways into the rows, and later the plants will put out roots sideways in search of water.

If the weather is very dry, however, or you are growing crops such as beans or melons or cucumbers, that require copious watering, you will either have to install an irrigation system or put up with moving the cloches to water them.

Plan your sowing or planting in strips so that, as the cloches are no longer needed on one crop they can be moved onto the next.

Beans

Colour guide on page 135

RUNNER beans are one vegetable that no self-respecting gardener should be without. Yard for yard, they produce an enormous crop of one of the most nutritious vegetables it's possible to grow. And they are not at all difficult if you take a bit of trouble over them.

Initial soil preparation is all important. They don't need a lot in the way of fertiliser because they make their own nitrogen, but they do like lots and lots of water. So, make sure they grow in a piece of land that has been well supplied with manure or compost in the lower levels.

Ideally, a trench should be dug in the autumn, organic matter incorporated, refilled and left to settle over the winter. But if you didn't get round to it, don't worry. There's still time for good preparation now.

Take out a trench one spade deep and about 18in (45cm) wide and fork as much manure or compost as you can afford into the bottom.

If you can't get hold of manure or compost, almost any organic matter will do. Spent mushroom compost, spent hops, wool shoddy, the inside of an old mattress, even screwed up newspaper, though this must be well wetted first.

After digging in the organic matter, refill the trench.

If your plot is small and you decide to grow your beans on "wigwams", manure a square of ground, rather than a trench.

Though beans will make their own nitrogen, give them a bit of fertiliser. Rake in 2oz per sq yd (60gm per sq m) of Growmore before sowing.

The supports for the beans should be set up before sowing. Bamboo canes are expensive but, looked after they should last for many seasons.

Alternatively, use bean poles, though these are not cheap either. Perhaps the cheapest way of doing it, though it is also the most troublesome, is to use wires and strings.

Put a 6ft (1.8m) post at each end of the row and stretch a wire tightly between them. Now put a stout peg 6in (15cm) either side of each post to take the bottom wire. Strings can then be run up between the wires.

If you decide to splash out and use canes or poles, start by setting the canes out along the row 10in (25cm) apart. They should lean slightly towards the centre.

Now set out the other row in the same way, 1ft (30cm) from the first. Cross the canes at the top and tie them together at the same height all the way down the row. To give added strength, it's worthwhile tying in a horizontal cane.

In small gardens, grow beans up canes arranged to form a "wigwam". This is probably a more convenient shape for the small plot and even looks quite attractive in the flower borders. But the crop is generally not quite as big.

Seed can be sown from the first week of May in the south to the middle or end of the month in the north. The art is to get the seeds to germinate and push through the soil just as the last of the frost is past.

Set two seeds 2in (5cm) deep at the base of each cane. When they show through and are growing well, the weakest seedling can be removed. But, just to be on the safe side, it's worth sowing a few extra seeds at the end of the row to replace any where neither of the two come up.

The soil should be quite moist enough still, but if not, give the seeds a good watering in.

If you have a greenhouse, or even space on the window-sill, you can raise your own plants inside. Sow the seeds in 3in (7.5cm) pots (peat or whalehide pots are ideal since they avoid root disturbance) of soil-less compost and put them in a temperature of about 55°F (13°C).

Dwarf French Bean

Soil. Though beans make their own nitrogen, they require a moist, water retentive soil, so should be grown on freshly manured land. pH — 6.5. Before sowing, apply 4oz per sq yd (120gm per sq m) of Growmore.

Sowing. Sow under cloches in March or in the open ground in late April to early May. Set the seeds 6in (15cm) apart in rows 18in (45cm) apart and 2in (5cm) deep.

Cultivations. Thin to 1ft (30cm) apart. Mulch and water if the soil is dry. In exposed situations, support the plants with pea sticks.

Harvesting. Pick regularly while the pods are still young.

Recommended Varieties. The Prince, Loch Ness, Masterpiece.

Broad Beans

Soil. They prefer a heavy, well-manured soil. pH. — 6.5. Apply Growmore at 3oz per sq yd (90gm per sq m) before sowing.

Sowing. For the main crop, sow in February or early March. Sowings can continue to April. Sowings can also be made in July for a catch-crop or in November to stand the winter for an early crop in the spring.

Sow 2in (5cm) deep in double rows 10in (25cm) apart. Place the seeds 2in (5cm) apart. Allow 2ft (60cm) between each double row.

Plants can also be raised in the greenhouse from a February sowing, hardened off and planted outside in April.

Cultivations. Hoe regularly. In exposed places, tall-growing varieties should be staked. When the plants are in full flower, remove the growing tips as a precaution against blackfly.

Harvesting. Pick regularly and when the beans are fairly young.

Recommended Varieties. Maincrop: Exhibition Longpod, Giant Windsor, Masterpiece Green Longpod, The Sutton (a dwarf variety). For autumn sowing: Aquadulce, Auadulce Claudia.

Pests and Diseases. Blackfly love broad beans. Pinch out tops and spray with lindane or resmethrin.

Broad beans ready to harvest.

Beetroot and cabbage

Colour guide on page 136

Beetroot

Like carrots they should not be sown on newly manured ground. The variety **Avonearly** is most suitable for sowing in April as it offers some resistance to bolting. They can be sown thinly and, as they develop can be pulled on attaining the size of a golf ball leaving the smaller ones to continue growing. If you require larger specimens, then it is better to space sow at stations about 4–5in (5–7.5cm) apart and thin out when large enough to handle, leaving the stronger plant at each station.

Assuming that fertiliser was applied in the preparation of ground, no further application is needed. The drills should be about 12in (30cm) apart, covering the seed to a depth of ¾in–1in (2–2.5cm). If your land is heavy then wait a bit longer before sowing.

Cabbage (Summer)

Soil. Plant on firm, manured soil. pH — 6.6. Apply Growmore at 5oz per sq yd (150gm per sq m) before planting.

Sowing. Sow in a seed-bed in March/April, ½in (13mm) deep and 6in (15cm) apart.

Planting. Plant out 18in (45cm) square during May or June.

Cultivations. Hoe regularly and water as necessary.

Harvesting. Cut when the heads are hard as needed.

Recommended Varieties. Minicole, Derbyday, Hispi, Greyhound.

Pests and Diseases. Flea beetles attack at the seedling stage. Control with HCH dust.

Cabbage Root Fly larvae burrow into stems at ground level, causing a bluish tinge, and eventual wilting and death. Use a soil pest killer around the plants within four days of planting.

Cabbage White Butterflies feed on the leaves making large holes. Control by spraying or dusting with derris as soon as they are seen.

Aphids attack most brassicas, but will also be controlled by the derris sprays.

Club Root causes thickening and distortion of roots. Control by rotating the crop. Some control is achieved by dipping roots in a calomel paste before planting.

Cabbage (Spring)

Soil. Plant cabbages on soil that was manured for a previous crop. pH — 6.6. Apply Growmore at 5oz per sq yd (150gm per sq. m) before planting.

Sowing. Sow in a seed-bed in July or August. ½in (13mm) deep and 6in (15cm) apart.

Harvest beets when they are still small.

Water cabbage seedlings before planting out.

Cabbage and cauliflower

Colour guide on page 136

Chinese cabbage, Pe-Tsai.

Planting. Plant 9in (22cm) apart in rows 18in (45cm) apart. Firm the roots well. Water well after planting.

Cultivations. Hoe regularly. Top dress with 2oz per sq yd (60gm per sq m) of nitrate of soda in March.

Harvesting. Cut every other plant for spring greens. Cut the remainder when they have hearted.

Recommended Varieties. Avoncrest, April, Early Offenham.

Pests and Diseases. See Summer Cabbage.

Cabbage (Winter)

Soil. As for Spring Cabbage.

Sowing. Sow in a seed-bed in May.

Planting. Plant firmly, 18in (45cm) apart with 2ft (60cm) between rows.

Cultivations. Hoe regularly and water as necessary.

Harvesting. Cut the heads when they are hard, as needed.

Recommended Varieties. Celtic, January Queen, Christmas Drumhead.

Pests and Diseases. As Summer Cabbage.

Chinese Cabbage

Soil. A moist, manured, rich soil is essential. pH — 6.5. Apply 2oz per sq yd (60gm per sq m) of Growmore before sowing.

Sowing. Most varieties will bolt if sown before July, though some new ones are resistant. Place the large seed 4in (10cm) apart in rows 12in (30cm) apart and ½in (13mm) deep.

Cultivations. Thin the seedlings to 8in (20cm) apart. Water copiously. When hearts begin to form, tie the leaves together with raffia.

Harvesting. Generally they are ready nine or ten weeks after sowing.

Recommended varieties. Sampan, Pe-Tsai.

Cauliflower

Soil. As for Summer Cabbage.

Sowing. Sow summer varieties under glass in January or February, or outside in a seed-bed in April or May. Winter varieties should be sown outside in a seed-bed in April or May.

Planting. Plant summer varieties 18in (45cm) apart in rows 2ft (60cm) apart from March to June. Plant firmly. Autumn varieties should be planted 2ft (60cm) square during late June and July.

Cultivations. Hoe regularly and water as necessary.

Harvesting. Cut the curds when they are white and fully expanded. If they are

Calabrese, carrots and celery

Colour guide on page 138

not needed immediately, break a few leaves over them for protection.

Recommended Varieties. Summer Cauliflowers, Mechelse Classic, All Year Round.

Autumn and Winter varieties: Flora Blanca, Autumn Giant, Walcheren Winter Thanet, English Winter.

Pests and Diseases. As Summer Cabbage.

Calabrese

Soil. As for Summer Cabbage.

Sowing. Sow in a seedbed in early April.

Planting. In late May, plant seedlings 20in (50cm) apart in rows 2ft (60cm) apart.

Cultivations. Hoe regularly and water as necessary.

Harvesting. Cut the centre flower before it opens. Then scatter a handful of Growmore around the plant. Harvest resultant sideshoots when they are about 6in (15cm) long.

Recommended Varieties. Express Corona, Green Comet.

Pests and Diseases. As Summer Cabbage.

Carrots

Soil. Do not manure, but apply Growmore at 1oz per sq yd (30gm per sq m). pH — 6.3.

Sowing. Start by sowing early, forcing varieties in frames or under cloches in early March. The maincrop sowings are made in succession from April to July. Sow in drills ½in (13mm) deep and 10in (25cm) apart.

Cultivations. Thin to 2in (5cm) apart. After two or three weeks, make a second thinning to 4–6in (10–15cm) apart.

Harvesting. Pull early carrots as they are required. Maincrops are lifted during the year as they are needed, and the final rows can be stored. Lift and cut off the top just above the root. Store in boxes of peat or sand.

Varieties. Early: Amsterdam Forcing (Amstel), Early Nantes, Early French Frame. Maincrop: Chantenay Red Cored, New Red Intermediate, Autumn King.

Pests and Diseases. Carrot Fly grubs burrow into the tops of roots. Dust seedlings with a soil pest killer, and do not leave thinnings lying about.

Celery

Soil. Deeply cultivated, rich soil is essential. Dig a trench 15in (38cm) wide and 18in (45cm) deep and work well rotted manure or compost into the bot-

Carrots after being correctly thinned out.

tom. Refill the trenches to within 6in (15cm) of the top, leaving the remainder of the soil on either side of the trench. pH — 5.8.

Sowing. Sow in a heated greenhouse in March. Prick out into boxes and harden off before planting.

Planting. Plant in June in double rows with 1ft (30cm) between plants each way. Water well.

Cultivations. Water copiously. Feed with a liquid fertiliser every two weeks. Start earthing up when plants are 1ft (30cm) high. Tie a collar of paper or black polythene round the stems and earth up in three stages with three weeks between each. Protect tops from frost with straw or cloches.

Harvesting. Start in November. Dig from one end, disturbing the other plants as little as possible.

Recommended Varieties. White Ice, Giant White, Giant Pink, Giant Red.

Pests and Diseases. Celery Fly larvae tunnel through leaves. Control by spraying with HCH.

Self-Blanching Celery

Soil. This crop needs a well manured soil but no trenches. pH — 5.8. Before planting apply Growmore at 4oz per sq yd (120gm per sq m).

Sowing. Sow in a heated greenhouse at the end of March. Prick out into boxes and harden off before planting.

Planting. Plant out in June in blocks of short rows, with 9in (23cm) between plants each way.

Cultivations. Keep well watered and feed with a general liquid fertiliser every two weeks.

Harvesting. Start cutting in September or October.

Recommended Varieties. American Green. Golden Self Blanching.

Capsicum, chicory and cucumber

Colour guide on page 139

A large chicory plant. The leaves can be blanched.

Capsicums can be grown in 'growbags'.

Capsicum

Soil. Grow on soil that was manured in the autumn. pH — 6.5 Apply Grow-more at 4oz per sq yd (120gm per sq m) before planting.

Sowing. Plants must be raised in a greenhouse. Sow in pots in March, and transfer to 4in (10cm) pots before hardening off.

Planting. Plant in a sunny spot in late May or early June. Start the plants under cloches, planting 18in (45cm) apart.

Cultivations. Pinch out the growing point when plants are 6in (15cm) high. Keep well watered and when the fruits start swelling, feed with a liquid tomato fertiliser every two weeks.

Harvesting. Start picking in August when the fruits are still green.

Recommended Varieties. New Ace, Canape.

Pests and Diseases. See tomatoes.

Chicory

Soil. They prefer a rich, freshly manured soil. pH — 6.5. Apply Grow-more at 4oz per sq yd (120gm per sq m) before sowing.

Sowing. Sow both forcing varieties and open-ground types in June/July, in ½in (13mm) drills 1ft (30cm) apart.

Cultivations. Thin forcing varieties to 10in (25cm) apart and open-ground types to 15in (38cm). Hoe and water as necessary.

Forcing. Start digging forcing varieties in November. Cut off the tops just above the ground and set upright in boxes of compost. Cover the boxes to exclude light and place in slight heat.

Harvesting. Outdoor varieties can be cut as soon as they have hearted. Forcing varieties will form a white 'chicon'. Cut these when they are 6–8in (15–20cm) long.

Recommended Varieties. Open Ground: Winter Fare. Forcing: Witloof.

Cucumber

Soil. They need a deep, rich, freshly manured soil and a sunny spot. pH — 6.3.

Sowing. Sow in a heated greenhouse in March/April in peat pots. Alternatively, sow two or three seeds 1in (2.5cm) deep in stations where they are to grow in May. Space them 3ft (90cm) apart. Thin to leave the strongest plant.

Planting. Harden off greenhouse raised plants and plant out in early June, 3ft (90cm) apart.

Cultivations. Hoe and water regularly. If growth seems slow, feed them with a general liquid fertiliser. Pinch out the growing point when the plant has seven

Leek and lettuce

Colour guide on page 140

leaves to encourage sideshoots. As fruits develop, lay them on a piece of wood or glass to keep them off the soil.

Harvesting. Start cutting in July. Cut regularly and do not let the fruits grow too big.

Recommended Varieties. Burpless, Baton Vert, Venlo Pickling.

Pests and Diseases. See Marrow.

Leek

Soil. Plant leeks on soil that has been freshly manured. pH — 6.3. Apply Growmore at 6oz per sq yd (180gm per sq m) before planting.

Sowing. Sow from late February to mid-April in a seed bed. Drills should be 1ft (30cm) apart and ½in (13mm) deep.

Planting. Plant in July, selecting the strongest plants. Make holes with a crowbar or dibber, 9in (23cm) apart with 15in (38cm) between rows. The holes should be deep enough so that only 2–3in (5–7.5cm) of the top of the plant protrudes. Do not refill with soil, but water in.

Cultivations. Hoe regularly, and water as necessary. Draw soil round the plants to blanch the stems in September.

Harvesting. Dig the plants from November as required.

Recommended Varieties. Catalina, Marble Pillar, Musselburgh.

Pests and Diseases. See Onions.

Lettuce

Soil. A rich, fertile, freshly manured soil is preferred. pH — 6.5 Before sowing or planting apply 4oz per sq yd (120gm per sq m) of Growmore.

Sowing. Start by sowing early varieties in the greenhouse in February. These can be planted outside in April. Outside, start sowing in early March and continue at two week intervals until July. Sow in drills ½in (13mm) deep and 12in (30cm) apart. For early crops outside, sow hardy varieties in September for overwintering.

Planting. Plant greenhouse raised varieties in April after hardening off. They should be set out in rows 1ft (30cm) apart with 10in (25cm) between plants. Throughout the spring and summer, thinnings from outside sown plants can be used to make another row, maturing slightly later.

Cultivations. Thin seedlings to 10in (25cm) apart as soon as they are large enough to handle. Hoe regularly and water as necessary.

Harvesting. Harvest as soon as they are ready, to prevent bolting.

Trim the leaves off leeks when planting out.

It helps, when planting out, to make a marked plank.

Lettuce

Colour guide on page 141

Lift seedlings by the leaf, never the stem.

A guard can be made out of wire mesh ...

... to protect against this damage by birds.

Recommended Varieties. For raising under glass: Fortune. For sowing outside in spring and summer: Avoncrisp, Windermere, Little Gem, Avon-defiance. For overwintering: Valdor, Winter Density.

Pests and Diseases. Slugs should be controlled with pellets. Greenfly can be a serious pest. Control with Resmethrin. Grey mould on the stems and leaves is a sign of botrytis, while a white powder on the underside of leaves indicates downy mildew. Both should be sprayed with thiram.

Onions

What cook could ever live without an onion in the kitchen? Of course, it would be unthinkable, so they are a "must" for every self-respecting vegetable plot.

Soil and Site

Ideally, onions like an open, sunny spot, but it will be possible to get a good crop from almost any part of the garden. Work in plenty of manure or compost in the autumn, and apply a dressing of Growmore at 4oz per sq.yd (120gm per sq.m), a couple of weeks before sowing or planting. Some gardeners use the same onion bed every year, but it is best to rotate the spot to avoid a transfer of pests and diseases.

Varieties

There are dozens of varieties and the final choice must be from experience and personal preference. Favourites are:

Hygro — a very high yielding variety which stores extremely well.

Solidity — A good variety for autumn sowing. The large, flattish bulbs store well.

Bedfordshire Champion — an older variety that often still outcrops the others. It also stores very well.

Sturon — one of the best to grow from sets. It produces large, well shaped bulbs and is less prone to bolting than many others.

Giant Fen Globe — an award-winning variety to grow from sets. It will produce very large bulbs of good flavour and keeping quality.

White Lisbon — still the best variety for spring or salad onions.

Barletta — a pickling variety of excellent flavour.

Senshyu — a good Japanese variety for late summer sowing.

Express Yellow — another Japanese variety that is very resistant to bolting.

Sowing

If you have a greenhouse, the easiest and best way is to sow seed in boxes and

Onions

Colour guide on page 143

transplant. If not, sow them outside either in the autumn or spring.

Under glass, the seed should be sown thinly in boxes of soilless compost in late January or early February. The earlier they are sown after late Jan. the bigger the bulbs are likely to be on harvesting. When they are large enough, prick them out into boxes and harden them off in a cold-frame before planting out in March, 6in (15cm) apart in rows 9in (23cm) apart.

Autumn sowing will produce large onions but the losses are often high. Sow in September in shallow drills 9in (23cm) apart and thin the seedlings to 6in (15cm) apart.

Spring sowing is more popular and easier. The crop will be quite satisfactory and it is therefore generally better than autumn sowing. Sow at the same distances apart in February or March as soon as the soil can be worked down to a fine tilth.

Onion sets are small bulbs that are planted individually 6in (15cm) apart in rows 9in (23cm) apart in February or March. This is an ideal way to grow onions in soil that is difficult to work early in the season.

Japanese onions are sown in early August and it is important not to delay the sowing date after about the 20th of the month. Sow at the same distances, but do not thin until the plants start growing again in the early spring. These varieties will also produce an early crop in late July or early August, if they are sown in the greenhouse in January.

Salad onions are sown fairly thickly in February or March and then in succession at fortnightly intervals until September. There is no need to thin the seedlings and rows can be as close as 6in (15cm).

Pickling onions are best sown thickly or they will form bulbs too large for comfort. Ideally, scatter-sow them in a band about 6in (15cm) wide. Sow thinly in March or April, and do not thin the seedlings.

Cultivation

It is essential to keep onions weed-free and, because they are fairly shallow rooting, this means hand weeding or very shallow hoeing. Make sure they do not go short of water, but cease watering after July to allow the bulbs to ripen, or they will not store well.

Harvesting

Contrary to normal advice, it is *not* a good idea to bend over the tops of onions in August to assist ripening. This often

Keep onions weed free.

The tops usually collapse when they are ready.

Onions

Colour guide on page 143

Onion sets can be started in trays to assist root growth.

leads to the bruising of the stem and the introduction of disease. Allow the tops to brown naturally, and then lift them slightly out of the ground to break the roots. Then, when the foliage has died down completely, lift the bulbs right out and allow them to dry in the sun in a warm, airy spot. A concrete path is ideal, or they can be laid out in a special 'cradle' made of wire-netting. When they are completely dry, remove the dead foliage and any surplus soil and skin and store them in netting bags, discarded stockings or in strings. They should be hung in a cool, airy, frost-free shed.

Pests and Diseases

Onion Fly will lay its eggs near to the plants and, once hatched, the maggots will burrow into the bulbs causing yellowing and wilting of the leaves. It is best to anticipate an attack by applying a soil insecticide such as *diazinon* (**Fisons Combat Soil Insecticide**) or *chlorpyriphos* (**Murphy's Soil Insecticide**) before sowing or planting.

Onion eelworm causes swelling and distortion of the leaves. It is rare these days because seed is treated against it. There is no chemical cure, so infected plants must be removed and burned. Do not use the soil for growing members of the onion family, peas, beans, rhubarb, or strawberries for at least two years.

Neck Rot is a storage disease. It can be avoided by growing good, hard bulbs and by drying thoroughly before storage.

White Rot shows as a fluffy growth near the base of the bulb. Control it by rotating the crop and applying 4% *calomel dust* before sowing.

Tree or Egyptian Onion.

Welsh onion or Ciboule.

Parsnips and peas

Colour guide on page 144

Peas

Soil. Sow on land that was manured in autumn. pH — 6.5.

Sowing. Sow hardy varieties in October/November, and others in succession from March to June. Take out a trench to a spade's width across and 2in (5cm) deep. Place the seeds 2in (5cm) apart in a double row with 4in (10cm) between rows.

Cultivations. Hoe regularly and water as necessary. Support with sticks or netting.

Harvesting. Pick regularly when the pods fill, working from the bottom of the plant.

Recommended Varieties. Hardy varieties: Feltham First, Meteor.

Earlies: Early Onward, Hursts Beagle.
Maincrop: Green Shaft, Onward, Kelvedon Wonder.

Pests and Diseases. Pea moth grubs burrow into pods and eat the seeds. Spray with HCH or Resmethrin ten days after flowering and again ten days later. Mildew causes white, powdery patches on leaves, especially in August and September. Do not let the plants dry out and spray with Bordeaux Mixture.

Parsnips

Soil. Fresh manure should not be used. pH — 6.3. Apply Growmore at 3oz per sq yd (90gm per sq m) before sowing.

Sowing. If the soil conditions permit, start sowing in February, though sowings can be made as late as April. Sow three seeds in stations 8in (20cm) apart. Drills should be 1in (2.5cm) deep and 18in (45cm) apart.

Cultivations. Hoe regularly and water as necessary.

Harvesting. Dig from October onwards. In the south, they can be left in the ground until needed, but in the north they should be lifted in November and stored in boxes of peat.

Varieties. Avonresister, Tender and True, Hollow Crown.

Pests and Diseases. Canker is the main trouble, causing the roots to crack showing orange cankers. Use canker resistant varieties.

Potatoes

Colour guide on page 144

POTATOES are the Englishman's staple diet. Certainly the average family spends more on potatoes than any other vegetable, so you can make a real saving by growing your own. And, while you may not improve much on the quality of main crop tubers, your new potatoes will taste far, far better.

Potatoes take up a fair bit of space in the garden, but even so, it is well worth while growing a few, even in the smallest garden. If you have a bit more room, they are an essential.

Nobody could deny that potatoes have their problems. And the biggest of these is virus. And, since there is still no known cure for virus, the sensible thing to do is to avoid it.

The Ministry of Agriculture has for many years, gone to great lengths to limit the spread of virus in this country, and one of the results is their scheme for certified seed. Virus is carried by aphids, so it is possible for a crop to be infected at any time. But the biggest risk comes from infected seed. To avoid this, potato seed is grown in remote parts of the country — mainly Scotland, west Wales and Ulster — where attack by aphids is less likely. Before the seed can be sold, it is inspected by Ministry experts and certified free from infection.

So, if you buy certified seed, you can almost guarantee that it will be clean.

Avoiding virus

But seed is expensive and many gardeners like to save their own from year to year. There is no reason why this should not be done, provided certain precautions are taken.

First, stick to varieties that have a resistance to virus diseases. Particularly leaf-roll and virus Y. This is particularly important if you live in a well populated area where there is a higher risk of attack from aphids from other people's gardens.

Make sure that you separate seed you have saved yourself from fresh certified seed. Grow them as far apart as possible leaving at least 50yds (46cm) between the two.

Regularly control aphids. If you have a bad attack during the season, it would be safer to use fresh seed the following year.

Groundkeepers — tubers that you miss when digging — can carry virus diseases, so make every attempt to dig thoroughly and lift even the smallest tubers.

Virus can also live throughout the winter in the soil, so you should practice rotation, growing the crop in a different part of the garden each year.

Finally, replace your seed with fresh certified stock every few years. The

Incorporate compost when planting potatoes.

frequency will depend on where you live and the amount of aphis problems you have. In some areas it is wise to use fresh seed every year, and, even in more isolated areas it is unwise to save seed for more than a couple of years.

Varieties

The National Institute of Agricultural Botany at Cambridge carry out regular trials on potatoes and their results are well worth attention when it comes to choosing varieties for the garden. Some of the varieties they recommend for general use are:

First earlies

Arran Pilot. A well known variety that is easy to obtain. It is slower to bulk than many other varieties but the yield at maturity is high. The tubers are oval and the flesh and skin white. Flavour is good when tubers are cooked straight after lifting. It is resistant to spraing.

Arran Comet. A very early and high yielding variety. It produces tubers with a white skin and creamy white flesh. It does not disintegrate on cooking and the flavour is excellent especially when boiled. It is particularly good in salads. Unfortunately it is susceptible to mosaic virus and to dry rot.

Home Guard. Early bulking but susceptible to drought. The tubers are somewhat small, white skinned and with white flesh. Flavour is good when boiled or in salads, but it does have a slight tendency to blacken after cooking. Shows some resistance to gangrene and tuber blight.

Pentland Javelin. Slightly later than some varieties but producing tubers of excellent quality. The flesh is very white and flavour is good both boiled and in salads. It is very resistant to virus Y and to mild mosaic viruses as well as cyst nematode.

Ulster Sceptre. One of the earliest varieties and it gives a high yield in most conditions. Produces tubers with white skin and flesh and flavour is good boiled, in salads and for chips. It is susceptible to gangrene, so handle the seed with care.

Maris Bard. This only has a provisional recommendation from NIAB, but results so far look very good. It is very early and high yielding, producing tubers with a white skin and flesh and a waxy texture. It is very resistant to virus Y but susceptible to powdery scab. Cooking qualities are as yet unrecorded.

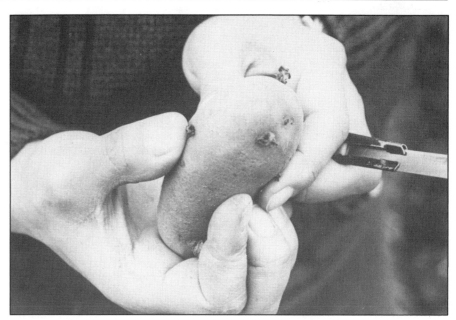

Seed potatoes should be 'chitted' before planting out.

For early potatoes plant in a large container.

Potatoes

Colour guide on page 144

Second earlies

Craigs Alliance. Produces a moderate yield of good quality tubers. The skin and flesh are white and the texture good. It is at its best from July onwards with excellent boiling qualities and good for chips and salad use. It is susceptible to drought but otherwise has no particular defects.

Red Craigs Royal. Yields of this variety are moderate and the quality good. Skin is red and flesh white with a good, close texture. It rarely discolours after cooking and the flavour is excellent when boiled. It is also good for chips and in salads. It is immune to mild mosaic virus but susceptible to virus Y and common scab.

Maris Peer. This moderately yielding variety produces mainly small to medium sized tubers of good quality. Tubers are white in skin and flesh and they rarely discolour after cooking. Excellent for boiling and good when roasted, chipped or in salads. They are susceptible to drought but resistant to blight, scab and skin spot.

Maincrop

Desiree. A high yielding, early maincrop variety producing a good proportion of large tubers. Skin is red and flesh pale yellow with a good texture. Cooking quality is excellent when roasted or chipped and good for boiling, mashing and jacket baking. Shows a good resistance to virus Y, but is susceptible to common scab.

King Edward. Produces moderate yields of the very highest quality but only under the best growing conditions. The skin is slightly pink and the flesh cream. It rarely discolours on cooking and is excellent when boiled, mashed or jacket-baked and good for chips or roast. Unfortunately it is susceptible to both drought and to wart disease and is very susceptible to virus Y.

Maris Piper. High yielding early maincrop variety. The tubers are of a uniform, medium size, with white skin and cream flesh. It rarely discolours after cooking, is excellent for jacket-baking and chips and good boiled, mashed and roast. It is very susceptible to scab and to slug damage and susceptible to drought. It is resistant to mild mosaic viruses and to one form of potato cyst nematode.

Pentland Crown. A very high yielding variety with white skin and flesh. Tubers are often large and the cooking quality fairly good. It is resistant to virus Y, leaf roll, and common scab, but susceptible to powdery scab and spraing.

Pentland Dell. A high yielding, early maincrop variety, with white skin and flesh. Texture is good and cooking qualities fairly good. It is very susceptible to tuber blight and spraing but immune to mild mosaic viruses. It is advisable to use well sprouted seed and not to plant too early in cold soils.

Pentland Ivory. A good yielding, early maincrop variety producing good sized tubers. A good multi-purpose variety being recommended for most culinary purposes. Very resistant to virus Y and moderately resistant to blight. Susceptible to spraing.

Majestic. A well known variety producing high yields of fair quality. Cooking qualities are fair, with a tendency to blacken. Its main recommendation is that it stores very well indeed. It shows some resistance to blight but is susceptible to scab.

Finally, just a mention of a very old variety that is being re-introduced. **Pink Fir Apple** gives a very high yield of long, narrow tubers. Perhaps their greatest advantage is that even though they mature in October, they retain the "new potato" flavour for a very long time, making new potatoes possible during the winter.

Since this is an old variety that has never been submitted for certification, there is no certified seed available.

Apply 'Growmore' before earthing up.

Radishes, shallots and spinach

Colour guide on page 145

Radishes

Soil. Best grown quickly, so a moist spot is best. The soil should be in good heart and fertile. pH — 6.5. Apply Growmore at 1oz per sq yd (30gm per sq m) before sowing.

Sowing. Sow thinly from the beginning of March to July at two week intervals. Sow in drills ¼in (6mm) deep and 6in (15cm) apart.

Cultivations. Hoe between rows and apply water in dry weather.

Harvesting. Pull as required, but remember that young roots have a milder taste.

Varieties. French Breakfast, Cherry Belle, Red Forcing.

Shallots

Soil. Plant these on the half of the plot that was recently manured. pH — 6.2. Apply Growmore at 4oz per sq yd (120gm per sq m) before planting.

Planting. Plant from February onwards, with a trowel so that the tops are just showing. Sets should be 6in (15cm) apart with 1ft (30cm) between rows.

Cultivations. Check after planting, that the sets have not been lifted by the birds. Hoe regularly.

Harvesting. When the leaves start to yellow in July, the bulbs can be lifted. Lay them on a concrete path for a few days until they are quite dry. Then store in slatted boxes.

Varieties. Dutch Yellow, Giant Yellow, Dutch Red.

Pests and Diseases. Onion fly larvae burrow into the bulbs. Control with a soil pest killer. Downy mildew may cause the tips of the leaves to die back and the leaves to become covered with a fine, grey growth. Control with zineb.

Spinach

Soil. A soil rich in organic matter and moisture retentive is preferred. pH — 6.6. Apply 4oz per sq yd (120gm per sq m) of Growmore before sowing.

Sowing. Sow in succession from March to July, in rows 1in (2.5cm) deep and 1ft (30cm) apart. Winter varieties can be sown in August and September.

Cultivations. Thin the seedlings to 6in (15cm) apart. Hoe regularly and water as necessary.

Harvesting. Pick young leaves regularly, always leaving some leaves on the plant.

Recommended varieties. Summer varieties: Longstanding Round, Sigmaleaf. Winter varieties: Greenmarket, Broadleaved, Prickly.

Pests and Diseases. Few pests att-

Set out shallots first to space them right.

123

Spinach beet, broccoli, squashes

Spinach beet.

ack spinach. Yellow patches and a grey mould underneath leaves are signs of Downy Mildew. Avoid by growing on well drained ground and spacing properly. C copper fungicide will help control it.

Spinach Beet
Soil. As Spinach.

Sowing. Sow from April to July in drills 1in (2.5cm) deep and 18in (45cm) apart.

Cultivations. Thin to 8in (20cm) apart. Cultivate as spinach.

Harvesting. Pull leaves regularly from the outside of the plant, always leaving some to grow on.

Recommended variety. Perpetual.

Sprouting Broccoli
Soil. See Cabbage.

Sowing. Sow in April in a seed bed.

Planting. Plant firmly in May or June, leaving 2ft (60cm) between plants and 30in (75cm) between rows.

Cultivations. Hoe and water as necessary. Mulch with peat or manure. Stake plants on exposed sites.

Harvesting. Sprouting should begin in February. Cut the centre shoot first and then cut side-shoots regularly for a constant supply.

Pests and Diseases. As Cabbage.

Vegetable Marrow and Squashes
Soil. Dig in plenty of manure or compost, as water retention is vital. pH — 6.0.

Sowing. Sow in peat pots under glass during April/May or outside from mid-May. Set two seeds where the plants are to grow in prepared "stations" 2ft (60cm) apart for bush marrows and 3ft (90cm) apart for trailing marrows and squashes.

Planting. Plant at the end of May or early June, 2ft (60cm) or 3ft (90cm) apart depending on whether they are bush or trailing varieties.

Cultivations. Never allow the plants to dry out. If growth appears unsatisfactory, feed with 4oz per sq yd (120gm per sq m) of Growmore.

Harvesting. Cut regularly when the fruits are young. For winter storage, allow a few to grow large. Let them ripen so that the skins are hard and cut them in late September. Hang in a cool, frost-free place.

Recommended varieties. Bush Marrows: Prokor, Smallpak, Trailing: Table Dainty, Long Green.

Squashes: Custard Yellow, Custard White, Vegetable Spaghetti.

Pests and Diseases. Slugs should be

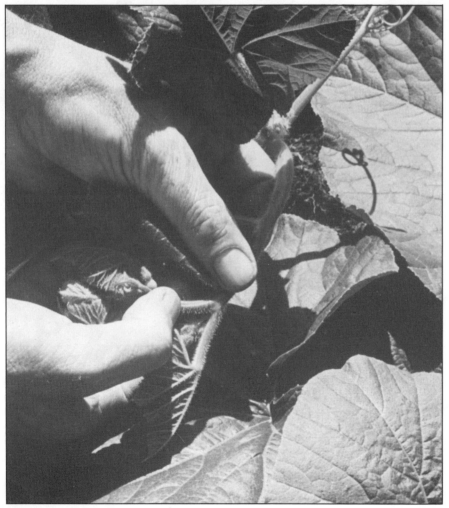

Small marrows form behind the flower.

Swedes and sweet corn

controlled with pellets and aphids with resmethrin.

Mosaic virus causes stunting and yellow patches. There is no control and plants should be removed and burned. Mildew often attacks in the autumn, generally due to the plants being dry.

Swedes

Soil. Swedes need a moist, un-manured soil. pH — 6.7. Apply Growmore at 3oz per sq yd (90gm per sq m).

Sowing. Sow in drills 15in (38cm) apart and ½in (13mm) deep in May or June.

Cultivations. Thin as soon as the first young leaves appear, to 1ft (30cm) apart. Hoe regularly.

Harvesting. Leave in the ground until required, but in very cold areas, it may be wise to lift and store them.

Varieties. Chignecto. Purple Top.

Pests and Diseases. Flea Beetle or Turnip Fly are likely to attack at the seedling stage causing small round holes in leaves. Dust with HCH. Brown Heart causes a browning of the inside of the root and is a symptom of boron deficiency. Water the soil with a borax solution.

Sweet Corn

Soil. Sweet Corn needs a sunny spot and a rich, freshly manured soil. pH — 6.6. Before planting, apply 4oz per sq yd (120gm per sq m) of Growmore.

Sowing. Sow in peat pots under glass in April, or outside in May. Outdoors, sow two seeds in "stations" 15in (38cm) apart with 2ft (60cm) between rows.

Planting. Plant in late May or early June. The plant is wind pollinated, so it is best to plant in blocks of short rows rather than in long rows. Set the plants 15in (38cm) apart in rows 2ft (60cm) apart.

Cultivations. Hoe regularly and water as necessary. A mulch of manure or compost will help retain moisture.

Harvesting. The "silks" or male flowers at the top of each cob will start to wither towards the end of August. When they do, test a seed or two by squeezing it. If the liquid that comes out is milky, it is ready to cut. Cut only as needed.

Recommended varieties. Kelvedon Glory, Kelvedon Sweetheart, First of All.

Pests and Diseases. Frit Fly larvae burrow into the growing point. Spray with HCH when the plant has two or three leaves.

Sweet corn is ripe when 'silks' wither.

Test for ripeness by squeezing, milk should flow.

Tomatoes

Colour guide on page 156

TOMATOES can be grown quite successfully outside in most parts of the country. With the introduction of the newer bush varieties, quite early crops can be obtained with a minimum of fuss.

Soil and Site

Choose a sheltered sunny spot for this tender crop. Tomatoes are gross feeders and will use a lot of water, so the site should be well prepared in advance by working in a generous quantity of well rotted manure or compost. Before planting, apply a dressing of tomato base fertiliser according to the maker's instructions.

Varieties

Decide first whether you are to grow bush tomatoes which need no staking or sideshooting and will produce good crops of flavoursome, small fruits, or the more conventional upright varieties. These will need more attention, and the rewards are bigger fruits.

Gardener's Delight is an old favourite, upright variety. It produces an abundance of small sweet fruits.

Outdoor Girl is a potato leafed type, also growing upright. The fruits are larger and well flavoured.

Alicante will fruit well outdoors and the flavour is excellent.

Sleaford Abundance is a popular bush variety, producing masses of small, sweet fruit.

Sub-Arctic Plenty is a newer variety having the advantage of early cropping. It is one of the best for direct sowing outside.

Pendulina is a new variety, very early and with a compact habit that makes it suitable for small gardens or even window-boxes and pots.

Sowing

Tomatoes are frost-tender, so they must be started inside. Sow the seeds in soilless compost in March. Allow about eight weeks between sowing and planting out.

Ideally, place the seed trays over a little gentle heat. When they are large enough to handle, they should be pricked out into small pots and given plenty of light and air. Put them in the cold frame in early May for hardening off.

If you have no greenhouse, it is possible to sow direct outdoors. The seed must be pre-chitted and fluid sown. This method is generally successful, but the fruits are usually later than from plants raised under glass.

Planting

Never plant tomatoes until all danger

of frost has passed. Indeed, even one cold night can chill the plants and stop them growing. Once this happens, it will be some time before they start to grow out again, and plants set out later will easily catch them up. In most parts of the country, the first week in June is early enough.

For upright growing varieties, put 4ft (1.20m) canes in first at 18in (45cm) intervals, and plant to them. Make sure the plants are watered well after planting. Bush tomatoes need no canes, and should be planted at the same spacings.

Cultivation

As upright varieties grow, they must be regularly tied to the stakes, or they may snap off. They must also have the sideshoots regularly removed. These shoots grow from the joint between the leaves and the stem, and must all be removed as soon as they are large enough to handle. When upright varieties have set three trusses of flower, pinch out the growing point.

A tomato ready to plant out.

Against a south or west facing wall is ideal.

Tomatoes and turnips

Colour guide on page 156

Tie tomatoes securely to canes.

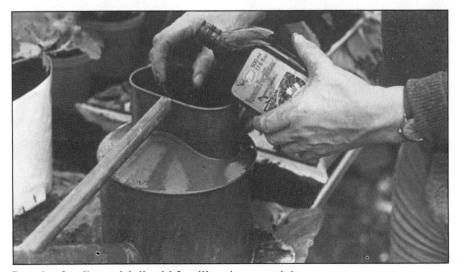

Regular feeding with liquid fertiliser is essential.

Both types should be fed as soon as the first flower truss has set tiny fruits. Use a liquid tomato feed at weekly intervals. The plants should be watered regularly, for they should not be allowed to wilt, and the rows must be kept weed-free.

Bush tomatoes will benefit from a mulch of peat or straw to keep the ripening fruit off the ground.

Harvesting

Pick the fruits when they are red and ripe and use them immediately. At the end of the season, the remaining·fruits can be ripened under cloches, or they can be removed, wrapped in paper and ripened in a drawer. This way though, they lose some of their freshness.

Pests and Diseases

Outdoor tomatoes escape many of the pests and diseases of those grown under glass.

Aphids are almost bound to attack and can be kept at bay with *resmethrin* (*PBI Sprayday*).

Potato Blight will also attack tomatoes and is controlled in the same way, by regular spraying with a copper fungicide from July onwards.

Virus diseases cause a yellowing and mottling of the leaves and a general decrease in vigour. There is no cure. Pull out the plants and burn them as soon as symptoms show.

Turnips

Soil. Turnips need a moist soil that has not been recently manured, pH 6.7. Apply Growmore at 3oz per sq yd. (90gm per sq m).

Sowing. Sow early varieties from February to May. For autumn and winter use, sow in June and July, 1ft (30cm) apart and ½in (13cm) deep.

Cultivations. Thin as soon as the first rough leaves appear to 6in (15cm) apart. Hoe regularly and water as necessary.

Harvesting. Pull early varieties when they are young and tender. Lift later varieties in October, cut off the tops just above the roots and store in boxes of peat.

Pests and Diseases. Flea beetle is a problem but is easily controlled with HCH dust.

Digging

1 When single digging, simply dig one spade deep and throw the soil forward to fill the previous trench.

4 When double digging, divide the plot in half and 'stitch' down the line with a spade.

7 Place a liberal dressing of manure or compost in the trench and dig it in to the full depth of the fork.

2 If you are using manure, spread it over the surface and scrape it into the trench as you dig.

5 It is important to keep all the trenches the same width, so mark them with a stick.

8 Measure out and dig the next trench, but this time, fill the first trench with the soil you dig out.

3 The trenches should all be the same width, and the spade should be kept upright for maximum depth.

6 Dig out the first trench and wheel the soil to the opposite side but the same end of the plot.

9 When you come to the end of the plot, simply turn round onto the other half and work back again.

Compost container

1 Bang in a post at each corner. Don't make the container bigger than 4ft (120cm) square.

4 Fix the batten securely with wire to one of the corner posts on the most convenient side for removal.

7 Beg, borrow or steal some old cardboard containers and slide them between the walls.

2 Measure the distance between the posts. Try to make it as 'shipshape' as possible.

5 Stretch the wire netting between the outside of the posts and securely staple it to each.

8 The container can now be filled with any vegetable matter that will rot down.

3 Staple the end of the wire-netting to a batten first. This will make the 'door' for easy removal later.

6 Now continue round, stapling it to the inside of the posts to form a sort of 'cavity wall'.

9 Build up the compost in 9in (23cm) layers sprinkling a proprietary compost activator over each layer.

Peat blocks

1 Wet the compost in a bowl. Overwetting is better than underwetting.

4 Place on a hard surface and press the plunger down to compress the compost. Then release the block.

7 Set out the blocks on the dampened mat ensuring that there is a small gap between each block.

2 Thoroughly mix the compost. When squeezed, it should hold together.

5 Lay out a sheet of opaque polythene on the staging. Old fertiliser bags are ideal.

8 Sprinkle the seeds onto a piece of card and, using a knife blade, put six seeds into each block.

3 Fill up the special blockmaker with compost so that it completely fills the cavity.

6 Watering is best done by capillary action, so use a special fibre mat. Wet it before placing the blocks.

9 There is no need to cover with compost. Simply place a piece of opaque polythene over the blocks.

Sowing

1 Fork over the soil, turning in annual weeds and adding manure or compost where necessary.

4 Decide how much general fertiliser is to be applied for each crop and spread the correct amount.

7 Seed must be sown thinly to avoid overcrowding. It is best to sprinkle it between thumb and forefinger.

2 If you are good at digging, you should be able to keep the surface level.

5 Now rake the surface level, working the soil to a fine tilth and raking in the fertiliser.

8 Cover the seeds with soil, making sure that you don't bury them too deeply by heaping the soil.

3 Seeds must be sown in firm soil, so go over the whole area, treading it with your weight on your heels.

6 Stretch a tight line across the plot and take out a shallow drill with the corner of a draw-hoe.

9 To ensure that each seed is closely surrounded by soil and not hanging in mid-air, tamp down.

Fluid sowing

1 Seeds are first placed on a moist tissue in a plastic box. Placed in a warm spot, they will soon germinate.

2 When the tiny first roots are the correct length, gently wash them off the tissue into a sieve.

3 Make up a mixture of wallpaper paste and carefully transfer the germinated seeds into it.

4 Paste and seeds are now poured into a polythene bag or a cake icing syringe ready for sowing outside.

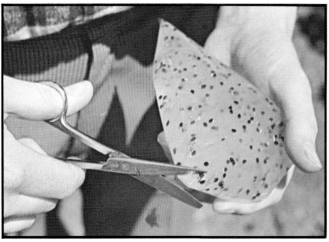

5 If a polythene bag is used, cut off the corner so that the paste and seeds can be squeezed out of the hole.

6 Make a drill in the normal way and gently squeeze a thread of paste into it. Cover with soil and keep moist.

Planting

1 For plants that need a firm soil such as the cabbage family, hoeing is often all the cultivation needed.

4 Never allow the tender roots of seedlings to be exposed to sun or wind.

7 Plants such as lettuce require looser soil and these are best planted with a trowel or fingers.

2 For other plants such as lettuce, loosen the soil with a fork removing weeds as you go.

5 Plant members of the cabbage family firmly, using a dibber. Bottom leaves should be at ground level.

8 Make sure that the soil is well firmed around the roots by pressing all round.

3 Lime or fertilise the ground if necessary and then stretch a tight line across the plot.

6 After planting, make sure the plants are firmed in really well by treading round them.

9 All plants need watering after planting. Most will still wilt but will soon recover.

Beans

1 Before sowing runner beans, set out the canes first, to a tightly stretched line.

2 The second row of canes are put in at an angle and about 12in (30cm) from the first row.

3 Tie the tops of the canes together and, for extra rigidity, tie another cane across the tops.

4 Sow two bean seeds against each cane. Later, the weaker seedling will be removed.

5 Don't forget to sow a few extra seeds at the end of the row to make up any failures later.

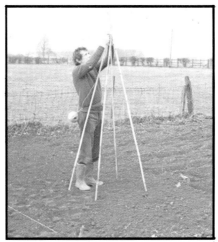

6 In a small space, beans can be grown up 'wigwams', though the crop is likely to be inferior.

7 For the earliest crop of french beans, sow them in large pots in the greenhouse or windowsill.

8 Cover pots with opaque polythene or glass and paper. Remove it when first seedlings show.

9 For an earlier crop of beans outside, sow them in the greenhouse and plant them out.

Cabbages

1 Brassicas are generally raised in a seed-bed in a spare corner of the garden.

4 Before planting, lime if you know it to be necessary, remove all weeds and rake level.

7 Using a dibber, set the plants so that the bottom leaves are at soil level and no lower.

2 Prepare the ground, in the usual way and sow thinly in rows about 6in (15cm) apart.

5 To minimise root damage, water the seed-bed well before lifting the plants when ready to plant out.

8 Firm them with the dibber at the side of the plant, take care not to damage the roots.

3 Cover the drills, tamp down lightly and make sure to label each row clearly and securely.

6 Though brassicas can be pulled out it is best to lift them with a fork, to avoid root damage.

9 After planting, water generously to settle the soil around the roots and revive the young plants.

Spring cabbage

1 Spring cabbage, like all brassicas, will do best on firm soil. So simply hoe off the weeds.

2 If the ground is really hard, just fork over the top few inches without disturbing the lower levels of soil.

3 All brassicas like lime. If you are planting following potatoes, or if your soil is acid, apply lime.

4 Whether the plants are your own or are bought in, cover the roots to stop them drying out.

5 Stretch a tight line and plant with a dibber, setting the plant's bottom leaves just at soil level.

6 To ensure that the soil is well firmed at the bottom of the hole, ram the dibber down near the plants.

7 Make sure that the soil is really firm around the plants by treading around them with your heel.

8 'Puddle' the plants in with plenty of water. This will help them to root quickly and will minimise wilting.

9 If birds are a problem, cut-up polythene bags tied onto canes are very effective.

Carrots

1 Stretch a tight line across the plot and draw a shallow drill using the corner of a draw hoe.

2 Sow the seed thinly. Put a little in your hand and sprinkle it out between thumb and finger.

3 Cover the seed with a little soil and then tamp it down with the back of a rake to firm lightly.

Celery

1 Celery and celeriac are both sown in the greenhouse, in March. Make sure the compost is evenly moist.

2 After watering it, rub it through your hands to remove lumps and to ensure that every part is wetted.

3 Fill a box with compost and lightly firm with your fingers, paying particular attention to the edges.

4 Use the levelling board to scrape off any excess compost to leave it level with the top of the box.

5 Again with the board, lightly firm the compost to leave a flat and level surface for sowing.

6 Sprinkle the seed evenly by placing a little in the palm of your hand and tapping it out with your finger.

Chicory

7 Lightly cover the seeds with a little more compost and then press lightly with the levelling board.

1 To force chicory, lift the roots and trim the tops to leave about 1in (2.5cm) of foliage.

4 Get an orange box from the greengrocer and line the inside with a few sheets of newspaper.

8 The box should now be placed in a spot where it will receive gentle bottom heat.

2 Trim off the bottoms of the long roots to ensure that they will fit into the boxes.

5 Place a little peat in the bottom. Alternatively, use old potting compost or garden soil.

9 Cover the box with glass and paper or a piece of opaque polythene. Check daily for germination.

3 The thonged side roots can also be trimmed to allow more roots to be packed in.

6 The roots can now be packed into the box as closely as they will go without touching.

Leeks

7 Fill round the roots with more peat or compost and work it down between them.

1 Leeks are best planted in May or June. Dig the ground over and then consolidate it by treading.

4 Using a marker board or a stick, make holes with the dibber, 9in (23cm) deep and apart.

8 Now take another orange box and pin some old opaque polythene round it to exclude all light.

2 Apply a dressing of Growmore scattered evenly over the surface at a rate of 4oz. per sq. yd.

5 If the plants have been grown inside, water the boxes first. Seedbeds will also need watering.

9 This box is placed over the first and they can then be forced in gentle heat in the kitchen.

3 Rake the area to produce a fine, firm tilth and to incorporate the fertiliser into the surface soil.

6 The roots are very long and unruly. To facilitate planting, trim them back with a sharp knife.

Lettuce

Marrow

7 To compensate for the plant's reduced ability to take up water, trim the leaves by a third.

1 When lettuce seedlings are big enough they should be transplanted. Water before lifting.

1 Marrows should be planted in well prepared soil, to which plenty of organic matter has been added.

8 Select strong young seedlings and simply drop one in each hole. There is no need to refill the hole.

2 Place a finger either side of the plants that are to remain, and carefully lift out those in between.

2 Before planting, water the pots well. If they are dry, removal of the pots will damage the young roots.

9 Now water each hole, washing a little soil around the roots. The holes will fill up with soil later.

3 Transplant them at between 6-9in (15-23cm) apart. Firm with your fingers, and water well.

3 Most plants will have been raised in whalehide or paper pots. These should be carefully torn away.

Marrow | Mushrooms

4 Set the plants in the prepared planting stations at about the same level they were in the pots.

5 Firm gently round the plants with your fingers, leaving a shallow depression to retain water.

6 After planting, give a good watering to settle the soil around the roots.

1 Build up the heap of manure or activated straw, until it is about 4-5ft (1.2m) high by 5.6ft (1.5-1.8m) wide.

2 The heap will need to be watered at first to start off fermentation with a hose or watering can.

3 Cover the stack to keep off rain, turn it every 6-7 days, watering if necessary.

4 Fill a box with the compost. Size should be at least 5in (12.5cm) deep. Place the spawn on top.

5 Alternatively if you are using 'grain spawn', this is scattered evenly over the entire surface.

6 In either case, the spawn is then forked well into the compost, ensuring as even a spread as possible.

7 Once sown, the compost should be well firmed. Leave at least 2in (5cm) of space for the casing.

8 The box can now be placed in a cool shed for about three weeks, or until the fungus forms a white 'mat'.

9 Meanwhile, mix up the casing. Use two parts by volume of sphagnum peat, to one of chalk.

10 This must be thoroughly watered, until it is quite moist, as this is the chief source of moisture.

11 Fill the box to the top with the casing material, and then replace it in the shed for a further 5-8 weeks.

12 Finally, small clumps of 'pinheads' will start to arise, followed by larger heads.

Onions

1 Onion sets can be started in the greenhouse. Fill a box with soil-less compost and firm lightly.

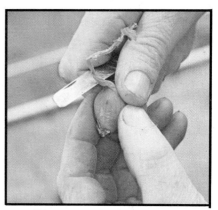

2 Trim the top of the sets to remove the dead remains of leaves to prevent birds pulling them up.

3 Place the sets in the seed trays over gentle heat. This will give them a good start in wet seasons.

Peas

Potatoes

1 Before sowing peas, dig the ground deeply and then firm it by treading with your weight on your heels.

4 Stretch a tight garden line, and take out a shallow, flat-bottomed drill using a spade.

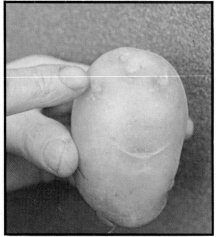

1 Chitting potato seed will improve the weight of crop. Look for the end with the most eyes.

2 Generally peas don't need a fertiliser dressing, but on infertile soil it could be worthwhile.

5 Sow the peas in a double row. Early peas in cold soil can be sown a little more thickly than normal.

2 Place the tubers upright in a shallow tray; the end with the most eyes in it should be uppermost.

3 Rake the soil down to a fine tilth, at the same time raking the fertiliser in to the top two inches.

6 Cover the drill with soil, and protect the emerging seedlings against birds with wire netting.

3 The trays should now be placed where they will receive maximum light but not too much heat.

Shallots

4 When lifting potatoes you will damage the tubers less, if you lift from the side of the row.

7 To clamp potatoes outside, start by building the tubers into a conical heap on a layer of clean straw.

1 The land for shallots should be prepared by deep digging incorporating manure or compost.

5 If the potatoes are for storage, lift them and lay them out in the sun for a few hours to dry.

8 Cover the heap with straw, and then throw a layer of soil over it, a few inches thick, to keep out frost.

2 In the early spring, as soon as the soil is dry enough, consolidate it by systematic treading.

6 The old haulm should now be carted away. It is best to burn it to kill off pests and disease spores.

9 Leave a 'chimney' of straw at the top to allow the heap to breathe, and firm the soil covering.

3 Shallots will benefit from a pre-planting dressing of a general fertiliser such as Growmore.

4 Trim the dead foliage from the tops before planting to prevent birds pulling out the bulbs.

7 When the foliage begins to die down, lift the bulbs carefully, raising them to break the roots.

1 If bare-rooted plants arrive when planting is impossible, heel them in by covering the roots with soil.

5 Place the bulbs about 6in (15cm) apart in rows set the same distance apart. Do not push them in.

8 In a few days, the bulbs can be lifted out of the soil completely and cleaned of excess soil.

2 Dig out a large hole, giving plenty of room to spread out the roots to their full width.

6 Now replace the soil, aiming to just leave the tip of the bulb showing above the soil surface.

9 Place the plants into shallow boxes, or lay them out on a path to dry before storing them.

3 To give the roots every chance of getting going straight away, fork over the bottom of the hole.

4 A little bone-meal sprinkled on the heap of soil you have dug out, will give the new roots a good start.

7 The hole can now be filled and trodden once more to make sure that the soil is really firm.

10 When planting container-grown trees, water the pot well first and then remove the plastic container.

5 Hammer in the stake and then set the tree against it, spreading out the roots to their full spread.

8 As a precaution against bark damage by rabbits and cats, fit a plastic tree guard round the stem.

11 Make sure that the tree is planted at the right level by setting a stake across the hole.

6 Cover the roots with top-soil, and work it between them. Firm with your heel as filling progresses.

9 All young trees must be firmly tied. Use a patent tree-tie or a pad of sacking and strong string.

12 In dry weather, container-grown plants may dry out. In the early stages water them.

Soft fruit

1 Before planting, eradicate weeds. Spray with Weedol for annuals, or Tumbleweed for perennials.

4 Before planting container-grown plants, give the pots a good watering, remove the container.

7 Blackcurrants are an exception to the rule. These should be set a little lower than they grew before.

2 Prepare the whole area well by double digging incorporating well rotted manure or compost.

5 Dig out a hole big enough to comfortably take the root ball. Sprinkle a handful of bone-meal.

8 Bare-rooted plants need plenty of room. The hole must be big enough to take the full spread.

3 If, when the plants arrive, the roots are on the dry side, soak them for a few hours in water.

6 It is important to plant at the right level. Most plants are set at the level they grew on the nursery.

9 Work a little of the best of the topsoil in around the roots with your fingers before refilling.

10 As refilling progresses, consolidate the soil around the roots with your heel to make sure it is really firm.

11 Raspberries are best planted in a trench previously prepared by digging in manure or compost.

12 After planting, mulch with manure or compost to help conserve water and reduce weed growth.

13 Pruning should be done a week or two after planting. Cut raspberries back to about 9in (23 cm).

14 With redcurrants, whitecurrants and gooseberries, reduce the previous season's growth by half.

15 Blackcurrants are grown on a stool, so they should be pruned right down to the ground.

Blackberries

1 Blackberries should be planted against training wires. Dig compost or manure into the hole.

2 To assist root formation, sprinkle a handful of bone-meal onto the pile of soil you have dug out.

3 Place the plant at the level it grew in the nursery and spread out the roots to their full extent.

Blackcurrants

4 Push back a little soil with your foot, at the same time holding the plant at the correct level.

5 As refilling progresses, firm the soil round the roots with your heel. Firm planting is essential.

6 After planting, the main shoot should be cut back to a bud about three buds from soil level.

1 Blackcurrants should be planted on well-prepared soil. Dig a hole big enough to take the full root spread.

2 Plant deeper than the plants were on the nursery, and prune back hard to encourage growth.

3 Soft fruit can also be planted at any time of the year provided the plants have been grown in containers.

4 After planting, firm well and water the plants in. They will wilt at first, but will soon recover.

5 New plants can be propagated from existing beds. Peg down runners with a wire 'staple'.

6 Alternatively, runners can be pegged into pots of compost for bringing inside for an early crop.

Pears

1 Pears will do well trained as espaliers up a fence or wall. Fix up stout wires before planting.

4 Dig a hole big enough for the full spread of the roots. Plant so that the rootstock is above soil level.

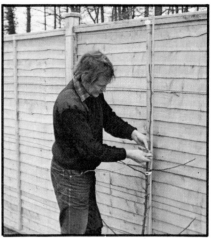

7 The main stem of the tree is now tied to a training cane which in turn is tied to the wires.

2 Prepare the whole area in the autumn, digging in plenty of well rotted manure or compost.

5 If the soil is heavy, lighten it with a little peat before refilling around the roots.

8 Treat the side branches in the same way, tying to a cane to prevent chafing against the wires.

3 Before planting the tree, check the roots for damage. Broken parts should be trimmed back cleanly.

6 As filling proceeds, it is important to firm the soil in layers not more than 6in (15cm) deep.

9 Prune the leader and the side branches by a third, cutting back to an outward facing growth bud.

Raspberries

1 Weedy land should first be thoroughly cleaned. Do this by spraying with weedkiller.

4 When the plants arrive, the roots may well be on the dry side. Soak them for a few hours.

7 Go along the row firming each plant in with your heel and at the same time making it upright.

2 As long before planting as possible, prepare the land well, working in manure or compost.

5 Set out the plants at the correct distances, leaning them against the back "wall" of the trench.

8 After planting, the canes are pruned back to about 9in (23cm) to encourage new growth.

3 Mark out the rows, and take out a trench one spade deep, trying to maintain a clean "wall" at the back.

6 Cover the roots with soil, making sure that the plants are set a little lower than at the nursery.

9 Give the row a good, thick mulch with well-rotted manure or compost to conserve moisture.

Redcurrants

Strawberries

1 When planting redcurrants, dig a hole large enough to take the full extent of the roots.

4 As refilling progresses, firmly consolidate the soil around the roots by treading every 6in (15cm).

1 Good preparation will pay dividends in the long run. Remove perennial weeds before planting.

2 Bushes should be grown on a "leg", so plant at the level they grew in the nursery.

5 Measure out for the next plant. Redcurrants need about 5ft (1.5m) between plants.

2 Raised beds will improve badly drained land. Soil dug out from the pathways can be used.

3 Before refilling, scatter a handful of bone-meal on the soil you have dug out. This stimulates root action.

6 After planting, prune the shoots back by about half, or harder still if growth has been weak.

3 Land must be consolidated before planting. Either allow for natural settlement, or tread firm.

4 Apply a dressing of fertiliser before planting. Do not use nitrogen at this stage or soft growth will result.

5 Rake the fertiliser into the top of the bed, at the same time making a fine and level surface for planting.

6 Make sure that the crown of the plant is not buried. Too deep planting may result in rotting.

7 Set the plants out to a line. They should be 18in (45cm) apart with 30in (76cm) between the rows.

8 After planting, settle the plants in with a good soaking. Plants should never go short of water.

9 To propagate strawberries, simply select a healthy runner from a good plant and peg it into the ground.

10 Alternatively, runners can be pegged into pots to avoid root disturbance when transplanting.

11 A mulch of straw between the plants will protect fruit from dirt and the attentions of slugs.

12 Birds seem to like strawberries as much as we do, so the crop will need protecting.

Fruit propagation

1 Propagate gooseberries from cuttings taken in September-October.

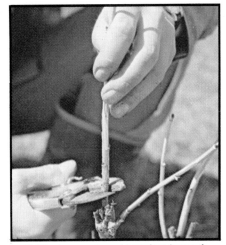

4 Blackcurrants can be taken in much the same way, but leave them until leaf-fall. Trim to below a leaf bud.

7 Raspberries are easily propagated by digging up suckers and replanting them.

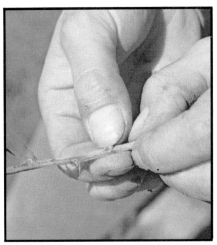

2 It has been common practice to remove some buds. This is no longer recommended.

5 The easiest way to plant the cuttings, after dipping in hormone rooting powder is down a spade.

8 Cut the root into pieces about 1½in (4cm) long, using a slanting cut at the top and straight at the bottom.

3 Insert the cuttings into a moist, but well drained soil, in the open about 6in (15cm) deep. Firm well.

6 On light soils, they can be planted so that only two or three buds are above the soil.

9 Insert the cuttings vertically, into boxes of compost, making sure that the lower end is the bottom.

Tomatoes

1 When direct sowing tomatoes, the seed must first be pre-germinated on a piece of absorbent paper.

4 When the gel is cool, the seeds should be stirred into it carefully, so roots are not damaged.

7 Pour into the drill a starter solution of liquid fertiliser and cover it with soil before sowing.

2 Place the container in a warm spot, and when the tiny radicles emerge, wash the seeds into a sieve.

5 Pour the gel into a special plastic bottle. Alternatively, a polythene bag can be used.

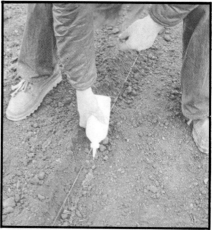

8 Pour the gel and seedlings into the drill and cover with soil. Water well afterwards.

3 In the meantime, make up a gel, using wallpaper paste, or preferably a special gel powder.

6 Prepare the ground in the normal way for sowing, but the seed drill should be about 2in (5cm) deep.

9 The drills should now be covered with cloches which can be removed when the plants outgrow them.

Frames

1 Prepare the frame for sowing, early in the season by keeping the glass closed and banking up with straw. Apply good dressing of fertiliser.

2 Just before sowing, rake the soil down to a fine tilth, also raking in the fertiliser. Ensure, too, that the soil is sufficiently moist.

3 Correct spacing is even more important when sowing in the frame than in the open ground. Always make straight drills, using a board or cane.

4 Sow the seeds at the appropriate depth, covering them lightly and firm the soil. Afterwards replace the glass, until the seedlings germinate.

Preserving | Freezing

1 Beans, and many other vegetables can be preserved in salt. Use only pure salt.

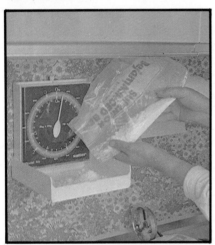

2 Weigh out the salt and the beans, using three times the weight of vegetables to one of salt.

3 Salt and vegetables are put in the jar in alternate layers, starting off with a layer of salt.

1 To freeze chops, interleave with foil so that they can be used individually.

2 Joint chickens if they are to be used for casseroles etc. Store drumsticks separately.

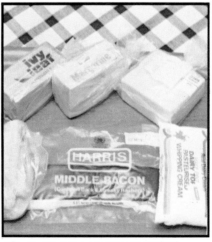

3 Perishable and vacuum packed food is best put into the freezer in small amounts.

4 Mushrooms should be wiped with a damp cloth, de-stalked and open frozen to avoid sticking.

5 Once they are frozen, they can be packed into separate freezer bags. Pack the caps and stalks separately.

6 To freeze cauliflower, cut into separate florets, blanch 3-4 minutes in boiling water.

7 Once they have been blanched, plunge into iced water to cool as quickly as possible.

10 To freeze liquids, place a freezer bag into a container and fill. Cream tubs and foil can also be used.

13 Citrus fruits can be sliced and frozen, or pulled into segments and frozen in a container.

8 Place the florets in seed trays or Hampster free flow trays and open freeze.

11 The procedure for meat dishes is similar. When frozen hard, remove from the carton to store.

14 To freeze left-over cream, whisk stiff and freeze in margarine tubs, or pipe onto foil and open freeze.

9 Tomatoes can be frozen whole, made into a puree and frozen like that, or even made into a soup.

12 It is best if fruit and crumble are frozen separately, pies are wrapped and pancakes interleaved with foil.

15 Small amounts of leftovers, purees, lemon juice and herbs can all be frozen in icecube trays.

Bean sprouts

1 Put a handful of Mung beans to soak in some tepid water. Place in the airing cupboard for 24 hours.

4 Fill the jar threequarters full with lukewarm water, shake vigorously for about one minute.

7 Each morning and evening, rinse, shake and drain until the sprouts are ready to eat in about three days.

2 Strain the beans into a fine mesh sieve and rinse. Put a tablespoonful in the bottom of a clean glass jar.

5 Drain the water through the muslin lid. Repeat the process – fill, shake vigorously and drain.

8 Wash thoroughly, removing the bean 'coat'. They can be eaten straight away or stored in the fridge.

3 Cover the mouth of the jar with a piece of muslin and secure tightly with a rubber band.

6 Make sure that the seeds are nicely damp but not lying in water. Place jar on its side in the airing cupboard.

9 The beans are delicious raw in salads or cooked in some of those mouth-watering Chinese recipes.

Fruit — planting

Colour guide on page 147

ALONG with trees, shrubs and lawns, fruit growing is one of the more permanent aspects of gardening. Apart from strawberries, twelve years or so is the very least one would expect to keep soft fruit and, if properly looked after, tree fruit can still be going strong after forty or fifty years.

This will only be possible though if thorough site preparations are carried out. Once the trees or bushes are in position, there is nothing you can do to improve the ground under them.

Soil Preparation

With the exception of strawberries and, on well drained land raspberries, double digging is vital for incorporating plenty of bulky organic matter and making sure that the drainage is adequate. Where only single digging is felt necessary, this must still be done thoroughly to break up the soil and add organic matter to it.

Only if the land is extremely acid will any lime need to be added as, although they will tolerate a wide variation, all fruits prefer a slightly acid soil.

Some fertilizer will be wanted to get the youngsters established and, although bone meal has been the time honoured material, a handful of Growmore well mixed into the planting position will do more good. It provides all three of the major plant foods and not just phosphates.

Planting

The most important factor when planting is to ensure that the plants are set at the correct depth. Apples, for example, must not be planted too deeply, while blackcurrants will do better planted deeper than they were on the nursery. Correct depths are explained fully in the cultural instructions for each fruit.

Generally though, the principles are the same.

Where it wasn't possible to get hold of enough farmyard manure etc to treat the whole area to be planted, you can get away with forking some into the bottom of the planting hole and mixing more with the soil you took out. Although this is something of a second best, it will at least ensure that the plants have the best possible conditions to start with.

When digging out the hole, be sure it is wide enough and deep enough to accommodate the root system when fully spread out and remember that roots are meant to grow downwards, not upwards, so leave a slight mound in the bottom of the hole.

Having set in the plant at the correct level, put back the soil, a little at a time, firming it down as you go.

Fruit — planting

Colour guide on page 147

Fruit trees must be staked in their early years to stop them blowing about in the wind and dislodging the roots.

If, after planting, you can give them a mulch of farmyard manure, straw or peat it will help a lot in conserving moisture during the first vital year.

Now that most fruit trees and bushes can be bought in containers, you can plant all the year round but, with traditional bare rooted material, these should only be planted in the dormant season, i.e. when they are leafless.

November and March are probably the best months for this but any time between these is perfectly all right so long as the weather is reasonable and the soil in good condition.

In the case of strawberries, we have a rather different routine. In order to get a good crop in the first year, planting should take place no later than September, and August is the ideal time. It isn't always easy to do this as the supply of young plants at that time of year is limited but it's worth paying extra and getting pot-grown plants. Bare rooted ones planted after September will only give a very small crop in their first year.

Aftercare

By far the most important job is to make sure that the newly planted fruit has adequate water in its first summer. Quick establishment makes all the difference to the success of the operation.

Another thing we can do is to give the plants a foliar feed as soon as the leaves are large enough to hold the spray. This gets them growing even sooner.

Strawberry planting.

Work the soil around roots of fruit trees.

Apples

Colour guide on page 147

BECAUSE these are undoubtedly the most popular fruit in Great Britain, a lot of research has gone into growing them. It is now possible for any householder, with no matter how small a garden, to grow at least a few trees.

Today we can grow apple trees against a fence with as little as a yard between each.

Soil and Site

Apples will tolerate a wide variety of soils from acid and sandy ones to heavy clays and alkaline chalk or limestone.

The one thing all these must have in common, though, is enough depth of fertile and well drained soil for the extensive root systems to work in. There must be at least 18in (45cm) of this; hence the need for double-digging.

There isn't usually a great deal we can do about the overall lie of the land in one's garden, but we can take steps to put minor faults right and so make the place more suitable for fruit.

The first is to provide adequate shelter from strong winds either by carefully choosing where you plant or by erecting a fence or putting in a hedge or windbreak to create a more hospitable environment. Not only will fewer fruits be blown off but pollination will be better as well.

There's very little we can do about the susceptibility of an area to spring frosts but it's as well to be aware of the risk and be ready to take action at blossom time.

A low lying garden surrounded by higher land is always likely to suffer and you can even get trouble on sloping ground if cold air cannot drain away to a lower point. A tall hedge can cause this problem if it prevents cold air escaping.

Apples need plenty of sun to ripen them and bring out the flavour so avoid planting them where they are in the shade. A south or west aspect is always best.

Pollination

Few varieties of apple will set a worthwhile crop if there is not another variety close at hand to pollinate them. This problem tends not to be so acute in towns as the gardens are usually smaller and, consequently, neighbouring trees are nearer.

Always have a look around before ordering apple trees and, if you can't see any others close by, plant more than one variety yourself and make sure that they are compatible. The table on page 167 shows which to choose to ensure adequate pollination.

Apples

Colour guide on page 147

Rootstocks

Today, no fruit tree is grown commercially from seeds or cuttings. The resulting plant would either not be true to variety or the habit of growth would be unpredictable.

All fruit trees are budded or grafted onto a ready-made root system called the rootstock.

There are many different types of these but, for garden purposes, we can restrict the number to three or four.

M9 produces a very small tree that comes into bearing quickly. However, good soil is essential and, because the roots are brittle, the trees need staking throughout their life.

M26 gives a slightly larger tree and is suitable for use where the soil is not good enough for M9.

MM106 is certainly the most useful stock for gardens with no varieties. The trees are of intermediate vigour and many different tree forms grow well on them.

It is vital when planting apples to ensure that the joint between the rootstock and the variety is above the ground and the tree roots above the stock or the beneficial, growth regulating properties will be lost.

Tree forms

With all these different rootstocks to choose from, it is now possible to grow apple trees of virtually any shape or size you want.

Here are some of the most common ones.

Standard. This is the largest tree of all and is really only suitable where space is unlimited as there is normally 5–6ft (1.5–2m) of trunk even before you reach the bottom branches.

Half standard. This also makes a fairly large tree but it can be useful for planting in a lawn or border as a specimen the 3–4ft (1-1.2m) trunk making it quite easy to mow or cultivate beneath.

MM111 is a good rootstock for half standards and, where more than one is to be planted, they should be about 20ft (6m) apart.

The pruning of these is the same as for bush trees.

Bush Trees. This is the smallest form of free-growing tree (lightly pruned and not trained) and is suitable for gardens where a traditionally shaped tree is wanted. It doesn't reach any great height if looked after properly and all picking and pruning can usually be done from the ground or at worst a set of steps, the trunk being little more than 18in (45cm) tall.

MM106 is the normal rootstock although, on really poor land. MM111

James Grieve on M27 rootstock.

Cordon grown fruit.

Stake trees well.

might be needed for its extra vigour.

Although it will vary with the strength of the variety, 15ft (4.5m) apart would be about right where more than one tree is planted.

There are two simple ways of pruning bush, half standard and standard trees; the easier being called the "Regulated System".

All this involves is keeping the trees open to the fresh air and sunshine by the removal, in the winter, of any small branches that are in the wrong place. These will normally be confined to those that are too tall, those that are crossing over others and any diseased, broken or otherwise damaged ones.

Bramley and Newton Wonder react

well to this form of pruning but many dessert varieties tend to overcrop and produce a lot of small fruits. For these, the "Renewal System" is better.

This is also a fairly light method of pruning and is aimed at the continual production of new shoots to replace old ones as they grow too large or bend down too much.

Apples

Colour guide on page 147

Cut out dead or decayed branches.

Clean up cuts with a sharp knife.

Dwarf Pyramids. These come somewhere between a bush and a cordon in that they are small and fruitful trees but no wires etc are needed for training.

Where the soil is good, M9 or M26 would be suitable rootstocks but, where it is questionable, MM106 is a safer bet.

The trees can be planted 3½–4ft (1–1.2m) apart with 6 or 7ft (1.8–2m) between rows. They will need staking throughout their lives.

Dwarf pyramids need special pruning "from birth" and, where a one-year-old is planted the main stem should be cut back to 20in (50cm) high and any side-shoots to 5–6in (12.5–15cm) after winter planting.

Once the central leader has reached about 7ft (2m) in height, it is cut out to the branch below it and no further leader pruning is required.

As this pruning involves a lot of shortening back of the side shoots, varieties that bear their fruit at the tips of the branches such as Worcester Pearmain and Laxton's Superb are better grown in another way.

Cordons. This is a popular and space-saving system in which the trees crop early in their life.

The same rootstocks and planting distances can be used as for the dwarf pyramids.

Two horizontal supporting wires will be needed either between stakes, in the open, or against a wall or fence. These should be 2–3ft (60cm–1m) and 5ft (1.5m) above ground. The trees should be planted at an angle of 45°.

One-year-old tip-bearing varieties should then be cut back by a quarter but all others should be left unpruned. The larger side-shoots on one-year-olds are pruned back to three buds beyond the cluster of leaves found at the base of the shoots.

The glory of cordons is that all pruning can and should be done in July and September.

Feeding

In common with most other fruit crops, apples need an all-round fertiliser to keep the balance between growth and fruiting, but the emphasis must be on potash.

Where growth is adequate, a tomato or rose fertiliser will give this but, where it is poor, more nitrogen will be needed and Growmore would be more suitable. Early spring is the time to apply it.

Burn all cuttings.

VARIETIES

For full pollination, choose two or more varieties from the same group.
X indicates varieties that will not pollinate.

Variety	Dessert or Culinary	Time of use	Pollinator class
George Cave	D	Aug	A
Discovery	D	Aug–Sep	B
Emneth Early	C	July–Aug	B
Worcester Pearmain	D	Sept–Oct	B
Grenadier	C	Aug–Sep	B
James Grieve	D	Sep–Oct	B
Fortune	D	Sep–Oct	X
Ellisons Orange	D	Sep–Oct	C
Lord Lambourne	D	Sep–Nov	A
Egremont Russet	D	Oct–Dec	A
Howgate Wonder	C	Oct–Jan	C
Sunset	D	Nov–Dec	B
Blenheim Orange	DC	Nov–Jan	B
Bramleys Seedling	C	Nov–Feb	X
Cox's Orange Pippin	D	Nov–Jan	B
Laxton's Superb	D	Nov–Feb	X
Malling Kent	D	Dec–Feb	B
Idared	D	Dec–Apr	A
Tydemans Late Orange	D	Dec–Apr	C
Lanes Prince Albert	C	Dec–Mar	C

Pears

Colour guide on page 151

ALL that has been said about apples with regard to soils, sites and pollination applies equally well to pears although they are rather more tolerant of poor soil conditions. Also, they blossom 1–2 weeks earlier, so frost protection is more important.

Rootstocks

Pears are grown on quince roots and the semi-vigorous **Quince A** is virtually universal. **Quince C** is more dwarfing but it is only used where soil conditions are exceptionally good and the fruiting variety is very vigorous.

As with apples, pears must be planted so that the union between variety and rootstock is a good 3in (7.5cm) above ground. If the fruiting variety is allowed to root into the soil, the vigour of the tree will be drastically increased at the expense of the fruit.

Tree forms

These are exactly the same as those mentioned for apples except that standards and half-standards are very seldom planted in gardens due to their potentially great size.

Bush trees are certainly the most suitable and manageable type of tree.

Planting and pruning

Quince roots being somewhat stronger than apple, the natural life of a stake put in at planting is usually all the support required. Plant at 12–15ft (3.5–4.5m) between trees.

The pruning of bush pears differs somewhat from that of apples as pears take longer to come into bearing. As a general rule, therefore, the less you prune them the better.

Following winter planting, a maiden tree is cut back to 30in (75cm) and any "feathers" (side shoots) are halved in length.

Next winter, the central leader and the side shoots wanted as main branches are pruned back by 1/3rd. Any other less vigorous shoots can be left to fruit providing they don't restrict the tree's growth.

By the following winter enough shoots should have grown to form the main branches and the central leader can be cut back to the branch below it.

The branch leaders and any other shoots you wish to keep for branches are cut back by 1/3rd.

Subsequent pruning is along the lines of the Regulated System except that light tipping of young shoots to form new branches will be needed to encourage side shoots.

Pear, Louise Bonne de Jersey.

VARIETIES

For full pollination, choose two or more varieties from the same group.

Variety	Dessert or Culinary	Time of Use	Pollinator class
Williams Bon Chretian	D	Sept.	B
Laxton's Forecast		Sept.–Oct.	C
Louise Bonne de Jersey		Oct.	A
Beurre Hardy		Oct.	B
Conference		Oct.–Nov.	B
Seckle	D	Oct.–Nov.	A
Doyenne du Comice	D	Nov.	C

All pears can be used for culinary or dessert purposes, but those marked "D" have a superior flavour for eating.

Plums

Plums

THE unreliability of these largely accounts for their lack of popularity but very good crops can be grown, particularly in the East, if conditions are right for them.

Soil and site

They like a deep fertile soil, preferably light with adequate amounts of nitrogen, potash and lime.

Plums flower earlier than apples and pears, so a sheltered and frost-free site is a big help.

Pollination

There are two things to consider here. First, the early flowering means that there are fewer pollinating insects about, so in cold springs they may be unreliable. But, pollination is helped by the fact that a few varieties will set a good crop with their own pollen. Where only one tree is wanted, therefore, choose a self-fertile variety.

Rootstocks

St. Julien A is the most suitable one for gardens. If **Myrobalan** is used, it will result in too large a tree for most sites.

Tree forms

Only the smaller types of tree should be grown.

Bush trees. Even with these, 12–15ft (3.5–4.5m) should be allowed between them.

They should be staked when planted but, once the stake has outlived its usefulness, it won't need to be replaced.

Pruning is best done in the spring so that the fungus disease "Silver Leaf" has less chance of infecting the wounds.

When planting a maiden tree, it should be cut back to 3ft (1m). Any "feathers" are left unpruned but those growing below 2ft (60cm) high will not be required for branches and are best shortened to 4–5in (10–12.5cm) in the summer.

Next spring, choose 3 or 4 well placed shoots of near equal vigour and cut them back by half. Remove all others.

In a year's time, shorten all shoots you want for branches by half and cut out any badly placed or crossing ones.

Repeat this in the fourth spring but, thereafter, only leader shortening (by about $\frac{1}{3}$) and the removal of unwanted shoots will be needed.

Dwarf pyramids. These should only need staking where the site is exposed. Trees are best planted 12–15ft apart. After planting, cut the maiden tree back to 5ft (1.5m) and any feathers by half. Remove any below 18in (45cm).

Growth has usually stopped by the second half of July and this is the best time to prune. In the first and all following summers, branch leaders should be cut back to 8in (20cm) and any new side shoots to 6in (15cm).

The next April, and every year thereafter, the central leader is shortened by $\frac{2}{3}$rds

Victoria plum.

Plums

Plum, Laxton's Delicious.

Plum, Denniston's Superb.

until it has reached about 9ft (2.7m) when it is cut back to 1in (2.5cm).

Fan trained. These need a lot of room — 15–18ft (4.5–5.5m) each.

A west facing wall or fence is best but an east or south one can be used for early maturing varieties. They should be equipped with horizontal wires 6–9 in (15–23cm) apart.

When growth begins in spring remove all buds that point towards or away from the wall. In July pinch out tips of unwanted side shoots, and then shorten these shoots by half after cropping.

Follow this routine until the required space is filled.

To encourage "fruiting spurs", any shoots that are not wanted as branches should be pinched back to 5–6in (12–15cm) several times during the summer and cut back to a fruit bud in the autumn. Any that are obviously too strong are best cut out when first seen. Once the space is filled, all growths are treated in this way.

Plum, Marjories Seedling.

VARIETIES

'SF' indicates that the variety is self-fertile and needs no pollinator, but will pollinate those in its group.

Variety	Dessert or Culinary	Time of Use	Pollinator class
Early Laxton	D	July/Aug.	B
Early Rivers	C	July/Aug.	B
Czar	C	Aug.	B.SF
Oulin's Golden Gage	D	Aug.	C.SF
Purple Pershore	C	Aug.	B.SF
Denniston's Superb	D	Aug.	A.SF
Victoria	DC	Aug./Sept.	B.SF
Cambridge Gage	D	Aug./Sept.	C
Severn Cross	D	Sept.	B.SF
Marjories Seedling	C	Sept./Oct.	D.SF

Peaches

THESE are hardier than one imagines but, in spite of this, it's best to grow them fan-trained against a wall or fence with a south or west aspect.

They respond well to plenty of organic matter in the ground but, in other respects, the soils and sites are the same as those recommended for plums.

As with plums, poor pollination and spring frosts are the greatest hazards so it usually pays to pollinate by hand using a bit of cotton wool. Drape an old sheet or some polythene over the trees when frost threatens.

Pruning

Forming a fan-trained tree is done in just the same way as it is for plums but, because peaches fruit only on last year's shoots, pruning for fruit once the fan has been formed, is different.

The system to adopt is as follows. Once the formation of the fan is advancing well, as many shoots of the previous season's growth as can be accommodated comfortably are tied into the wires. From the base of these shoots a number of new ones will start to grow in the spring. Allow up to two of these to develop and tie them in. Also tie in the leading bud on the existing shoot if there is room for it.

Where the developing fruit has a shoot growing from its base and where there isn't room for the leader to grow, pinch these back to 2in (5cm) and later, any further growth they have made to 1in (2.5cm).

After fruiting, the shoots that bore fruit are cut out to leave the one or two retained at the base to take their place.

Thinning

Following a good blossom "set", the fruit will need to be thinned. This is done in two stages. When they are about the size of a marble, thin them out to one every 4–5in (10–12.5cm) and later, when something like a walnut in size, to one fruit every 9in (23cm).

Varieties

In order of ripening, **Duke of York, Early Rivers, Rochester** and **Royal George** are all good but **Peregrine**, ready in early August, is probably the best all-rounder.

Peach, Peregrine.

Peach, Prince of Wales.

Peach blossom.

Fruit pruning

PRUNING is a job which can be done over a longer period than most — from leaf fall in autumn to bud burst in the spring.

Judging by the results in many gardens it is usually neglected and so the full benefits of having fruit are lost.

The typical neglected tree, say, an apple or gooseberry, is usually particularly obvious in winter when the leaves have fallen because the centre is overcrowded with shoots and branches. It follows from this that fruit is difficult to pick, usually small in size because there is too much of it, often of poor colour because of lack of light getting in to the bush and possibly affected by disease because of the crowded conditions and limited air movement in the centre. All these can be improved by pruning. Simply starting with tidying up the tree or bush often gives a big improvement.

Broken branches

Any broken or damaged shoots should obviously come out. Small cuts are made with sharp secateurs, large ones with, preferably, a special pruning saw with a coarse blade on one side and a fine one on the other. A handyman's saw will do, except that it is often broad and may not fit into some of the small spaces on trees.

When taking out a large branch, remove it back close to the one which is to be left in the tree so that it will heal over quickly and cleanly. Leaving a long snag invites die back and provides an entry for further problems.

Where the branch to come out is a heavy one it can break halfway through if it is cut from the top side only, sometimes stripping the bark down and making a large wound. If this is likely to happen, start by cutting upwards on the underside of the branch at an angle to correspond with the angle of the downward cut. Then the branch should snap off cleanly under its own weight. To make a perfect job, trim the rough sawn surface smooth with a knife and to be extra careful paint large cuts (over say 1 in (2.5 cm) diameter) with a special bituminous wound-protecting paint such as P.B.I. Arbrex. This resists any organism which tries to enter the wound through the cut.

A start has been made by cutting out broken and damaged branches — including any that have been rubbing against their neighbour. If you have to choose the one to remove, leave in the one which is least damaged and best placed in the tree. A little thought at this stage, trying to visualise the effect of taking out one branch or the other, is worth a lot of regret afterwards that the wrong one has

been removed. The ideal arrangement for branches is to be spaced out like the spokes on a wheel and by aiming for this, each branch will have the maximum amount of space, light and air.

Next look for any dead or diseased wood and cut this out. Do not bother at this stage with small shoots, otherwise you can find you have spent time on details when the whole branch has to come out because another part of it has something wrong.

Having tidied up your neglected tree by pruning out dead, diseased, damaged and broken branches, it should already be looking more open and much less crowded, particularly in the centre.

This may be just the moment to stop pruning this year! Judge this by looking at what lies on the ground and comparing with what still remains in the tree. If more than say, $\frac{1}{8}$ to $\frac{1}{4}$ of the tree has already gone, leave the rest of the tree alone. Otherwise, the reaction to hard pruning can be a lot of unwanted growth and cropping can be reduced. This especially applies to a tree which is growing vigorously, but the chances are that one which is not making very much growth can, with benefit, be pruned fairly hard and will not grow too strongly.

If in doubt about how much to take off a neglected tree, better to spread the job over two to three seasons and bring it round to better shape, improved fruit size, increased colour and less disease, in a gradual fashion. At least a start has been made and the tree should already look a lot tidier as a result of this "good housekeeping".

Where the tree is already of good shape and fairly open, the main need may well be for a reduction in the complicated spur system on which the fruit is carried. Over a period of time these tend to become large and complicated and there are too many in the tree, so that it tends to produce a heavy crop of small fruit. In this case, thin out the spurs so they are smaller in size.

Pruning on its own, of course, is not the only treatment required by fruit and you may want to continue the job with a winterwash and feeding.

Raspberries, blackberries and loganberries

Colour guide on page 148

Raspberries

A popular crop nowadays as they freeze well.

Soils and fertilisers. They dislike cold and wet soils but, being surface rooting, respond well to mulches of farmyard manure which is more important than depth of soil. Potash is needed so an annual dressing of a tomato or rose fertiliser is necessary. Where growth is poor, this should be replaced by Growmore.

Propagation and planting. Due to their extreme susceptibility to virus diseases, it is always wise to buy in fresh and clean stock when replanting.

Plant the canes during the dormant season 18in (45cm) apart and with the roots about 3in (7.5cm) deep. Now cut them down to 9–12in (23–30cm) high.

Support. The canes will need this and the simplest form is a single strong wire, 4–5ft (1.2–1.5m) above the ground, strained between posts.

Pruning. The usual way is to cut the fruited canes right out soon after picking and tie in the new ones for next year. In exposed areas, though, the old canes can give some winter protection and the job can be left until early spring.

Autumn fruiting varieties should not be pruned till February when all growth is cut to the ground.

Varieties. Summer fruiting — **Malling Promise** and **Glen Clova**. Autumn fruiting — **September** and **Zeva**.

Blackberries and Loganberries

Both are well worth growing if you like them and have the room. Loganberries are the easier to handle and they take up less room.

Soils and fertilisers. Beyond a deep and moist root run, they have no particular preference but both will benefit from an early spring dressing of Growmore.

Propagation and planting. Both are easily propagated by tip-layering. When a young cane is about 1yd (1m) long, it is bent down and the tip buried 6in (15cm) deep. This will root and produce a young plant that is fit for severing and lifting the following autumn or spring.

Final planting distances vary. Loganberries should be 7–8ft (2–2.5m) apart. Weaker varieties of blackberry will need 8–12ft (2.5–3.5m) and vigorous ones 12–15ft (3.5–4.5m).

Blackberries are often bought container-grown and after planting need pruning back.

Strawberries

Colour guide on page 153

STRAWBERRIES are one of the easiest fruits to grow. Certainly the quickest to come into production, say, 40 weeks to cropping from an August planting, and so they should be in every garden as an introduction to fruit growing.

Buying plants

The main ingredient in the recipe for successful strawberry growing is the choice of planting material. If this is healthy and of a good variety, you can almost guarantee a crop. With early planting (August or early September) for outdoor culture, there is every chance of a good crop in the first year after planting.

The magic word is *"certified"*. The scheme for certification, run by the Ministry of Agriculture in post-war years, means plants have passed two inspections in the growing season. The certificates cover trueness to name and freedom from diseases, particularly viruses. These are very damaging to strawberries, reducing vigour and cropping.

Certification is mainly for commercial producers but the best garden suppliers can also provide certified runners and they are well worth searching out. Those available in August will have been lifted before their second inspection and cannot be sold as certified. But if entered for certification they must have originated from certified stock and will still be well worth having in preference to uncertified plants.

Bed preparation

Having made sure what you are planting, other aspects of strawberry growing are quite simple and show how easy it really is.

Any good garden soil will suit, but a well-drained one, rich in humus will give best results. A dressing of garden compost or well-rotted manure plus sulphate of potash at $\frac{1}{2}$oz per sq yd (15gm per sq m) and bonemeal at 2oz per sq yd (60gm per sq m) well worked in before planting could often last right through the three, or at the most, four crops you should expect before the bed is due to be replaced.

These apparent limited requirements for fertiliser result from runners, during propagation accumulating a lot of the nutrients required later on in life. Then mature plants in a well-drained soil will usually find the rest.

Propagation

The point about healthy runners for planting cannot be stressed enough. Do not try to propagate plants unless they are healthy (growing vigorously and

Strawberries in the traditional 'pot'.

Strawberries

Colour guide on page 153

Keep the fruits off the ground with straw.

Strawberries grown in a barrel.

cropping well). Only in the first year after planting certified runners will you be safe in propagating your own.

Runners are produced freely by established plants, usually from late June onwards, and will take root wherever they are in contact with moist soil for sufficiently long. Often such plants need help if the runners are to root quickly and well enough to be separated from the parent plants and moved on to their own roots by, say, mid-August. It is easy to lift your own runners in September and later, but this is rather late in the season for best results in the following year.

So to speed things up, put a stone or make a peg to hold down the runner near to the first plantlet. Remove any growth beyond it. Often the soil is hard and dry from walking down the rows picking fruit, so cultivate the soil before rooting starts and keep it moist.

A better practice is to grow the mother plants in isolation, that is, as far apart from fruiting beds as possible. Do not allow them to produce any fruit but devote all their energy to runner production.

For the least check of all in moving runners, dig holes out round the mother

RECOMMENDED VARIETIES

Name	Description	Season of Production
Baron Solemacher	An alpine strawberry with fruits small in size but of characteristic sub-acid flavour. This variety is only propagated from seed sown in spring or autumn and does not produce any runners.	June/October
Cambridge Favourite	A widely-grown variety in commerce, heavy cropping, of average flavour unless the fruit is allowed to ripen on the plant. Can also be grown under cloches. A regular and heavy cropper tolerant of virus diseases.	late June/mid-July
Cambridge Prizewinner	Perhaps the best variety for production under cloches. Fruit large, conical and of good flavour. Average crop yields.	mid-June
Gento	Fruit sweet of slightly musky flavour. A variety which is regularly grown for its long season of production. Removal of blossoms in June tends to concentrate crops in the autumn.	June/October
Grandee	A very large fruited and vigorous variety with rather soft flesh and a slightly sweet acid flavour.	mid–late June
Redgauntlet	This variety produces large fruit which is dark red in colour and only of fair flavour. Of main interest is the ability in many seasons to produce an autumn crop.	mid-late July
Royal Sovereign	The 'Cox's Orange Pippin' of strawberries, of slightly sharp flavour. Very susceptible to disease and yields are often not heavy. Best if grown some distance from other varieties since this variety is very susceptible to virus diseases, carried by other varieties without showing it.	late June/early July
Talisman	A hardy, late variety of good flavour. As beds age the size of fruit tends to fall off and in some situations it is necessary to grow this plant as separate crowns rather than allowing them to form a matted row.	mid–late July

Low net cages keep out the birds.

STRAWBERRY PRODUCTION

Fruit Produced	Production Method	Plant Spacing	Notes
Extra early, say, late April —earlier than this is uneconomic	Heated greenhouse	2 plants round the edge of a 5in (12.5cm) pot or follow instructions for Verti-strawb or Tower pot	Chilling needed to stimulate flower formation
Very early, early–mid May	Unheated greenhouse		
Early, late May–early June	Planted outdoors covered with glass cloches or polythene mid–late February	According to cloches usually in pairs or rows 2ft (60cm) apart with 9in (23cm) between plants	Plant pot-grown runners mid–late August. Glass gives 7/10 days earlier production than polythene
Mid-June	Outdoors	4ft × 9in (122cm × 23cm)	Plant early August for maximum crop in the maiden year.
Normal crop, say, late June/mid-July	Outdoors	2ft 6in × 1ft 6in (75cm × 45cm)	Plant September to early October. With later planting than this de-blossom in the first year. Extend season by choice of varieties.
September/October	Outdoors, covered with polythene to ripen fruit at the end of the season	2ft 6in × 1ft 6in (75cm × 45cm)	Varieties like Redgauntlet capable of producing an autumn crop in many seasons or general varieties for autumn cropping.

Strawberries

Colour guide on page 153

plants and sink pots to their rims in these holes. Fill the pots with compost and peg the runners down as already described.

For quicker results, take the first young plants which are produced at the end of each stolon from the mother plant. Prepare a pot of compost as already described and stick the young plants into the compost around the rim of the pot. Water this well in and cover with a polythene bag. Then keep the pot in a warm place. Roots will start to form in 3 to 5 days according to temperature and the plants should be well enough rooted in 14 to 21 days to be ready for planting out.

Do not forget to "wean" them away from the "hot-house" conditions inside the polythene bag. As a first stage, take it off and when the plants have got over that change of conditions, plant the pots outside for several days to get them used to being outside before knocking the contents of the pot out and separating individual plants.

For very early planting, raise a single plant in each pot.

Planting

Strawberries are fussy about depth of planting. Too high and they never seem to establish and grow well. Too deep and the centre of the plant, the *crown*, seems to be always cramped and does not develop new leaves quickly. On wet soil it may also rot. Plant them so the crown of the plant is just at soil level after it has settled. Time of planting and spacing are shown in the table.

For early planting, expect some difficulty in finding pot-grown plants which will be expensive because of the trouble involved. These earlier crops will, however, produce more fruit if properly tended. Later runners are cheaper but plants put out in September will produce later and lighter crops. Indeed, for plants put out much later than this it is usually advised not to allow them to carry any crop in the following season, but to remove the flowers. Rather than taking this as a "rule of thumb" it is better to judge whether the plants seem sufficiently large to be able to carry the crop before taking this drastic action.

Early planting with high soil temperatures means watering will be necessary until the plants are established. Weeds also will be encouraged with watering under high temperature conditions in late summer and these need to be controlled either by shallow cultivations or chemically.

There are many new systems for the cultivation of strawberries.

Blackcurrants

Colour guide on page 150

Soak roots before planting.

Birds are very fond of blackcurrants too.

A very profitable crop for the land they occupy, with a life expectancy of about 15 years. Extremely rich in Vitamin C.

Soils. A wide range is tolerated, their only real dislikes being thin sandy ones and shallow soils overlying chalk, both of which can be improved.

Site. The early flowering of blackcurrants (usually in the first half of April) makes them particularly susceptible to spring frosts so, where these occur regularly, you ought to think twice before planting unless you can take precautions.

Windy sites should also be avoided as they will have far fewer pollinating insects.

Propagation. Unlike tree fruits, all soft fruits are grown on their own roots without the need for budding or grafting.

Blackcurrants are propagated from 8–10in (20–25cm) long cuttings of the present season's growth taken in October. These are firmed into the ground 8in (20cm) apart with only the top two buds showing.

They will have rooted by next autumn but are best cut back and left for another year to strengthen.

Only use healthy shoots from disease-free bushes for cuttings.

Planting out. Following thorough ground preparation, the young bushes (2yr olds are best) are planted a minimum of 5ft (1.5m) apart and, preferably, 6ft (2m). Autumn is the time for this and the bushes should be planted 1in (2.5cm) or so deeper than they were previously so that the base of all the stems is just underground.

Pruning. Blackcurrants only fruit well on wood less than four years old so an abundant supply of new growth each year is vital. After planting therefore, cut all the young shoots right back to ground level. This will test your nerve but is important for a strong bush.

The bush will not fruit that year, but will make strong shoots for fruiting the following year.

After fruiting, each shoot that has

borne fruit should be cut hard back, either to a young shoot low down or to its point of origin. This should be carried on throughout the bush's life.

Manures and fertilisers. Blackcurrants are gross feeders and need abundant supplies of nitrogen. Every spring the bushes should be given a dressing of a fertiliser rich in this and if possible, a mulch of farmyard manure. On light soils, a further dose of fertiliser straight after picking is very beneficial.

Varieties. New, improved varieties are appearing quite frequently and, although it doesn't always pay to plant one up before a track record has become established, **Ben Lomond** has been consistently good. **Jet** is also to be recommended. The much older **Baldwin** is reliable and crops well but is very frost sensitive.

Redcurrants and gooseberries

Colour guide on page 153

Bonemeal should be added at planting time.

Open containers with a knife to avoid disturbing the root ball.

Red and White currants

Not too widely grown, but, if you like them, well worthwhile as the fresh fruit tends to be pricey.

In every respect the cultivation of the two is the same.

Soils and sites. Although water-logging is not tolerated, they don't need a rich soil and are nowhere near as greedy as blackcurrants though they do share their susceptibility to frost.

Propagation. Because redcurrants are grown on a short trunk (leg) as opposed to a stool like blackcurrants, the 10in (25cm) long cuttings taken in October should have all but the top 4–5 buds removed. The cuttings are set in the ground so that these buds are clear of the soil.

A year later, cut back the resulting growths by half and, after another year, the bushes are ready for planting out 5–6ft (1.5–2m) apart. The new shoots should again be cut back by half.

Pruning. Redcurrants fruit best on "spurs" formed on a permanent framework of branches. Although lateral shoots can be cut back in the winter to form these, a better time is in the summer just before the fruit starts to ripen.

They can also be grown as cordons — very useful where space is scarce. In this case, the 2yr old bush is pruned to leave only two wide-angled shoots. These are shortened to 6in (15cm) each and the resulting leaders are tied to vertical canes 1ft (30cm) apart. Summer pruning is as for bushes.

Varieties. Red Lake and **Laxton's No 1** are the best redcurrants, while **White Versailles** is the best white.

Gooseberries

There are two definite uses for these. Those wanted for cooking or preserving are picked at the end of May whilst those to be eaten as dessert are left another month to ripen.

Soils and sites. Thin, sandy or strongly alkaline soils are disliked so these will need improving, but sites that are suitable for currants will also be fine for gooseberries.

Propagation, planting and pruning. As for redcurrants except that the pruning of fruiting bushes and cordons is only done in the winter.

Varieties. Leveller (dessert) and **Careless** (dual purpose but mainly culinary) are the two main ones but **Keepsake** (dessert) is more tolerant of poor soils.

Fruit — pests and diseases

Colour guide on page 255

PESTICIDES — a collective term for insecticides and fungicides — are indispensable in the garden but should always be used as a last resort.

Gardeners have one great advantage over farmers and growers. They grow on a small scale. Where a farmer needs a massive tractor equipped with sophisticated spraying equipment, or indeed even a helicopter, to control his caterpillars, for example, the gardener can pick them off by hand.

And this should always be the first line of attack. Keep the garden and the greenhouse as clean as possible and keep a constant weather-eye open for the first sign of attack. Often a pest can be effectively controlled by simply removing it physically before it has a chance to spread.

But eventually, the time must come when more drastic measures must be used. But even then, you can reduce the extent of the pest problem and use less chemical by catching it early. It's a useful exercise to take a walk around the garden every evening, just to check on your plants' state of health. That way, as soon as you detect the first sign of trouble, you can whip out the sprayer and nip the little blighters in the bud.

Don't forget those all-important preventative sprays in your spraying programme. There are some pests and diseases that are not apparent until the damage has been done. Perfect examples here are potato blight and codling moth on apples. The first sign of blight is a blackening of the leaves followed by complete collapse of the plants. By that time, the spores will have spread not only to other plants but down to the tubers as well. The first sign of codling moth is that nasty little maggot in the fruit — and we all know what it's like to find half of one of those! Both these pests and a few others *must* be stopped before they start by spraying before they arrive — just in case.

These days, there is a vast armoury of insecticides and fungicides with which to fight just about any foe you are likely to meet. In fact, the choice is perhaps a little too wide for comfort. Go into any garden centre and take a look at the pesticide shelves and you'll come out thinking that you need a veritable chemist's shopful of bottles, puffers, powders and potions. Take heart. It's not nearly as bad as it looks. In fact, you'll get away with about half a dozen different chemicals, even less if you keep your garden clean and tidy and do the recommended picking-off at the first sign of trouble.

But don't get carried away by the

Regular spraying is sometimes unavoidable if crop yields are not to suffer.

desire for convenience. It may at first sight, be an ideal situation if you could find just one insecticide to control every pest in the garden at one go. But if you do that, you will undoubtedly be storing up trouble for yourself. The snag with complete obliteration of every insect pest is that you must at the same time also destroy the insect friends.

Use a powerful wide-spectrum insecticide at fruit blossom time, for example, and you'll also kill all the bees. Then you

won't need to spray against maggots in the fruit because there won't *be* any fruit. There are also many insect predators who will do a remarkable job of controlling some pests without doing any damage to your plants. The best example of this is our friend the ladybird, which devours greenfly at an amazing rate. Killing off ladybirds will very quickly result in a rapid build-up of greenfly.

A few insecticides will only kill one type of pest. These should always be

Fruit — pests and diseases

Colour guide on page 255

Grease banding an apple tree against pests.

PESTS AND DISEASES

Pests affecting all fruit crops

Pest	Principal control chemical	Suggested control where other pests are also present
Aphids	Rapid	Fenitrothion (Fentro) A systemic insecticide
Caterpillars	Fenitrothion (Fentro)	Sybol 2
Sucker	Lindane	Fenitrothion (Fentro) A systemic insecticide
Capsid Bug	Fenitrothion (Fentro)	Sybol 2

Pests affecting specific fruits

Apples and pears

Red Spider Mite	A systemic insecticide	Sybol 2
Apple Sawfly	Lindane	Fenitrothion (Fentro)
Pear Sucker	Malathion	Fenitrothion (Fentro)
Codling Moth	Fenitrothion (Fentro)	

Mildew and scab can be controlled by Benlate, Nimrod T and other systemic fungicides.
Spray every two weeks or so from pre-blossom till mid-July.

Plums and peaches

Red Plum Maggot	Fenitrothion (Fentro) in late July
Peach Leaf Curl	Dithane 945 or Copper Fungicide 1. As the buds are opening 2. During leaf-fall

Black and redcurrants and gooseberries

Big Bud Mite (Blackcurrants)	Pick off infected buds in the winter
Red Spider Mite	A systemic insecticide Sybol 2
Gooseberry Mildew (also attacks currants)	Nimrod T or Benlate
Leaf Spot (mainly blackcurrants)	Nimrod or Benlate
Grey Mould on fruit	Benlate or Captan
Gooseberry Sawfly caterpillars	Fenitrothion (Fentro)

Strawberries

Red Spider Mite	A systemic insecticide or Sybol 2
Grey Mould on fruit	Benlate or Captan

Raspberries, blackberries and loganberries

Aphid and Leaf Hopper (both spread virus)	A systemic insecticide
Cane Spot	Benlate or Thiram
Grey Mould on fruit	Benlate or Captan

With the exception of strawberries, all the above fruit can be treated with tar oil winter wash (Mortegg) during the dormant season which will greatly reduce the numbers of aphids, Apple Suckers, Raspberry Moths and Red Plum Maggots. In addition, it will kill all the moss and lichen on trees and bushes.

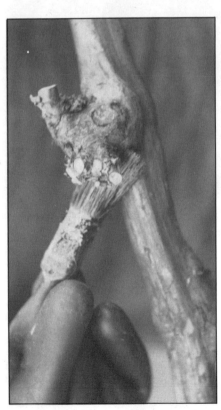

Tar oil kills many fruit pests.

used if that pest is your only problem.

Insect pests can be conveniently divided into four categories, depending on how they attack the plants. Generally, their method of attack will determine the chemical treatment to use.

Suckers

These are perhaps the greatest problem in the garden and are very widespread. They attack the plant by sucking the sap and can be even more dangerous because they spread virus diseases. **Aphids** — greenfly, blackfly and whitefly — are the most common in this category and there are few years when any garden will escape their attentions.

Borers

Some insect pests will bore into stems, leaves, fruits and buds of many plants. **Codling moth** and **chrysanthemum leaf miner** are good examples. They are difficult to control once they are inside the plant tissue.

Eaters

Perhaps the most dramatic of all insect pests are those that simply devour the foliage and other parts of the plant. **Cabbage white butterfly** caterpillars for example, can strip the leaves of all plants in the cabbage family in a very short time. The function of caterpillars is simply to eat. And very good they are at it too! Since they have a very simple structure, they are not generally killed by the majority of insecticides. Most attack the nervous system, but this is so basic in caterpillars that they are not affected. Different sprays, then are necessary.

Soil pests

These are generally borers or eaters but they live below soil level. Some are specific to one type of plant — like **cabbage root fly or carrot fly** — while others, like **cockchafers** and **slugs**, will eat almost anything.

Diseases

Diseases are caused by bacteria, fungi, viruses or by a deficiency of an essential plant nutrient. Generally, it is safe to say that fungus diseases are very difficult to cure but fairly easy to check and maintain at an acceptable level. It is generally much better to use preventative sprays than to wait until an attack occurs.

Bacterial diseases are rather more difficult. Often, the first symptoms are a slimy, rotting mess and by that time, the only thing to do is to throw the plant away. In woody plants a spread of the infection can often be prevented by cutting back to healthy wood.

Virus diseases still remain something of a mystery. Not enough is known about them yet to be able to recommend a control. Again, the only remedy is to pull up the plants and burn them. With both virus and bacterial diseases, a strict rotation of crops will help prevent re-infection.

Nutrient deficiencies often cause symptoms that are easily mistaken for disease. Bitter pit in apples is a good example. However, the remedy is not at all as simple as it may seem. Often, the deficiency in the plant is caused not by a lack of one particular element but by an excess of another, or simply by lack of water. In the main though, these physiological disorders can be avoided by good cultivation techniques.

Use clean seed and planting material, buying certified plants or seed wherever applicable. There are many varieties of plants now that have been especially bred for disease resistance. Use them wherever there is a likelihood of pest or disease.

In the vegetable garden, a yearly rotation of crops will help to break the life-cycle of some pests and diseases. Never grow the same crop on the same piece of land two years running.

Remember, too, that a healthy strong plant will always stand a better chance of survival, than a weak one. So feed and water your plants regularly, giving them enough room to benefit from plenty of light and air.

Even though a last resort, chemicals will almost certainly be needed at some time in the season. The list opposite should control most pests and diseases you are likely to come across.

Application

Insecticides and fungicides can be applied in three forms. For pests and diseases that attack the above-ground parts of the plant, either a dust or a liquid can be used. Liquids are undoubtedly to be preferred. They are easy to apply uniformly through a sprayer and can also be mixed with some foliar feeds or with other pesticides (though only on the maker's recommendation).

Dusts tend to be more difficult to apply and rather wasteful. They are useful, however, if no sprayer is available.

Soil pests are controlled either with a powder or, more recently, with insecticide crystals. Since these break down more slowly than powders, they will give a more sustained control.

Though most liquid insecticides and fungicides are in concentrated form, needing to be mixed with water before

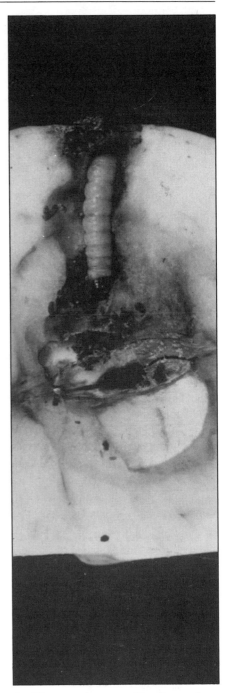

Codling moth caterpillar in apple.

application, a new method has just been introduced by ICI. They have devised a method of concentrating the active ingredient into granular form. This means that it is now possible to buy insecticides in small sachets containing a pre-measured dose. They are available in pint or gallon sizes and only need mixing with the appropriate amount of water. It looks like a very handy and safe method.

Harvesting and storage

MOST of the August maturing fruits are, in fact, better if they are picked before they are quite ready to fall as they are usually very ripe before they do. As the season progresses into October and, possibly, November, then varieties have to be picked before they are ripe and are suited for longer-term storage.

When to pick

First, when to pick the fruit? You are usually well on the way to an answer to this question if you know the name of the variety. Then it has a known season of use and you will have some idea of when to harvest it.

It is more difficult when you do not know the variety and then you have to try the 'unhooking' test. This means at intervals of not more than a week, going round the trees and trying to pick the fruit off. This is best done as if you were unhooking it from a peg.

With the fruit in the palm of the hand, lift and twist. If the fruit is ready to be picked then it will part from the fruiting spur. If it does not seem to come off the tree readily, then it should be left a bit longer.

Any rougher treatment than this can lead to various problems later. Fruit without stalks does not keep well. Equally, if fruiting spurs are broken off the tree then they are left with an injury, however small, and diseases can sometimes attack them. Certainly, one of the sites from which next year's crop might be carried has been removed.

Try this test first on fruit which is on the sunny side and the outside of the tree. Such fruit is the first to ripen and if you only have a small number of trees then it is well worth picking over the fruit so that you harvest from each tree in a total of, perhaps, ten days. This means that each batch of fruit is taken from the tree in prime condition.

The fruit at the top ripens first followed by that on the outsides — sunny side before shady side. Last of all is the often green fruit on the inside of the tree.

It is obvious that some fruit is much better coloured than others. The fruit which is shaded from the sun usually remains green and looks relatively unattractive, especially where the variety is capable of producing good skin colour in full sun. The only way round this is to prune the tree in the winter to open it up so that light is let in to more parts of it.

What to store

When thinking about storage, of course there are culinary ways of storing fruit such as bottling, in jam or as apple rings or puree in the freezer. However, apples and pears store well under correct conditions without this additional trouble as long as a few rules are obeyed. Fruits to store should be:—

1. Of a variety suitable for storage
2. If anything, under mature rather than over mature
3. Not too large for the variety
4. Unblemished
5. Undamaged

From the moment of picking all fruit starts to decline. The period over which this takes place is partly controlled by the variety but also by the conditions of storage. So, if the variety was slightly under mature when it is put in to store then it has a correspondingly longer useful life in store. The lower the temperature within reason at which the fruit is stored, the longer the life of the fruit.

Over-large fruit does not usually store very well. Often the 'king' fruit of a truss, that which is formed from the first open flower and is usually the largest fruit on the truss with a prominent rib next to the

RIPENING GUIDE		
VARIETY	WHEN TO HARVEST	WHEN TO USE
APPLES		
Discovery	Mid-August/Mid-Sept.	
Worcester Pearmain	Early Sept./Mid-Oct.	Use straight from the
James Grieve	Early Sept./Mid-Oct.	tree, or do not attempt
Laxton's Fortune	September/October	long-term storage
Ellison's Orange	September/October	
Lord Lambourne	Late Sept./Early Oct.	Use late Sept./Mid-Nov.
Egremont Russet	Early October	October/December
Sunset	Mid-October	October/December
Cox's Orange Pippin	Late September	December/January
(long-term storage)		
Cox's Orange Pippin	Early October	November/December
(short-term storage)		
Laxton's Superb	Mid-October	November/February
Bramley's Seedling	Early October	November/January
Newton Wonder	Mid-October	November/March
Lane's Prince Albert	Mid-October	December/March
PEARS		
William's Bon Chrétien	September	Use straight from the
		tree, or do not attempt
		long-term storage
Conference	Late September	October/November
Doyenné du Comice	Mid-October	November

stalk, is the sort of fruit to use fairly quickly.

Turning next to blemishes on fruit, obviously some types of damage are worse than others. It has already been said that fruit without stalks does not keep well.

Diseased fruit is not good for long-term storage. Both apple and pear scab which appear as brown marks on the fruit surface can often spread in store, especially under humid conditions. On the other hand, damage done by the 'Capsid' bug is not progressive. It takes the form of corky raised areas on apples and can easily be removed in preparation for cooking.

The question of damage is to some extent under the control of the gardener. It is probably too extreme to talk of picking apples and placing each one individually on a bed of cotton wool in a basket. Certainly careful handling is needed and some varieties, like **James Grieve** apples are very susceptible to bruising with individual finger marks to be seen on badly handled apples. The idea of cupping fruit when picking it is done partly with a view to saving undue pressure being put on the skin of the apple.

It should be placed carefully into the container and not in such a way that the stalks of other fruit or rough edges of the container can cause injury. Such damaged fruit is, of course, perfectly usable but not suitable for storage where it will deteriorate and rot and the trouble will spread to other fruit.

Storage conditions

In looking to storage conditions one can perhaps learn something from the days of the large, old, private garden. Then the fruit store was often windowless or with north facing windows, and the floor level sunk below the level of the surrounding ground. The door was on the north side and the roof was often thatched!

All these factors contributed to producing cool, dark, even conditions in which the fruit could be kept for a long time. Humidity was often maintained by damping the floor and the fruit was frequently placed in oiled, paper wraps on special shelves. There are not many houses that can afford these sort of facilities! However, attempt to copy them as far as possible.

First, try to find somewhere which is cool. As long as the temperature does not fall below freezing point the closer apples are kept to this temperature, then the longer they will keep. Certainly, steady temperatures in the range of 35–40 deg F (2–4 deg C) are best. The power of the sun should not be underestimated and, as far as possible, the room chosen for storage should not be one in which the sun can reach, especially in the middle of the day.

Humidity also is important. If the fruit is kept in a dry atmosphere then it will tend to lose moisture to the atmosphere and shrivel. Nobody likes shrivelled fruit so it is worthwhile going to some trouble to look for humid conditions.

Even to store fruit in new boxes may not be a good idea because they can be made of dry wood which itself cannot draw moisture from the air and this in turn will dry it out so that the fruit loses moisture.

Faced with new boxes, leave them out in the rain or spray water over them so that they have absorbed moisture before using them for fruit storing.

Often a garage is a good place to store fruit, though bear in mind that it is capable of absorbing strong smells from the surrounding air.

Freezing

Colour guide on page 158

IF you have a productive garden or an allotment, you really *can* save money by freezing your own produce.

Instead of throwing away those excess vegetables you can't eat immediately, pop them into the freezer and use them out of season when prices are generally high.

Or why not grow specifically for the freezer? By choosing the right crops and the best varieties (most seedsmen's catalogues will tell you which varieties freeze best), even a small vegetable and fruit garden can keep you in garden produce all the year round.

And your freezer will also enable you to buy other food in bulk at very advantageous prices, so there is little doubt that you'll soon recoup the initial outlay.

Choice

Choosing a freezer is very simple because they are all similar. The most important factor is shape.

A chest freezer is cheaper to run than an upright because the cold air doesn't fall out when the door is opened as it does with an upright. Consequently the upright has to be defrosted more than the chest freezer. A chest freezer needs defrosting once or twice a year and an upright 2–3 times.

Fridge/freezers are also very popular. They are ideal for small families or as a second freezer — perhaps for those with a large freezer in the garage.

Do not buy a large freezer and keep it half full, because a full freezer is much cheaper to run than a half full one. A simple way to calculate the size required is to allow 2 cubic ft per person in the family plus 2 cubic ft for the cook. So for a family of 4 that would be 10 cubic ft. But if you can accommodate and afford a larger one go for a 12 cubic ft, especially if you have got a lot of garden produce to freeze.

If your freezer is to be kept in the garage look for one with a lock on it. Also you can get some freezers with a battery operated alarm that rings when the temperature rises. For those kept inside, a red light comes on when this happens.

In an upright freezer it is a great deal of help if the shelves and baskets are on runners that can be pulled out so you can

Open freezing Courgettes.

Freezing Rhubarb.

see what is at the back of the shelf rather than having to take everything out.

Using the freezer

Most people keep their freezer in the garage or utility room. Wherever you keep yours, make sure it is dry and as cool as possible. If it is kept in a warm place the compressor will work overtime, so it will cost more to run and it will need defrosting more frequently.

If the freezer is kept outside, make sure it is in a dry place. If the cabinet gets damp, in time it will rust which will shorten its life.

To get the best results when freezing always start with foods that are at peak freshness. Do not freeze something that has been knocking about in the kitchen for a couple of days and expect it to come out fresh. Freezing doesn't work miracles — it just stops the biological clock. In other words food can only come out of the freezer as good as it went in.

Freezing does not kill bacteria and germs — they are just dormant at the low temperature. To kill them food must be blanched or cooked.

Remember too, that freezing dries food, so it is important that it is wrapped and sealed to prevent loss of moisture. "Freezer burn" may occur if foods are not wrapped properly. This is when the tissue of the food dehydrates completely and goes spongy. It can be seen when polythene bags or other freezer wraps become punctured. Red meat goes pink, and fish and chicken go white. The food is perfectly safe to eat but you won't be getting produce at its best and therefore value for money.

Never put warm foods in the freezer as this would cause excessive frosting so always make sure foods are completely cold. Freeze them until frozen hard, in the fast freeze compartment of the cabinet. Wherever possible spread the packets out as they freeze quicker than when pressed together. Once frozen they can be stored in the main part of the cabinet.

Always label and date foods so that you can use them in rotation.

The temperature inside your freezer should be kept static at 0° F (−18° C), so try not to cause any fluctuations.

Freezing

Colour guide on page 158

Herbs such as mint and parsley freeze well in ice cube trays.

Freezing strawberries.

Methods of freezing

Foods can be frozen in a number of ways either cooked or uncooked.

Open freezing

This is the most popular method of freezing. It is particularly suitable for chops, fish fillets, vegetables, fruit, decorated dishes and small cooked foods such as sausage rolls, buns or cheese straws.

The food to be frozen is spread or placed in the freezer. When frozen hard it is wrapped in a polythene bag or put in a rigid container, sealed and stored in the freezer. The advantage of this method is that the foods stay separate and any number of portions can be used as desired. Peas, raspberries, strawberries and other small fruits or chopped vegetables are ideally frozen by this method. It is also sometimes known as "free flow", implying that the foods can be virtually poured from the container.

Remember that watery foods expand on freezing and many fruits will burst their skins. So your currants, raspberries and strawberries will look super while frozen, but as soon as they thaw they will collapse. So "pour" them straight into pie dishes or fruit salad to prevent them breaking up too much.

Freezing in Syrup

The most common use of this method is the freezing of soft fruit A sugar syrup is made by dissolving sugar in water and then boiling for 2–3 minutes. The amount of sugar depends on the fruit to be frozen, but for medium strength syrup 1lb of sugar to 2 pints of water (450gm per litre) is used.

All fruits can be frozen by this method including fruits that discolour such as apples, plums, apricots and peaches. Add 2 tablespoons of lemon juice to help prevent discoloration.

Pack the fruit in rigid containers and pour over the cold syrup, leaving ¾in headspace. Crumple a piece of greaseproof paper and lay it on the surface of the syrup to prevent the fruit rising out of it. Put the lids on the containers and freeze. Defrost just before use leaving the fruit in the syrup to prevent discoloration.

Puree Method

Fruit and vegetables can be frozen successfully by this method. Soft fruits can be mashed very lightly with a fork and frozen. Harder fruits such as apples, rhubarb, etc can be cooked until they fall apart. Spinach, carrots and parsnips can also be frozen by this method. Most vegetables will need pureeing in a blender for freezing by this method, but it is not necessary with fruits as they go very watery.

Dry Sugar Pack

Fruit to be frozen by this method is placed in the base of a rigid polythene container and covered with a layer of sugar. These layers are continued until all the fruit is used. You will need approximately 6oz caster sugar to 1lb (330gm per kg) of fruit.

Vegetables

Choose vegetables that are young and fresh and freeze them as quickly as possible. Most vegetables need blanching before freezing, because they contain enzymes which develop off-flavours and spoil the texture of produce while it is in the freezer. Blanching in boiling water kills the enzymes.

To blanch vegetables prepare them for cooking by slicing or trimming and dip them in small amounts in fast boiling water for the required time. The time depends on the texture and shape of the vegetable, but it should be long enough to kill the enzymes but not long enough to cook the vegetables. Sliced carrots will take longer to blanch for example, than spinach or broccoli.

As soon as the vegetables come out of the boiling water they should be plunged into iced water to stop them cooking. The boiling water can be used for all your vegetables but the iced water needs changing as soon as it becomes warm. For blanching times see the table.

Vegetables with a very high water content do not freeze well. This is because on freezing the water expands and forms ice particles. These break the vegetable tissues so that when they thaw they collapse. If these vegetables are made into soups they will freeze satisfactorily.

Fruit

Choose fresh produce that is in peak condition. Avoid bruised or over-ripe fruit.

Only wash soft fruits if it is really necessary — most soft fruit is clean and can be frozen as picked. Wherever possible freeze soft fruits by the open freeze method as this is the quickest way and most of these fruits come all at once.

Skin or peel other fruits and prepare them for eating or cooking in the usual way. See the table for individual freezing instructions.

If fruits need to be skinned before freezing, plunge them into boiling water for 30 seconds, place them in cold water until they can be handled.

Blanch carrots in boiling water before freezing.

Aubergines can also be frozen.

189

Freezing

Colour guide on page 158

VEGETABLE FREEZING GUIDE

CROP	PREPARATION	BLANCH AND COOL	PACK
ARTICHOKE GLOBE	Cut off stalk, remove outer leaves	Blanch three at a time; 6 minutes small, 8 minutes large	Pack each in a polythene bag
ASPARAGUS	Grade according to thickness, wash and trim to even lengths and scrape lower part of stem	4 minutes thick stems 2 minutes thin stems	Tie in 4 oz bundles; pack in polythene bags
AUBERGINES	Peel and cut into 1in slices	3 minutes	Open freeze for free flow pack then put in polythene bags
BEANS, BROAD	Pod and grade	2 minutes small 3 minutes large	Open freeze for free flow pack then pack in polythene bags
FRENCH	Top and tail, leave small beans whole, cut others into 1½in lengths	3 minutes whole 2 minutes cut	Open freeze for free flow pack then put in polythene bags
RUNNER	String, top and tail, slice thickly diagonally	2 minutes	Open freeze for free flow pack then put in polythene bags
BEETROOT	Use small beetroots, cook until tender, cool, peel and leave whole or slice	None	Pack whole in polythene bags; pack sliced in rigid container
BROCCOLI & CALABRESE	Trim to even lengths with compact heads and cut off any tough stalks	2 minutes thick stems 1 minute thin stems	Open freeze for free flow pack then put in polythene bags
BRUSSELS SPROUTS	Peel trim, wash and grade	4 minutes medium 3 minutes small	Open freeze for free flow pack then put in polythene bags
CARROTS	Scrub small carrots and scrape large ones, slice or dice large ones	3 minutes small whole 4 minutes thick slices	Open freeze for free flow pack then put in polythene bags
CAULIFLOWER	Break into florets of even size, wash in salted water	3 minutes	Open freeze for free flow pack then put in polythene bags
CELERY	Trim, scrub and cut into ½in slices, cut off any foliage	3 minutes	Open freeze for free flow pack then put in polythene bags
CELERIAC	Wash-trim and scrape slice fairly thinly	6 minutes	Open freeze for free flow pack then put in polythene bags
CORN ON THE COB	Use young corn. Remove husk and silk, cut off stem	4–6 minutes, cool	Pack individually in polythene bags. NB. this is the only vegetable that needs to be thawed before cooking
COURGETTES	Cut in half if small or 1in slices if large	1 minute, cool	Open freeze for free flow pack, put in small quantities in polythene bags
KOHL RABI	Trim and peel, leave small ones whole and cube large ones	3 minutes whole 1 minute cubed	Pack in polythene bags
ONIONS	Peel and leave whole or cut in ½in slices	2 minutes slices 6 minutes whole	Open freeze whole small onions for a free flow pack and put sliced onion in two polythene bags or a rigid container
PARSNIPS	Use young ones and peel, leave very small ones whole and cube others.	2 minutes cubed 4 minutes whole	Open freeze for free flow pack then put in polythene bags
PEAS	Use only young peas and pod	1 minute	Open freeze for free flow pack; put in polythene bag
PEPPERS	Leave whole or dice having cut out stem and seeds	No need to blanch whole 2 minutes diced	Freeze colours separately. Pack whole in polythene bags and diced in bags or rigid containers. Red and green types
POTATOES CHIPPED	Deep fat fry until tender but not brown — drain	None	Open freeze for free flow pack then put in polythene bags
TOMATO PURÉE	Simmer slowly in own juice until tender, reduce to purée and sieve	None	Pack in small polythene containers or freeze in ice cube trays and then pack in polythene bags
TURNIPS	Choose young roots. Trim and peel, leave small ones whole and cube larger ones	4 minutes small 2 minutes cubed	Open freeze for free flow pack then put in polythene bags

Other methods of preserving

Colour guide on page 158

General principles

ALTHOUGH many people have freezers, there is now a return to some of the older forms of preservation — bottling, salting and drying.

Fruit is more usually bottled than vegetables, because it has a higher acid content so "Putrefacture" bacteria are prevented from forming.

Vegetables *can* be bottled but the process is far more complicated and lengthy and can be dangerous.

Salting is a much simpler way of preserving vegetables although it is only suitable for a few types. Beans and cabbage can both be salted successfully, and as both of these are not at their best after freezing, this method can be very helpful.

One of the oldest forms of preservation is drying. In many countries fruit and vegetables are left out in the sun to dry naturally. Unfortunately this would be a long practice in this country, but nevertheless it is possible.

Successful bottling depends on efficient sterilisation. This is to kill any yeast cells and spores of mould present on or in the fruit and to deactivate any enzymes which cause ripening, which in time leads to rotting.

The most common bottles to use are those with a clip top and those with a screw band fitting such as the well-known Kilner jars. It is essential to use bottles in good condition, chipped rims or lids or perished rubber rings will not give you an airtight seal.

The bottles should be really clean — if they are at all dirty it is best to sterilise them by putting them in cold water and bringing it to the boil. After 5 minutes of boiling they can be drained and used.

Fruit can be bottled in both water and sugar syrup, but you get a much better flavour if syrup is used. The fruit does rise in syrup which is a bit off-putting, but don't let this deter you.

Salting beans.

Other methods of preserving

Colour guide on page 158

As a general rule use 8oz (225gm) of sugar to 1 pint (½ litre) of water although the amount can be varied to individual taste. The 8oz (225gm) amount allows approximately 4oz (100gm) of sugar to 1lb (450gm) of fruit. If fruit is very tightly packed in bottles then use a heavier syrup, ie one containing more sugar.

To make the syrup, dissolve the sugar in half the amount of water, then boil the mixture for 1 minute. Then add the remainder of the water and leave to cool. If the syrup is very cloudy it can be strained through muslin.

Bottled plums

One of the most successful fruits to bottle, are plums and the method for these is the same as for apricots, greengages and other fruits with stones.

Remove the stalks and wipe the bloom off the skin. Halve and remove the stones or leave the fruits whole.

Pack the fruit into the jars without bruising. Make sure there isn't more than 11oz (300gm) of fruit or less than ¼pint (150ml) of liquid in a 1lb jar, otherwise a longer processing time is necessary. The syrup can be added hot or cold depending on the method of bottling chosen.

Slow water bath

Use cold syrup and pour over the fruit before sterilising. Place a piece of wood or a wire tray in the bottom of a large saucepan — the jars must not touch the base of the pan.

Place covers on the jars of fruit and stand them in the pan. Add enough cold water to come right up to the top of the jars. Heat the water slowly up to 180°F (80°C). This should take approximately 90 minutes. Keep the water at this temperature for 15 minutes. Remove the jars from the water and tighten the lids. Place them on a wooden surface and leave them to cool.

Quick water bath

Use hot syrup and pour over the fruit before sterilising. Bottle as above, but fill the pan with warm water and heat until simmering, taking 25–30 minutes. Keep at the temperature for 10 minutes (20 minutes for halved plums) and finish as above.

Using a pressure cooker

Use boiling syrup and pour it over the fruit before sterilising. Use hot water in the pan and 5lb pressure. Heat the pan until the pressure is reached. Time for 1 minute (3 minutes for halved fruit). Cool the bottled fruit in the pressure cooker for 10 minutes before opening the pan. Finish in the usual way. For further information see the instruction leaflet provided with your pressure cooker.

Choosing a greenhouse

Colour guide on page 234

A traditional wood-sided greenhouse.

TO the keen gardener, a greenhouse is not a luxury. It's an absolute essential. Not only will it extend the scope of this fascinating pastime throughout the whole year, but it will increase his range and dramatically improve his chances of success in the outside garden as well.

Used properly, this is unquestionably the most versatile and useful piece of gardening equipment you can own. It can provide you with all the plants you need outside at a fraction of the cost of buying them in, it can produce valuable food crops at times when shop prices are at their highest, and it can fill your house with cut flowers and pot plants for relatively little outlay. And it can pay for itself in just a couple of years.

Granted, greenhouses these days are not cheap. But never have they been such good value for money. Developments in the commercial world have been followed closely by designers and manufacturers of home greenhouses to produce a range of products that are better than they've ever been. Modern materials and design not only give us greenhouses we can afford, but they also provide the optimum in growing conditions.

But their very versatility means that choosing just the right house for the job you have in mind is a perplexing and important decision. And you *must* get it right first time.

An aluminium frame lean-to conservatory.

193

Choosing a greenhouse

Colour guide on page 234

A seven sided greenhouse is ideal where space is limited.

Wide doors are a useful feature.

Types

You may wish to specialise in pot plants, to use the house only for food production, to grow only one type of cut flower, or you may prefer to try your hand at a bit of everything.

Before you buy your greenhouse, try to come to that decision because it will affect the type of house you buy.

Leaving aside plastic houses and special shapes for the moment, there are basically three types of house available.

Those that are boarded half-way or are designed to sit on a brick wall are tailor-made for growing plants on a staging all round the house.

Brick or timber will hold much more heat than glass which loses it relatively quickly. So, in areas where light is not needed, it will reduce running costs considerably to use a 'solid' material. This type of house is ideal then, for the pot-plant specialist.

But plants grown in the borders or in pots or growbags on the floor of the house will need lots of light early on in their lives. So a glass-to-ground model is essential. If you wish to grow tomatoes or carnations etc, you'll need glass right down to the ground.

And for the gardener who wants a bit of each, there is a type just for you. This is the "hybrid" of the two types already mentioned, with glass-to-ground on one side and half timbered on the other.

Shape and size

The essence of a good garden is that it is an attractive place to look at and to

A hybrid model. (See text).

Where there is no room at all . . . a plant frame.

relax and work in. So any buildings must fit in with the general layout. Unless you have a very large garden and can afford to hide buildings away, this can be a problem.

But don't be put off by the look of an empty house. Fill it with plants and it will look different again.

Perhaps the easiest way to visualise what your greenhouse will look like erected in the garden, is to mark out the size with half a dozen canes. Often the house looks much bigger on the show-site than it will when it's set in the garden and surrounded by plants.

Naturally, your final choice of design must be a personal one, but you should be aware of the types available.

Certainly the most popular shape is the normal rectangular, apex roof house. These are available in wood or aluminium and even with a green or white plastic coating. Aluminium will fit in almost anywhere, but some gardeners with "old-fashioned" gardens shun their shiny, modern appearance. Here, the softer lines of a cedarwood greenhouse would be more appropriate.

If your garden is very small, you may prefer to have one of the more recent hexagonal designs. These will fit in with most small garden layouts and do not have to be positioned in any one direction to catch the full sun.

The size of house will, of course, depend on you. However much room you have, you will inevitably find that you don't have quite enough. So, go for the biggest you can stretch to. You'll soon fill it up.

Another space saving shape, the 'Gazebo'.

Choosing a greenhouse

Colour guide on page 234

Increasingly popular, for cost reasons, a polythene house.

Plastic houses

Plastic is a material that has revolutionised our lives over the past 50 years. And no less in the garden. Following closely on the success achieved by commercial growers, several manufacturers now produce houses covered in sheet plastic.

They have met with a mixed reception from gardeners. Certainly they have some disadvantages that are not relevant to the commercial man, but, once you get used to the slightly different growing techniques necessary, they will produce first class results.

Perhaps the biggest disadvantage for the small gardener is that they are not as aesthetically pleasing as their glass equivalent. Polythene does always look like polythene and, short of hiding it with planting, there's not much you can do about it.

They are also a little more difficult to control.

Polythene tends to collect condensation and this can cause the problem of an over-humid atmosphere and subsequent disease. But that's just a case of getting used to providing a mite more ventilation than you would in a glass house.

On the other side of the coin, they will allow absolute maximum light admission and, above all, they are very cheap. It is necessary to replace the polythene cover every couple of years, but even then, it will be many years before the cost catches up with that of a conventional house.

196

A 'solar' heat-retaining house.

Aluminium

When aluminium houses first appeared on the market in any quantity, more than a few sceptics were quite convinced that it wouldn't catch on. Now, aluminium houses outsell timber ones by a long, long way. And with very good reason.

They are relatively cheap, they are light and easy to erect, they need no maintenance and, above all they provide very good growing conditions.

Have a look at the cross-section of an aluminium glazing-bar, and you will see that, because of the "T"-shaped section, it is immensely strong. So, not only can the bars be relatively narrow, letting in more valuable light, but less of them are necessary. This means that the panes of glass can be bigger, so even more light is admitted. The criticism has been levelled, that this extra expanse of glass increases heat loss. True, of course, but the extra heating required is so minute as to be unnoticeable and a very small price to pay for the extra light.

Timber

Painted softwood houses are fast disappearing because of the difficulty of getting hold of decent, seasoned timber and because of the annual maintenance needed.

But cedar and redwood houses are still about, and very good they look too. Unfortunately, the price has rocketed in the past few years, so they are not cheap. But they will greatly complement any garden layout and provide very satisfactory

If you can afford one, a 'Victorian' conservatory.

197

Choosing a greenhouse

Colour guide on page 234

A 'Solardome', space-age light efficiency.

growing conditions too. They will not admit quite as much light as aluminium.

They are, in fact, virtually maintenance-free though an annual coat of cedar treatment will keep the timber in prime condition and greatly enhance the appearance.

What to look for

Before you buy a greenhouse, either have a look at a few actually erected, or ask the makers four important questions. The four points to look for are these:

Construction. Check first of all that the erected and glazed greenhouse doesn't "rock" in any direction. Obviously, any greenhouse can be pushed over if you push hard enough, but a gentle shove should show how solid it is.

In aluminium houses, check that there are sufficient angle brackets and stay bars to keep the house solid even in strong winds.

Make sure that the doors and ventilators fit well and slide or open smoothly. There should also be a complete absence of draughts when they are closed.

In timber houses, check that the boarding is free from knots which tend to drop out when the timber dries. The fittings and screws should be anodised, galvanised or be made of brass.

Light admission. In winter, light admission is far more important for good plant growth than is heat. So, go for a house with large panes — not less than 24in (60cm) wide — and with a minimum of superstructure. Obviously, here a balance must be made, since the house must be sturdy enough to withstand high winds and heavy snow.

Good ventilation is important, above and below.

The 'autovent' opens and closes the vents automatically.

Ventilation. Adequate ventilation should be standard. Some manufacturers offer extra ventilation at extra cost, so check that the standard equipment is adequate. If not, you must add the cost of extra vents when comparing prices.

It's easy to check that the house has sufficient ventilation. Open a ventilator as wide as it will go. Then measure the area of the opening — that is the two triangles at each side and the rectangle in the front. Add these areas together and multiply by the number of vents in the house. This will give the total area of ventilation. It should be not less than one sixth of the total floor area.

Cost. The same rules apply here as to any commodity and in these difficult times who doesn't know only too well the "rules" for shopping around. Very simply, you are likely to get what you pay for. It is often a false economy to go for the cheapest. But it is well worth shopping around even when you have decided on the model you want. There is fierce competition these days in the greenhouse market, and you may well be able to find a retailer who is prepared to cut his price a bit to make a sale.

Plastic greenhouses are a bit of an exception to the "false economy" rule. They are considerably cheaper than glass, and if you feel that one will fit your bill, you will certainly save money in the short term. And for the new gardener who has a lot of other expenses, they provide an excellent "stop-gap" solution.

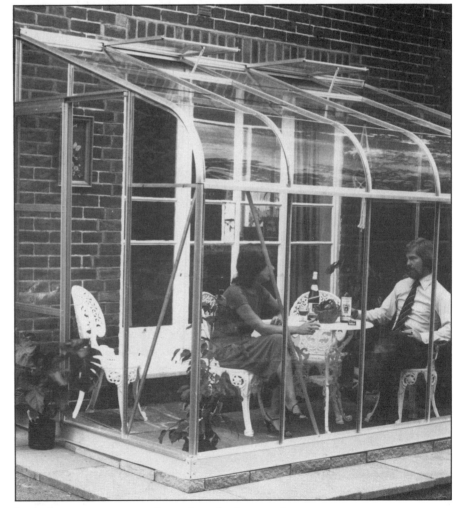

A modern conservatory is perfect for house plants.

Greenhouse heating

HEATING a greenhouse has always been a vexed question. The gardener must balance the advantage against the winter fuel costs of keeping the greenhouse at the correct temperature.

Usage

This is the first consideration. If you are only thinking of growing summer crops, or ornamentals, in any case, then there is little or no point in buying a heater. The annual round of bedding plants, tomatoes, perhaps a cucumber plant, chrysanths, etc, will be perfectly coped with, in a cold house. However, there are many pot plants which can be very easily raised from seed, to flower in mid-winter, as long as they receive a minimum of heat. In addition, many vegetable crops can be grown as well, at a time when they are either completely unobtainable in the shops, or so expensive as to be not worth buying. These include winter salad crops, beans, spinach and carrots (baby carrots, not the great big tasteless stumps that often pass for carrots). Most of these will only require a minimum of heat, providing frost can be kept at bay.

As far as starting your summer seeds off early is concerned, a propagating case will not only be cheaper to heat, but will also provide far more suitable conditions for germination.

What Sort!

Accepting the fact that we will probably have to make do with lower temperatures, what then is going to be the best form of heating. Electricity has always been the most convenient form of heating, in that it is relatively simple to install a power cable to the greenhouse. Electrical heaters are usually, small, light and easy to handle, control is straightforward, there is no mess or cleaning out to do, and there are no problems with fumes or condensation. Electricity has also been the most expensive form of heating — until recently, when oil has overtaken it in cost.

Undoubtedly, the most efficient form of heating is a hot water pipe system, fed from a boiler outside the house. However, if you have only got a six by eight (1.8 x 2.4m) greenhouse, then it is not likely that you will want to have a separate boiler, and in any case, the cost of buying and installing this sort of equipment would mean that it would be many years before the system would pay for itself. Boilers can be fuelled by solid fuel such as coke, coal, smokeless and even wood burning boilers are becoming popular again, which is fine, as long as you have a source of wood available. The

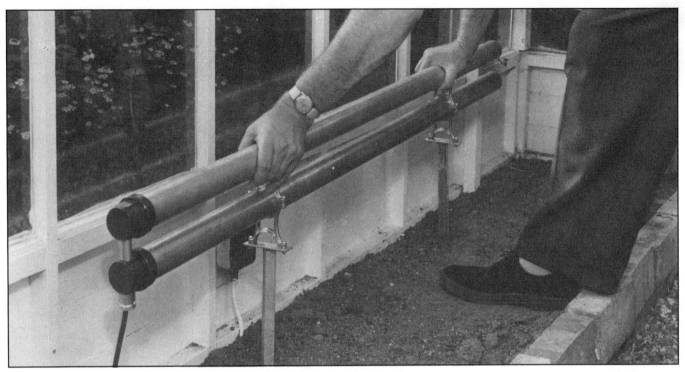

There is great variety of choice when it comes to heating a greenhouse,
electric above, ducted air below.

Greenhouse heating

Electricity is expensive but often most convenient.

other form of boiler burns oil, and with the current oil situation this has become extremely expensive.

There is one heater on the market that burns waste oil. This is the oil that nobody knows quite what to do with, when they change the oil in the car. Garages have plenty of it to spare, and it is probably one of the cheapest systems to run. However, it may well cost well over a hundred pounds to install.

The other two main methods of heating a greenhouse are gas, natural or bottled, and paraffin. In the past, gas has been a good, clean, cheap way of heating, which has become very acceptable as a method of heating a greenhouse, since the demise of coal gas. Unfortunately, rising costs again, mean that it is no longer the cheap alternative that it used to be, though it is probably still a lot cheaper than electricity.

Paraffin is also rising in price, and has probably doubled its cost in the last twelve months. However, it is still about the cheapest fuel there is. The problems attached to paraffin are more to do with the running of a paraffin heater in a greenhouse than the cost. It is essential to keep the heater very clean and running at peak efficiency, otherwise toxic fumes can be given off. The other factor is that it is essential to maintain quite a lot of ventilation, otherwise there can be big problems with damp, and this is often at odds with having a heater on in the first place.

Size of heater

Without getting too technical, it is difficult to explain fully, how to calculate the size of heater you will require. Electrical heaters are measured in kilowatts, in just the same way as domestic heaters. Fortunately, people have worked out a scale to give you the size of heater you will require to heat a particular size of greenhouse, giving you a known temperature lift.

As an example, to give a temperature lift of 20°F, which is all you will require in most winters, to keep the frost at bay, in a 6×8ft (1.8×2.4m) greenhouse, you will need a 1½kW heater. Double the size of the house, to a 12×8ft (3.6×2.4m), and the heater needed to maintain the same temperature lift will only need to be a 2¾kW. If the house is a lean-to, or is half boarded, then it is possible to take off about ¾kW from the size of a free standing, glass to ground house.

With paraffin or gas heaters, it is slightly more difficult to work out. The amount of heat is worked out in B.T.U.s (British Thermal Units), which are worked out in a somewhat complicated way. However, as a guide, if you can work out the floor area of the house in sq ft, and then multiply this figure by 1.4 and then multiply this figure by the required rise in temperature, the answer will be the amount of B.T.U.s required.

For example, our 6×8ft (1.8×2.4m) house will have a floor area of 48sq ft. We want a temperature lift of 20°F, so we multiply these two figures, 48×20 and then multiply the result by 1.4. The calculation is then a straightforward 48×20×1.4, and the answer is 1,344, which is the amount of B.T.U.s required. Most heaters will be marked with the amount of heat put out by that model, which can then be checked against the figure you have calculated.

Ease of use

Undoubtedly the easiest heating system to use is an electric one. The small, fan heaters that are free standing in the middle of the greenhouse, simply plugged in and switched on, are simplicity itself. They can be left to their own devices for long periods, need no regular maintenance that you can carry out and as long as they are run within the manufacturers specifications, there should be no problems at all.

Gas is similar, except that if you are using bottled gas, you will have to check that the container isn't empty, quite regularly — and change it whenever it does become empty. Paraffin will need checking every day to make sure that there is sufficient fuel, but then you will need to be in the greenhouse every day, during the winter and early spring, in any case, to make sure that ventilation, disease control, humidity, and all the other paraphernalia are all in order. Depending on the temperatures to be maintained, the temperatures outside and, most important, the size of the tank, it will probably need re-filling every two or three days.

If you decide that a hot water pipe and outside boiler are a better bet, for other reasons, remember that these may need stoking, ash clearing or riddling at least once a day, and they may also require cleaning out thoroughly, regularly. In addition, if you decide on a wood burning stove, it may well be the case that you will have to chop the wood as well (this can be a very relaxing way of spending Sunday afternoon, if you go at it with the right attitude), and it does keep you fit!

Larger greenhouses need more economic systems such as this 'Hotbox'.

Greenhouse equipment

Staging the modern way, plastic trays and metal tubes.

IF you own a greenhouse, there are certain pieces of equipment you simply can't do without. As you get more enthusiastic, there will be lots of other accessories you'll want to buy, but let's look first at the essentials.

Staging

Unless you decide to grow only in the borders on both sides of the house, some form of staging is essential. Certainly it is possible to put pot and boxes on the floor of the house and dispense with staging altogether. But this generally results in thin, drawn seedlings and for the gardener, a permanent stoop! No, for comfort, ease of working, and short, sturdy plants you can be proud of, you need some sort of bench about 3ft (1m) high.

Of course, the handyman can knock up a length of staging himself and save money into the bargain. But there are several very good, ready-made units available that will save you a lot of time and trouble and will last a lifetime. Most are made of aluminium which has the advantage that it is easy to keep spotlessly clean and will not harbour pests and diseases. They are child's-play to erect and surprisingly good value for money.

Before choosing, decide what you will grow and how you are going to grow it. If, for example, you intend to use the staging for boxes of bedding plants or vegetables, you will be better with a flat bench. You can always cover it with a sheet of polythene and a strip of capillary matting to reduce the labour of watering.

If, on the other hand, you are using the house for the growing and display of ornamental pot plants, you may well prefer a staging incorporating a fixed "gravel-tray". This can be filled with gravel or expanded clay granules for a very decorative effect. This type is also useful if you wish to grow tomatoes in large pots on the staging, on a modified "ring-culture" system.

Whichever one you decide on, it is essential to make sure that it is perfectly level when you install it. This is particularly important if you intend to fit a capillary mat. And, to make sure that the legs don't sink into the soil with the quite considerable weight of pots and boxes, set them on a piece of paving slab or a square of concrete.

Thermometers

Most gardening pundits, when describing the culture of a particular plant will quote an average, optimum temperature. While it is important to try to achieve something near these recommended temperatures, any greenhouse gardener who also has to do a day's work and who goes to bed at night, will know how difficult it is to keep to them. Particularly in the spring and autumn when nights are cold and days often quite warm, temperatures under glass can fluctuate wildly. In order to avoid harmful fluctuations, it is essential to know not only the temperature before you go off to work in the morning and when you come back at night but also the maximum and minimum temperatures reached while you were away, or in bed. That way, you can anticipate them to some degree and adjust the heating and ventilating accordingly.

So, a thermometer that records maximum and minimum temperatures is essential. If that sounds a bit scientific and expensive, rest assured that they are surprisingly simple and quite cheap. All that happens, is that the mercury in the thermometer tube pushes up a couple of small floats which will stick at the highest point, so recording both the highest and the lowest temperatures since last set.

Watering cans

It goes without saying that every plant you grow in the greenhouse is going to need artificial watering. What is not so obvious is the best way to do it.

In the height of summer, use a hose. Lots of water is needed, so this saves labour, and when temperatures are high, plants don't generally object to a cold shower. But in the winter, watering has to be strictly controlled. Slop too much about and you invite all sorts of trouble from fungus diseases. And apart from that, tender young seedlings are not going to thank you for an icy drenching. So, a watering-can is the answer. Fill up the can each day after watering, so that the water will warm to the greenhouse temperature before you next need it.

And you should use a can that is easy to control. Those tubby, fat models with a short spout are fine in the garden, but virtually useless in the greenhouse. Better by far to invest in one with a long, almost horizontal spout that will reach right across the staging to the plants at the back, without slopping water over everything else. These are also perfectly

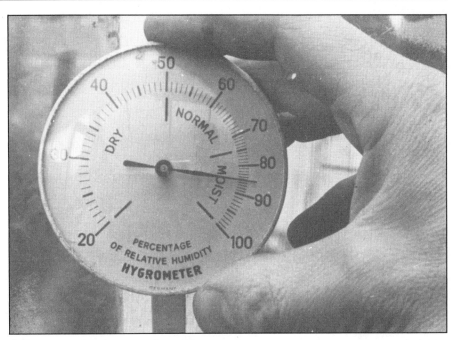

A hygrometer measures humidity.

Soil humidity can be measured too.

Greenhouse equipment

Always read the instructions first.

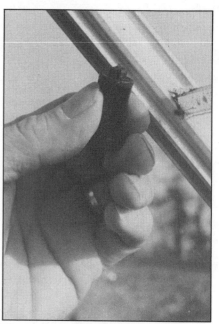

These fix to the glazing bars.

balanced so that you can control the flow easily.

Ideally you should buy one with two roses — a coarse and a very fine.

Long spouted cans are available in steel or plastic. But do not use the same can for watering weed-killer on the garden path and for giving precious seedlings a drink. However well the can is washed out, there must always be a slight risk of damage from residues, reserve a can especially for the more noxious chemicals.

Thermal screens

A thermal screen is the latest "in" word for greenhouse insulation. Even simple screens can save you a lot of money over the winter. They will certainly pay for themselves in the long run.

Greenhouse insulation using polythene sheeting attached semi-permanently to the glass is nothing new. And some of the materials used, especially those consisting of hundreds of "bubbles", are very effective.

This "bubbly" material is stuck to the glass or fixed to the glazing bars, forming a very effective insulating layer. They are cheap and efficient, but they do have one snag. They reduce light, albeit minimally, at a time of the year when every bit of light possible is of the greatest value.

This snag can be easily overcome by using the material only at night when heat loss is at its greatest and there is no need to worry about loss of light. Of course, it would be a great performance

They must be tight.

to stick up and take down the material every day. But what about using the same blinds that are used in the summer for shading?

There are now one or two blinds available that fit on the inside of the house. They can be pulled down at night and released during the day thus saving heat and expensive fuel without sacrificing any of that valuable light. They may not be quite as efficient as a continuous polythene sheet, because heat can escape around the edges. But they will certainly reduce fuel bills considerably.

Polythene sheeting can be fixed in various ways to the glazing bars or direct to the glass. You can use the small metal "Norry-bolts" for fixing to the bars and Sellotape adhesive pads to stick the sheeting direct to the glass. Both are effective and relatively inexpensive.

With these few essentials you'll be able to grow a wide range of subjects in your greenhouse. Once you get gripped by the "greenhouse bug", however, there are several other bits and pieces that you will not want to be without.

Light is not much reduced by this 'bubble' material.

Greenhouse equipment

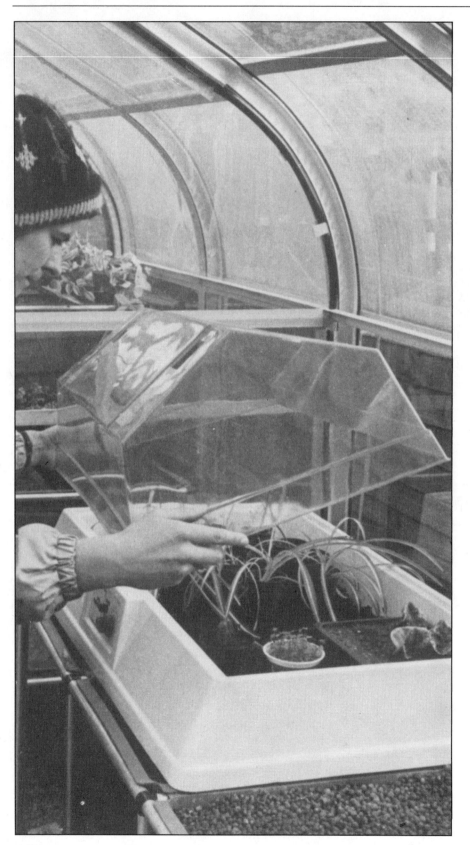

IF you have visited a garden centre in spring, you may have noticed how many propagators are on sale these days. All of them claim to be the best, the most economical to run, save you lots of money in the long run, and all the other advertising slogans that we have all come to recognise.

Are they really worth while? Will you, in fact, be able to use them? Will they save any money at all? Which one is best? All very confusing, indeed, to the casual observer!

The main principle behind all propagators is the fact that a plant requires a close, humid atmosphere until its root system is strong enough to keep it growing healthily. This applies to seeds as well as to cuttings, which have no roots at all, and a large leaf area to support. Obviously, it would be possible to provide these conditions in a greenhouse, but as the young plants are not likely to take up much room this would be a bit wasteful.

Propagators work because the atmosphere immediately around the plants can be kept very humid, and the temperatures can be raised by one means or another, but only over a small area, so that heating costs are kept to a minimum. Important in these days of high heating costs. Both seeds and cuttings have optimum temperatures at which they will germinate or root, quickest, and with the most chance of success. In many cases, this is best applied as bottom heat. This means that whilst the air temperature need not be very high, the temperature at soil level should be considerably higher. Where the plants are in a confined space, it is ideal, as the heat pushed in at the base is sufficient to warm the air slightly, keeping it nice and humid as well.

Heat sources

The heat can be applied in many ways, but in most cases, it consists of soil warming cables, which are electrically heated. These have the added advantage that the heat can be very carefully and accurately controlled by means of a thermostat. On an even simpler scale, no heating is built in, and the case is simply stood on a heating pad, or placed over a domestic heater. These propagators are probably the cheapest on the market, and for raising seeds, it is amazing what results you can achieve, just by putting the box on top of your central heating boiler. Of course, if you are thinking of propagating more exotic material yourself, or some of the more difficult woody plants, such as lilac, then you will need more sophisticated equipment. This,

Although more expensive a heated propagator is ideal.

really, is the key to deciding the sort of equipment you require.

Obviously, if you feel that you are likely to be raising the odd coleus cutting during the course of a year, then a polythene bag over a pot of compost, placed in the kitchen windowsill will be all that you will require. On the other hand, how much more interesting to raise all your own plants from seeds or cuttings? In which case, you will require more equipment, up to an automatic mist unit, over a heated bench, to raise tree and shrub cuttings.

Different plants will respond differently to different conditions, both from seed

and from cuttings. Most of the commoner seeds will germinate readily and quickly at a temperature of around 45–50° F (7–10° C).

However, more exotic varieties may require a temperature of anything up to about 70°F (21°C) before they will germinate properly.

Cuttings are a different matter altogether. Many of our hardy herbaceous and shrubby plants will develop new roots quite readily even if planted outside. Others require at least the head of the cutting to be covered, if only for the effect of reducing the water loss from the leaves. Some prefer a little bit of warmth

at the base of the cuttings before the roots will initiate, and yet others require quite considerable heat before they will do anything other than go mouldy.

The only way to find out, other than by trial and error is by looking up the requirements of the subject, in a relevant book. However, if you are that interested, this is where the real fun of gardening can lie. There is nothing more pleasing than to be told by some learned fellow that such and such is very difficult to propagate, and then to prove him wrong by producing far more plants than you have got room for. This is quite possible, even with the simplest equipment.

Greenhouse equipment

One of the main points to watch when propagating plants, either by seeds or by cuttings, is the hardening off process, after roots or germination has taken place. This is when the majority of fatalities occur!

Obviously, the young plant has been formed in ideal conditions, with protection from water loss, temperature drop, etc. To suddenly withdraw this protection may mean that the plant gives up the ghost before it really has a chance. So there must be some means of gradually introducing the young plants to cooler, drier air in whatever equipment you are using. This is a point to look out for when buying a propagator, even if it is only a ventilator at the top of the cover. This can be kept closed until the plants are ready, when it can be opened for longer periods each day, until finally after a week or so, the cover can be removed completely.

Types

What, then, are the main types of propagators that are available? In general, they tend to be more sophisticated versions of the polythene bag over a pot. That is, they consist of a rigid, clear plastic dome, covering a seed tray or similar container. To be used in conjunction with these, are a number of electrically heated pads, which can be placed almost anywhere. The case complete with top on, is then stood on the pad, which provides sufficient bottom heat.

One step up from this is the full case, which can be made of glass or plastic, and which contains its own soil warming cables. These are usually covered by a layer of sharp sand or grit.

At the top end of the field, we have the mist propagation units, which until recently were considered to be the last word in propagation. Whilst they are very useful for a number of subjects which are particularly difficult to root from cuttings, recent research is showing that in many cases, as good results can be obtained without using mist. This is not the actual rooting, which admittedly is faster and surer, but failure seems to occur at the weaning stage, when the plants, raised under ideal conditions, find it very difficult to adjust to harder conditions. Again, there are fitted heating cables in the bench containing the mist unit.

The one thing that all these propagators have got in common, is a reliance on an electricity supply. If you have not got, or cannot supply electricity in the greenhouse, it is probably better to get one of the cheaper models that can be put on the central heating boiler in the kitchen.

Apart from electricity paraffin may be used to heat a propagator.

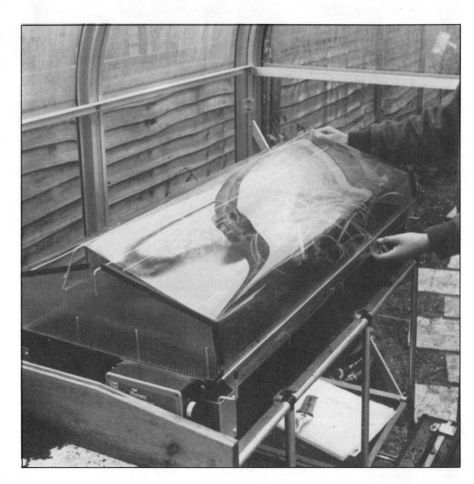

Greenhouse basics

Suggested Growing Programmes

The Productive Greenhouse

For a fully productive house growing only food crops, buy a glass-to-ground model and install a portable staging on one side and one end.

January to June

Use the staging to produce and grow on vegetable plants for planting outside. Bear in mind that plants will need to be "hardened-off" before planting, so you'll need a coldframe.

Use the border to grow lettuce sown last autumn, french beans, radish and salad onions.

June to September

Use one side of the border for tomatoes and the other for peppers and aubergines. It is quite possible to grow cucumbers and melons in the same house as tomatoes, but stick to the more vigorous F varieties.

September to January

Keep the tomatoes cropping as long as possible. Raise a "short-day" variety of lettuce in pots or soil blocks for planting when tomatoes finish. When the crops in the other border are finished, plant with a late crop of tomatoes or lettuce.

The Ornamental Greenhouse

For a house which is to be used for growing ornamental crops only, it is better to buy one that has a wall of wood or brick.

January to April

The staging will be needed to produce the summer bedding. Sow seeds, start off tubers, grow on geranium and fuchsia cuttings. Towards the end of April, these can go out in the frame to harden off.

May to September

The summer display will be in full show. Pelargoniums, fuchsias, begonias and many annuals such as petunias which can be quite happily grown in a pot. Watering, feeding, damping down and providing shade will be the main jobs.

Start off plants that are to be grown from seed for winter colour.

October to December

Bring in stock plants of dahlias, chrysanth. stools, canna roots, and other half-hardy perennials and store them in boxes of peat under the benches.

On the bench, many pot plants can be brought on to flower for Christmas — primulas, cyclamen, and azaleas.

Greenhouse basics

Large seeds and pelleted ones can be spaced carefully.

The Mixed Greenhouse

Most people with a small greenhouse in the garden will be wanting to grow a few vegetables as well as some pot plants. For this purpose, it is ideal to have a house with glass to the ground on one side.

January to May

The staging will be used for the production of vegetables and bedding plants from seed. The border can be used for starting off chrysanth. stools or the tail end of a winter crop of lettuce.

June to September

Whilst it is possible to grow cucumbers in a mixed house, tomatoes are a far easier crop to accommodate. An F variety will give a more guaranteed crop. The benching will accommodate pot plants for the house, and there should be room to start off the plants required for winter decoration.

October to December

Clear the border of the tomato plant residues and plant up with a short-day lettuce variety, or include other salads such as radish or spring onions.

Half-hardy perennials will be in boxes of peat under the benching, and the winter flowering plants can be grown on, on top.

Remove dead growth regularly in the greenhouse.

Sowing

Colour guide on page 47

Mass production helps.

It is important to sow thinly so that each plant has its full quota of light, air and nourishment leading to sturdy growth. A really good start in life will help plants to produce expected results in due course.

It is sometimes a puzzle to know how deeply to sow seeds. Certainly it is possible to sow too deeply. An old, but still reliable rule, is that seed should be covered by its own depth in soil — the smaller the seed the less the covering. Some items need the merest sprinkling of compost to be placed over them.

A few, including begonia, lobelia, gloxinia, and streptocarpus need no covering — simply press the seed into the moist surface of the compost.

Once the seed is sown, the pans or boxes can be covered with polythene bags. Alternatively, the older method of placing a sheet of glass over the container and turning it each day to get rid of condensation is good practice. Remove all coverings as soon as germination takes place, otherwise seedlings can be ruined.

Whether the actual raising of seedlings takes place on the staging or in a propagating frame, the containers must be looked at daily so that if the surface soil becomes dry it can be watered, preferably by the immersion process.

Flat wooden trays are still best for large numbers of seeds.

Greenhouse basics — sowing

Colour guide on page 47

There are a great number of seed block types. Or, you can make your own, see page 131.

Use a soft brush for fine seeds.

This means lowering the pot, pan or tray into a pail of tepid water so that it soaks upwards until dampness covers the surface. Then withdraw the containers slowly and stand them to drain. Seeds vary greatly in the time they take to germinate and it sometimes happens that there may be a week or more difference between various subjects.

"Transplanting or pricking out", is an important and necessary operation in a seedling's life and one over which every care should be taken.

Many of us tend to do this job too late and often in a hurry. Every effort should be made to prick out all seedlings just as soon as they are big enough to handle. It helps the busy gardener if seed sowing is staggered a little, so that all pricking out can be gradually done, instead of very many seedlings being ready for moving at the same time. For very tiny seedlings such as begonias and lobelia, the use of a pointed label to lift out the little plants minimises the possibility of damage to the delicate roots.

Potting on

Propagation from cuttings requires the same care and attention to detail as the raising of plants from seed. The gardener

Seedlings ready for potting on.

should ensure he uses only the healthy, short-jointed cuttings, free from signs of pests, disease or disorders. As with seeds, plants of tropical origin will need higher temperatures to induce the cuttings to root. They will root most readily where there is bottom heat in a propagating case with a fairly high humidity.

As seedlings and rooted cuttings develop, they will need "potting on". This expression means that when the plant has filled its pot with roots it should be moved to a bigger size. But never use unnecessarily large pots. Apart from not looking right, the soil in large pots containing few active roots is liable to become sour, while a lot of root room often means a lot of leafy growth with fewer flowers (or crops in the case of edible plants).

Quite mature plants can be removed easily by inverting the pot and tapping the rim on the bench. Support the plant with the other hand by passing the stem through the fingers. Never pack the compost hard, just sufficient to make it moderately firm.

While for the first potting many gardeners do not use crocks at the bottom of the pots, but rely on coarse peat or leaf mould, for the second and later pottings,

Never use too large a pot when potting on.

Greenhouse basics

Try not to damage the roots when potting on.

Label carefully when they are all potted up.

drainage holes should be covered with pieces of broken pots, etc. This is to ensure that there is a free passage for excessive water to drain away.

If the plants are to be automatically watered by a base irrigation method, crocking is not needed — just some coarse peat to prevent the soil running through the hole. Never fill the pots to the rim, but leave about ½in (13mm) between the rim and compost surface, to allow for hand watering.

Watering

When to water and how much to give, are questions that sometimes cause concern. Overwatering must be avoided since it causes root rot, a condition from which plants hardly ever survive, whereas they often make remarkable recovery from a parched and wilting state.

Ideally, the compost should be kept just moist to the touch — so feel the soil with the fingers before applying more water. Plants just making a little new growth require very little moisture, particularly where a good peaty compost has been used. More water will be needed by

Water well after potting.

plants growing in sandy soil which does not hold moisture so well.

Water should not be directed over the centre of plants that tend to rot at the crown if it remains wet — particularly cinerasias and primulas. Care is also needed in the case of begonias, gloxinias and cyclamen, for moisture lodging at the top of the tubers can easily cause rotting.

There is still much to be said for the old fashioned way of testing the need for watering. Simply tap the pot with a little wooden mallet or with the knuckles. Clear ringing tones indicate the need for water, a dull, low sound means the soil is moist enough.

Since fuel is now so expensive there are more gardeners using a cool greenhouse than a hot house. A very wide range of plants can be grown where, the temperature can be maintained around 50–55° F (10–13°C) during the daytime, and about 40–45° F (4–7°C) at night. With the coming of spring, warmth will naturally increase both by day and night.

It is always better to maintain a fairly even temperature, rather than one which rises steeply in the day and falls abruptly at night-time.

An automatic watering system.

Food from the greenhouse

ALTHOUGH it is unlikely that many gardeners will use a greenhouse entirely for the growing of food crops, there has always been considerable interest in raising vegetables under glass. Experiments during the last war have taught us that all kinds of glass structures can be used to grow edible crops. Certainly cloches and cold frames have proved their value in this connection.

The type of glasshouse usually described as the Dutch Light greenhouse, which is composed of large sized sheets of glass edged with a light frame of wood, is most useful in that it admits all possible light, especially if it is sited north and south.

The soil in any greenhouse border must be in a healthy state and fertile, being well moved and manured, with good drainage assured. Taking crops alphabetically, the following are well worth growing from seed where some heat can be provided.

Aubergines. The "Egg Plant" is an annual which will germinate freely in a temperature of 60° F (15°C). Gradually pot on the plants until they are in the 7in (18cm) size and then give the same cultivation as for tomatoes. Pinch out the growing point when the plants are 6in (15cm) tall and restrict each plant to 4 or 5 fruits. Once the fruits begin to swell feed with liquid manure.

Beetroot. This makes a welcome addition to early salads. Choose a globe variety and sow in the greenhouse border providing a temperature not more than 50° F (10°C), plenty of light and ample watering. Soil containing plenty of humus matter helps to keep the beetroot tender and of good colour.

Carrots. The short or round varieties will grow rapidly if sown in little beds of rich soil in the warm greenhouse. The roots can be pulled as they mature. Some gardeners intercrop carrots between newly planted cauliflowers.

French Beans. This is an important greenhouse crop in both the dwarf and climbing forms. The dwarf varieties can be grown in pots or boxes which, if necessary can be placed on the staging. Two of the best varieties for this purpose are Masterpiece and The Prince. Do not sow too many seeds in each pot. To secure a heavy crop two plants in a 6in (15cm) pot, three in the 7in (18cm) size and four in an 8in (20cm) pot is sufficient. Use a good compost made up of half fibrous loam, the other half being leaf mould, decayed manure, plus a good sprinkling of seaweed fertiliser.

Climbing French beans are best planted in the "floor" bed so that they can

Aubergine plants.

grow tall and carry their pods nearer to the glass and in full light. Supports will be needed and vertical strings can be fixed to strands of wire, one of which is placed just above soil level, the other nearer the "roof". Double rows 15in (38cm) apart, with 3ft (91cm) between double rows gives sufficient room.

A temperature around 60° F (15°C) should be provided. Anything less than 50° F (10°C) is too low. Water should be applied as necessary, preferably in the morning so that the foliage is dry by nightfall. This minimises the possibility of mildew.

Well nourished soil is needed for a good crop, and additional feeding with liquid manure during cropping will increase yields as well as the regular picking of the pods before they become old.

Peppers or Capsicums. These can be grown in the same way as tomatoes. Sow seed in temperature of around 60° F (15°C). Move the seedlings to 3in (8cm) pots and subsequently to bigger sizes according to growth or they can be grown in the greenhouse border. Overhead sprayings with water are beneficial and hand pollination usually leads to a heavier yield. Reliable varieties include Californian Wonder and the newer F.1 hybrids Canape, Ace and Mospa.

Potatoes. These are hardly likely to be seriously considered as a crop for greenhouse culture. Even so, it is possible to provide an extra early dish of new

Food from the greenhouse

Lettuce is grown on a large scale under tunnels.

Early Radishes can be grown under glass.

potatoes by planting one of the early varieties such as Home Guard, Arran Pilot and Foremost in pots. Plant tubers that have been sprouted for some weeks, one in each 9–10in (23–25cm) pot containing a mixture of loam, decayed manure and leaf mould. In early spring place the tubers 1in (2.5cm) deep in the half filled pots and then as growth develops top dressings of fairly rich compost can be added. Give frequent sprays of a liquid insecticide to reduce possibility of the appearance of greenfly. Lift the plants as soon as the foliage shows signs of leaf discoloration.

Peas. If grown under fairly cool conditions it is possible to obtain a very early crop of peas in pots or the greenhouse border. In both cases use dwarf varieties such as Little Marvel or Kelvedon Wonder. The 10in (25cm) pots will take six

Early potatoes in a pot.

seeds. Sow them 1½in (4cm) deep round the inside edge of clean crocked pots filled two thirds of their depth with a mixture of loam, leaf mould and silver sand plus a sprinkling of lime.

Stand the pots on a shelf near the glass and as growth proceeds add more compost. A day temperature of 65° F (18°C) is sufficient. For border culture fork over the surface soil and sow the seeds 2in (5cm) deep in staggered rows, providing twiggy sticks. Avoid a close dry atmosphere and give ventilation and water as necessary.

Radishes. These can be grown successfully in the greenhouse so long as there are adequate supplies of organic matter in the soil. If the roots dry out they will become hard, stringy and hot flavoured. French Breakfast, Sparkler and Cherry Belle are all suitable for under glass culture.

A small but tasty harvest.

Food from the greenhouse — tomatoes

Colour guide on page 156

Pinch out shoots here.

Tomatoes

Careful treatment of tomato plants always pays and the grower who keeps in close contact with them, anticipating their needs will obtain the best results.

Many disappointments arise when planting is carried out too early in the year. It is advisable to ensure that the soil temperature is not less than 55°F (12°C). When it is lower, new roots develop very slowly and become susceptible to soil borne diseases. If the air temperature is not at least 50°F (10°C) the plants will remain stationary and may take a long time to recover. In a cold greenhouse it is best to delay planting until well into April — in northern districts wait until the end of that month.

Once the plants are in their fruiting quarters watering must be done with care. At first, give just sufficient water to keep the ball of soil moist but once the plants start to grow well and the roots extend they can be watered more freely and over a wider area.

Where there is a deep "floor" of rich soil, the plants can be placed in a 6in (15cm) furrow. This deeper planting will allow an extra truss of fruit to develop — a great advantage, particularly in smaller greenhouses.

With both early and late tomato plants, it is important to ensure that the first truss of flower sets fruit, otherwise the plants will be leggy and become unbalanced.

Aids to fruit setting include the provision of a fairly moist atmosphere, the slight shaking of the plants or their supports just as the flowers open, which will distribute the pollen, or a fruit setting hormone spray can be used.

Keep the soil drawn towards the lower parts of the stems so that additional roots form. These will greatly help in ensuring continued production.

Tomato plants from earlier sowings

Pot grown plants can be put into growbags.

will now be growing quickly and should be kept properly supported by canes or strings. Remove sideshoots cleanly without leaving stumps, which if left, can easily result in the entry of disease spores or mildew.

A tip which works well, is, when the plants are about 15in (38cm) high, thoroughly spray each one with a solution made by dissolving $\frac{1}{4}$oz (7gm) of powdered sulphate of iron in 1 gal (4.5 litres) of water. This should be applied fairly early on a dull day. Such a spraying prevents leaf scorch and at the same time hardens growth and helps the plants to withstand attacks of fungus and other diseases.

If it becomes necessary to buy plants for early cropping, select good coloured, short jointed specimens about 8–9in (20–23cm) high. Avoid leggy speciments or those that have been kept out of the greenhouse and exposed in shops or garden centres.

To secure plants for placing outdoors at the end of May or early June, sow seeds about the middle of March using a heated greenhouse where it is possible to maintain night temperatures of between 60–65° F (15–17°C) Place the seeds individually 1in (2.5cm) apart in pots or boxes of seed compost, covering them with up to $\frac{1}{8}$in (4mm) fine sifted soil. After watering from overhead, using a can with a fine rose, cover the pots or boxes with glass and paper removing them once the seeds germinate.

Good varieties for outdoor growing include **Alicante, Ailsa Craig, Harbinger** (early), **Moneymaker, Outdoor Girl** and **Sweet 100**. The latter bearing quantities of small sweet 1in (2.5cm) diameter fruit.

Tie the plants as they grow.

Food from the greenhouse

Other crops

Cucumbers will need attention when the first flush of fruit lessens in quantity and sub-laterals appear. These will need stopping and tying to wires or other supports. The second flush of fruit will soon appear followed by a third, but less in quantity than the first crop. Some of the older, now useless leaves can be removed to allow young growths to develop.

Male flowers should not be left on the plants or the fruit will be bitter. Any flowers growing on the main stems should also be removed, for usually they form poor, club-shaped cucumbers. There are of course, now available, a number of so-called all female F.1. hybrids.

Young roots appearing on the surface soil should be mulched with rich compost, but never allow manure to touch the stems or they will rot. A top dressing of nitrogen-rich fertiliser will encourage a good crop over a long period but should not be applied before early May, otherwise there will be too much vigorous growth and less fruit.

Melons sown about the middle of the month can be planted out in the warm greenhouse in late April. Good varieties include **Hero of Lockinge** — of round shape with netted skin and pinkish flesh, and **Charentais**, a cantaloupe which has a "quartered" shape, and pink, richly flavoured flesh.

Sow two seeds in each 3in (8cm) pot of John Innes seed compost, subsequently removing the weakest seedling from each pot.

Earlier raised melon plants can now be moved to their prepared fruiting positions. Single stems from each plant should be tied to bamboo canes.

Carrots can be sown in March for an early crop. By gentle forcing, succulent roots will be ready for pulling in May. A minimum soil temperature of 50°F (10°C) is needed and this can be obtained by using electric soil warming cables or hot beds made from fermenting strawy manure and leaves. Such a bed should be at least 10in (25cm) deep and be covered with a 6in (15cm) layer of good rich fine soil.

Sow thinly, take out any weeds as soon as they appear, and thin the seedlings so they finally stand about 2in (5cm) apart. During very cold weather the frames should be covered at night, using mats or similar material. **Amsterdam Forcing** and **Early French Frame** both force

Melons may need netting.

well while **Early Nantes** and **Early Scarlet Horn** succeed under both greenhouse and frame culture.

Peach trees in the greenhouse must not be forced into growth too early or there will be some risk of damage to the blossoms. By the middle of March it should be safe to give less ventilation which will raise the temperature, except on very fine days when air can be admitted freely until mid afternoon. On such days the trees can be sprayed with water. Newly planted trained trees having shoots up to 2½ft (75cm) long can have the central shoot cut back to six buds and the other shoots can be shortened. Flowers on older trees will need hand pollinating.

Container grown plants

1 Prepare the ground well before planting — add some peat to a well dug soil, apply general fertiliser.

4 Remove the wrappings carefully so as not to damage the roots which cling to the sides of the pots.

7 Label the different plants according to the plan, making sure that you use an indelible ink marker.

2 Give container grown plants a good watering before planting them out in the border.

5 Take out a planting hole large enough to accommodate the root ball and place peat in the bottom.

8 Water in well. On sloping sites make a hollow around the base of the plants for it to collect.

3 By following the planting plan, lay out the plants in position, spacing evenly avoiding straight lines.

6 Set the plant upright in the centre of the hole, backfill with soil and firm in well with your fingers.

9 Top dress with peat or an organic mulch to help conserve moisture and keep down weeds.

Fruit cages

1 Before starting to erect the fruit cage, carefully read and understand the instructions.

4 The positions of the uprights can now be seen. Make a hole for each with the special tool provided.

7 It is important to paint the tops of the tubes with oil before fitting the joining pieces.

2 The upright supporting tubes on this cage have plastic end stops that must be hammered in.

5 The tool is banged down to a mark so that, when the tubes are inserted, they are the right height.

8 Before re-assembling the 'roof' pieces on to the uprights, slide on the plastic hooks for the netting.

3 The next step is to lay out and connect the tubes that form the 'roof' of the cage.

6 Now assemble the connecting pieces, inserting the plastic flanges to repel water.

9 Now, piece by piece, the 'roof' tubes are disconnected and fitted to the uprights.

10 If you are using the optional door, fit it together now, and slide the hinges over the upright.

13 The netting is anchored at the bottom with metal 'tent-pegs' pushed into the ground at an angle.

1 Remove all fuel from the engine and tank before storing. Or it will stagnate, causing starting problems.

11 The side netting is now stretched all round the assembled structure and fastened to the top hooks.

14 Now the special roof-netting is placed on the top and stretched down over the sides.

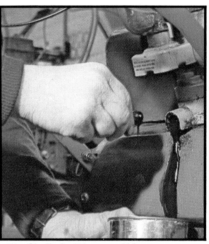

2 Similarly, it is a good idea to remove the oil, if the engine is a four-stroke.

12 To fix one end of the netting to another, special plastic 'G' shaped hooks are provided.

15 Finally, fasten this netting to the side netting, again using the special 'G' shaped hooks.

3 Another straightforward matter is to remove the sparking plug and clean it with a stiff wire brush.

Mower clean

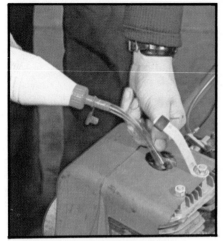

4 A drop of lubricating oil in the cylinder head, before replacing the plug will help to keep out rust.

7 With rotary and the Flymo type of mower, remove the blades and check if they have been damaged.

10 Where the motor is battery driven, remove the battery, charge it, and store in a frost-free shed or garage.

5 Cables (NOT electrical cables) also rust up, and a drop of oil will stop them from becoming stiff.

8 Check that the rotor is evenly balanced. File it down to balance, or take it to a service depot.

11 With cylinder mowers, too, it is essential to clean the cutting parts very thoroughly.

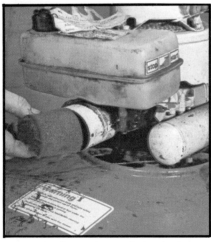

6 Remove and clean the air-filter on all fuel driven motors. If your machine has a paper filter replace it.

9 It is very important to thoroughly clean out under the cowling whilst the grass is still soft.

12 It is a difficult job to take out and replace the cylinder to be sharpened, but it will save money.

13 Once the cylinder has been returned, it must be refitted very carefully — for competent mechanics only.

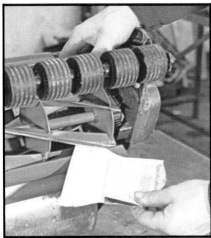

14 The chain must be tightened until there is about ¼in (6mm) play, at the tightest point in the circuit.

15 Once refitted, adjust the blades so that they turn freely, but will cut a piece of paper at every point.

Miniature gardens

1 Wash and dry the bottle before use. A handful of gravel in water swilled round the bottle will act as a scourer

2 Put in a layer of gravel to improve the drainage. Followed by a layer of compost 2-3in (5-7.5cm) deep.

3 Arrange the plants in the bottle. Use only as many as the container will accommodate.

4 Firm the plants in gently with your fingers making sure that the rootballs are adequately covered.

5 To water the bottle garden hold a jug or can at the rim allowing the water to run down the glass.

6 Ready to display! Using a glass sweet jar enables even children to make a bottle garden.

Narrow necked bottles

1 Having chosen a suitable bottle, the drill is the same as for a wide necked one.

2 Use a cardboard funnel in order to pour in the gravel and sand.

3 Do not forget to add a small amount of charcoal to keep the compost 'sweet'.

4 Fashion a trowel and fork from kitchen utensils tied onto canes. Plant near the edges first.

5 Position the plant into the hole, cover the roots and gently firm the soil around them.

6 After planting — water just enough to make the soil moist. Aim at the rim so water runs down the sides.

Bowl gardens

1 Select a group of plants that have similar care requirements — Avoid too much variety.

2 Ideally your container should be at least 3-4in (7.5-10cm) deep and lined with a layer of crocks.

3 Knock the plants out of their pots and arrange them with a watering space.

Bark trough

1 Line a free standing trough-shaped piece of cork bark with sphagnum moss, packing it tightly.

2 Arrange plants such as these Bromeliads 'Tank plants' along the trough.

3 Using a mist hand sprayer water daily. Regularly add a liquid feed. Ideal for a centrally heated room.

Log box

1 Cut a V-shape from the rim to the entrance hole of a Blue-tit nesting box. Line with sphagnum moss.

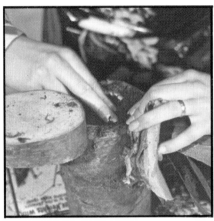

2 Arrange the fronds (leaves) to make sure that none are trapped and firm the rootball.

3 Use a hand mist sprayer to water and regularly apply a liquid feed. Close the lid and hang them.

Trees from seed

1 Seed can be sown indoors, in pots, at any time of year. They should be covered to about their own depth.

2 Labelling clearly and permanently is very important, particularly until the seedlings appear.

3 Some seed needs chilling before it will germinate. Mix the seed with moist sand, place in refrigerator.

T budding

4 Outdoors, sow the seed in drills, ½-½in deep, in spring. Seed that needs chilling can be sown in autumn.

7 Grow them on for two to three years, before planting them where they are to grow.

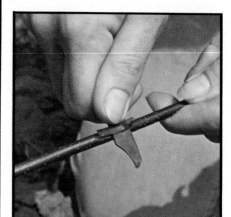

1 Starting ½in (13mm) below the bud, peel a thin slice of bark until the knife has just passed behind.

5 Germination will be quite erratic, even within one batch of seed, but be patient.

8 Conifers are best grown in pots so that the rootball is not disturbed when planting out.

2 Use the blade of the knife to strip away the bud complete with a sliver of bark. Use straight away.

6 Pot them on into individual pots. Outdoor sown seedlings should be thinned to give them more room.

9 It is essential to firm the soil really well, after planting, and ensure that it stays moist.

3 The finished bud ready to be inserted. Handle it by the stump left when the leaf was removed.

Chip budding

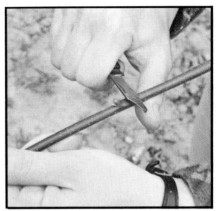

1 Make a short sloping cut at 45 deg. into the budstick, about ½in (13mm) below the bud.

2 Starting ½in (13mm) above the bud, peel away a thin layer of bark with the bud, until the two meet.

3 The 'chip' will then fall out. Handle it by the leaf petiole stump as for T budding.

---

4 To prepare the rootstock, first make a horizontal cut in the bark, about a third of the way round.

5 Make the vertical cut about 1in (2.5cm) long to meet the centre of the horizontal cut.

6 Use the point of the knife to open up the T to make it easier to slide the bud inside.

7 Push the bud well down into the T, as far as it will go, using the stump of the leaf stalk.

8 Cut the spare bark from above the bud so that it is level with the horizontal cut of the T.

9 Tie the bud in very firmly with tape or raffia, making sure the bud is not covered over.

Greenhouse erection

1 Choose the site and mark out the area, making sure the corners form right angles.

4 Take a matching 'chip' out of the rootstock. Start with a sloping cut at 45 deg. into the stock.

4 The protruding angles which act as a footing to the base, should be covered with soil to anchor it.

5 Slice down to remove a thin flap of bark 1in (2.5cm) above this, to meet up with the first cut.

2 The site should be level from corner to corner diagonally. Rake and tread the ground until it is firm.

5 Make sure that the base is level and firm. For extra anchorage in exposed areas, pave the area.

6 Lodge the bud 'chip' into the notch that has been formed in the stock. Tie in with polythene tape.

3 The type of base supplied for use on the open ground is made up of four sections which are bolted together.

6 Construct the greenhouse. Lay out and bolt together the pieces of the side sections.

234

7 Construct the end elevations. Choose at which end you are going to put the door.

10 When the sides and ends are firmly secure, put the ridge into place. Tighten all nuts and bolts.

13 Place the supplied sealing strip in the grooves around the glazing bars, so the glass fits snug.

8 Erect the end and sides of the house. Bolt the pieces together and secure it to the base.

11 Construct the ventilator section of the roof and place into position along the ridge.

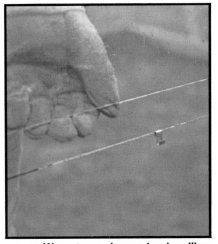

14 Wear strong gloves when handling glass. Glaze the house according to the plan supplied.

9 Make sure that the entire structure is 'square'. Choose a calm, dry day to erect the greenhouse.

12 Place the rest of the glazing bars along the ridge. Leave the right gap for the glass to fit.

15 Fasten the glass into place with the clips. Do not start to glaze unless you can complete in one day.

Fuchsias

Fuchsia Royal Purple. An old variety, but still one of the brightest.

Fuchsia megallanica Versicolor. This is the variegated form of the hardiest of all fuchsias.

1 Line the basket with moss, or polythene. Fill with a good compost.

2 Remove plants from pots and arrange in the basket, trailing over at the edge.

3 Cut one or two holes in the polythene for drainage, and trim the surplus away.

Fuchsia cuttings

1 New plants can be raised from cuttings of overwintered plants. Make them about 3in (7.5cm) long, or about three pairs of leaves.

2 Trim the base of the cutting, just below a leaf node, and remove the lower leaves. Always use a sharp blade to ensure clean cuts.

3 Dip the ends of the cuttings into hormone rooting powder, immediately if possible. If not, keep moist until they are to be inserted.

4 Insert the cuttings into a seed and cutting compost in a pot or box, depending on the numbers required, to about 1in (2.5cm) deep.

5 The compost should have been moist to start with, but even so, water the cuttings in well, to wash the compost round the bases.

6 Finally, cover the pot with a polythene bag, supported on sticks, and seal it with a rubber band. Alternatively, use a propagator.

Chrysanthemum cuttings

1 To avoid the spread of virus diseases, remove the cuttings by snapping them with your fingers.

4 After trimming the cuttings, dip the bases in hormone rooting powder to assist rooting.

7 In either case, water in each batch carefully, using a can with a fine rose. Label each batch.

2 Trim the bases of the cuttings, to just below a leaf joint, and remove the lower leaves.

5 If you have only a few cuttings of each variety insert them round the edge of a 3½in (9cm) pot, 6 to a pot.

8 Once the cuttings are well rooted, in two to three weeks, they are ready for the first potting up.

3 Again to avoid the transmission of virus diseases, sterilise the blade after each cutting has been done.

6 For larger batches of cuttings, insert them into boxes or beds. Make a hole first, with a dibber.

9 Once the first pot is full of root, pot up the young plants. Harden off in cold frame.

10 A stepped wedge is useful to gradually increase the amount of air given.

11 By the time the second pot is full of roots, they are hard enough to plant outside.

12 These are recently planted earlies, each one staked and tied individually.

Rooted plants

1 Plants will arrive wrapped in polythene bags and wood-wool. Remove them with great care.

2 Separate the individual plants and very gently tease out the roots before potting them up.

3 They can be potted straight into pots. They need good drainage at all stages so crock the pots well.

4 Use John Innes potting compost No. 1 or a soil-less compost. It is important that it should be moist.

5 A little flagging will not hurt, but shade from hot sun and spray over the top with clear water.

6 Alternatively, the plants can be potted into a deep box, and potted on later. About 4in (10cm) apart.

Carnation cuttings

1 Carnation cuttings should be selected from halfway up the plant, choose short-jointed shoots.

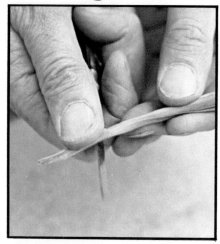

2 Prepare them by trimming just below a leaf joint. Use a sharp knife or razor-blade.

3 These cuttings are ideal — strong, short jointed, about 3in (7.5cm) long and without a flower bud.

4 Prepare the pots by crocking them well to provide good drainage, and filling to within 1in (2.5cm) of the top with compost.

5 Dipping the end of the cutting into a hormone rooting powder will speed the rooting process. Shake off excess powder.

6 Set the cuttings around the edge of the pot, making sure that the compost is well firmed.

7 Give the cuttings a really good watering to prevent wilting and to settle the compost around them.

8 Cover with a polythene bag to retain humidity and place the pot in a warm, shaded place.

Pelargoniums

Ivy leaved Pelargonium

Regal Pelargonium

Double flowered Zonal Pelargonium

Foliage variety of Zonal Pelargonium

Pelargonium cuttings

1 When taking cuttings, cut just above a leaf node, the new shoot will appear near the end.

4 If Jiffy '7s' are used, it is necessary to firm them well around the cutting base, to avoid an air pocket.

7 When taking leaf axil cuttings, trim to just above and just below the node, leaving one leaf and its bud.

2 Trim the cutting to about 2-3in (5-7.5cm) removing all but the last pair of leaves and stipules.

5 The cuttings should have rooted within two weeks, and can then be potted up.

8 Split the stem lengthways, using a sharp knife to ensure that the cut is absolutely clean.

3 Insert the cuttings into a good seed and cutting compost, free draining and open, to encourage rooting.

6 A 3in (7.5cm) pot is large enough for this first potting. Use a light potting compost at this stage.

9 This cutting is then inserted in a light compost. Treat cut surfaces with a fungicide.

Stem and leaf propagation

1 Remove any leaves that are in the way. Make an upward slanting cut below a leaf joint, 1½in (3cm) long.

4 Pack the polythene with sphagnum moss (peat will do) and press it firmly around the wound.

7 Select a mature, healthy leaf of Begonia rex. Trim the stalk and, on the underside cut across main veins.

2 Open the cut carefully so that you do not break the stem and apply hormone rooting powder.

5 Make sure that the moss is moist otherwise the cut area will dry out and thus will not produce roots.

8 Lay the leaf cut side down on the compost and secure with pieces of bent wire.

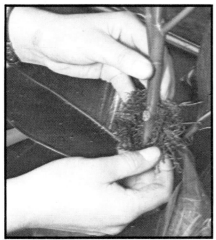

3 Place a polythene tube over the cut and secure it. Hold the cut apart with moist sphagnum moss.

6 Seal the top of the polythene. Rooting will take 8-10 weeks at 65degF (18degC).

9 Alternatively, cut into small squares each with a section of main vein present, and insert upright.

Cacti

Stenocactus multicostatus

Lithops bella

Lobivia var

Epiphyllum 'Hollygate'

Propagation

1 Sow seeds thinly in a special cactus compost. Distributing the seeds from a fold of paper will help.

2 Water by gently immersing the seed tray in a tank of water until it soaks through to the surface.

3 Carefully remove a piece of stem from the variety you wish to graft (the scion).

4 Using a knife, slice the base of the scion to provide a clean cut surface to bond with the stock.

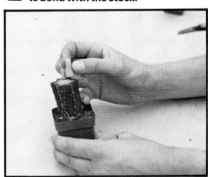

5 Place the scion on the stock. A rubbing movement excludes the air and ensures a good union.

6 Secure the scion to the rootstock by 'pinning' it with spines from another cactus.

Echinocereus pentalophus

Houseplants

1 Scrape the hard 'crusty' compost and any algae from the top of the pot and top dress with compost.

4 To stake tall growing plants choose unobtrusive stakes and ties. Avoid damaging the roots.

7 Cut down on NPK feeding during winter, if a boost is necessary use a house plant liquid feed.

2 Wash smooth leaved plants with rain water to remove dust which will block the 'breathing pores'.

5 Green plastic coated wire rings are an excellent unobtrusive tie which are strong and durable.

8 Water only when the compost feels dry, water from the top and empty the saucer when it drains through.

3 To get your mirror in those smooth leaved plants, use a dust repellent leaf shine in aerosol or liquid form.

6 Climbing and trailing plants can be effectively supported by a frame, round which they can be trained.

9 In centrally heated rooms where the atmosphere is very dry, spray the foliage to create humidity.

Varieties

10 Because Cyclamen corms are prone to rot, remove dead leaves and flowers from the corm.

13 Increase the humidity by setting the plant in a bowl of peat which should be kept continually moist.

Dieffenbachia picta. (Dumb Cane).

11 To control mildew and prevent rot, dust the corm and stalk bases with green sulphur.

14 To improve the 'microclimate', place several plants in a tray of gravel.

Regal Pelargonium

12 Use a specific control for any pest infestations and remember to read the instructions.

15 Place a bell jar (or the like) over plants that enjoy humid conditions, such as saintpaulias and ferns.

Sansevieria. (Mother-in-law's tongue).

Varieties

Pilea cadierei. (Aluminium Plant).

Azalea indica.

Ficus elastica (Rubber plant)

Codiaeum pictum. (Croton).

Cyclamen persicum.

Asparagus plumosus nana

**Euphorbia pulcherrima.
(Poinsettia).**

Chrysanthemum.

**Begonia masoniana (Iron Cross
Begonia)**

Hedera canariensis (Canary Ivy)

Cineraria multiflora hybrid

Sinningia speciosa (Gloxinia)

Calceolaria 'Gay Cluster' strain

Aechmea fasciata (Urn Plant)

Hyacinthus orientalis hybrid (Hyacinth)

Saintpaulia ionantha (African Violet)

Aphelandra squarrosa louisae (Zebra Plant)

Maranta leuconeura (Prayer Plant)

Houseplant care

Plants rarely need repotting in the winter, in spring wait until roots show through the pot.

All plants 'breathe' through their leaves, so make sure the pores are not clogged, by regular cleaning.

Some plants, such as cyclamen are best watered by immersing the pot in a bowl of water.

Azalea

1 Carefully remove dead leaves to keep the plants looking their best and help prevent disease attack.

4 Pinch off dead flowers to keep the plants flowering longer and free from fungus diseases.

7 Climbing plants look more elegant and grow more strongly if tied properly to good supports.

2 Keep a watchful eye out for diseases and treat with a suitable fungicide at the first signs.

5 Feed plants regularly during the growing season with a liquid feed or fertiliser spikes.

8 Spray foliage plants, except those with hairy leaves, with 'Leafshine' to keep them glossy.

3 Greenfly and other pests can be a nuisance too. An aerosol spray is a handy way to deal with them.

6 More plants are killed through over watering than anything else. A moisture meter can help.

9 Revive tired looking ferns with a steam bath. Place the pot above a bowl of boiling water.

Summer bedding

1 Whilst it is not strictly necessary, it is a good idea to give the ground a light dressing of balanced fertiliser before planting.

2 This can be forked into the soil as it is broken down, to give a good, fine tilth, in which the plants can easily establish.

3 The plants should not be dry but it is a good idea to water them before planting, to avoid root damage.

4 As they are required, knock them out of the box, being very careful to cause as little damage as possible.

5 In the case of plants such as lobelia and alyssum do not divide them into individual plants. Make small clumps.

6 Plant them immediately, to a previously worked out planting plan. Make sure the soil is well firmed round the roots.

Bulbs

1 When planting bulbs in bowls or pots, use a special bulb fibre, and make sure it is moist beforehand.

2 If a handful is squeezed, it should remain as a block, but there should be little or no run-off.

3 Plant tulip bulbs with the flat side to the edge of the bowl to prevent bunching.

4 Hyacinths too can be planted just touching, 3 or 4 to a bowl. Always keep the same colours together.

5 Cover the bulbs so that the nose is just showing, and then place the bowls somewhere cool and dark.

6 Prepared hyacinth bulbs can also be grown simply by sitting them on a jar of water, in a suitable position.

1 When planting the bulbs outdoors, it will pay to prepare the border as you would for bedding material.

2 Space the bulbs according to what they are. If mixed with spring bedding, plant that first.

3 Plant with a trowel, making sure that there is about 2-3in (5-7.5cm) of soil covering them.

253

Bulbs

1 If you are 'naturalising' bulbs in the lawn or other grass, the best way of placing them is to throw them out.

2 Where they land, they can be planted, to form informal groups. Make a dibber hole for crocuses.

3 Daffodils can be treated in the same way, except that they will need a bigger hole.

1 Summer bulbs, such as gladioli can be started off in trays, under glass, to give earlier flowering.

2 Alternatively, they can be planted in informal groups, directly in the mixed border.

3 Yet again, for cut flower, they can be lined out in a drill, at the front of the vegetable plot.

4 Begonia corms can be started off as early as February, under glass, in the pots in which they are to grow.

5 For bedding out in May or early June, start them off in trays of moist compost, in gentle warmth.

6 For early flowering, cover the tray of corms, and place it on a propagation bench.

254

Garden pests and diseases

Grapevine Powdery Mildew (Uncinula necator).

Hollyhock Rust (Puccinia malvacearum)

Rose Black Spot (Diplocarpon rosae)

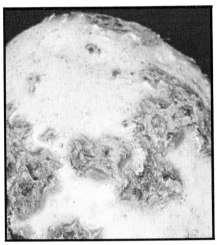

Potato Common Scab (Streptomyces scabies)

Currant Leaf Spot (Pseudopeziza ribis)

Honey Fungus (Armillaria mellea)

Clubroot (Plasmodiophora brassicae)

Potato Blight (Phytophthora infestans)

Grey Mould (Botrytis cinerea)

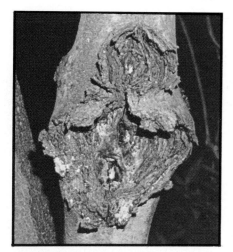

Ash Canker (Nectria coccinea)

Damping Off (Rhizoctonia solani)

Virus

Rose Greenfly (Macrosiphum rosae)

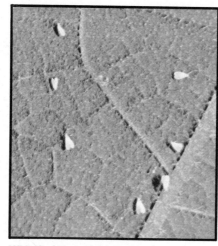

Whitefly (Aleyrodes brassicae)

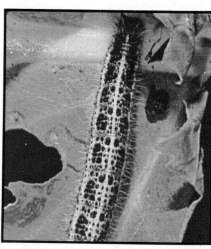

Cabbage White Caterpillar (Pieris brassicae)

Vine Weevil (Otiorehynchus sulcatus)

Woodlice (Oniscus asellus)

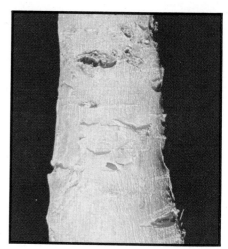

Carrot Fly (Psila rosae)

Ornamental plants under glass

Colour guide on page 242

AS with the garden, what most people want from the ornamental greenhouse is colour all the year round. Well, by a selected programme of seed-sowing, there should hardly be a week when you do not have something in flower.

Auriculas

The beauty of the auricula growing under glass will be showing up during April. Anyone who hasn't had the pleasure of examining these florist flowers close up is in for a treat. And one can understand the enthusiasm of the auricula specialists whose National society stage shows in the North, Midlands and the South during May.

Many of the varieties seen at the shows are raised by the amateurs themselves and it is not easy to obtain them unless you are a member and in a position to do a bit of "swapping and changing".

There are a number of fine varieties available from the nurseries who specialise in alpines, half-a-dozen which could form the basis of a collection.

Show Auriculas — recognised by the "meal" on flowers and foliage.

"Chloe" — green-edged and producing plenty of off-sets for propagating stock.

"Teem" — grey edged.

"Lovebird" — grey edged.

Alpine Auriculas — smooth green foliage without meal and with light or gold centres to flowers.

"Argus" — deep maroon with light centre.

"Kingcup" — rich crimson with gold centre.

"Joy" — rich velvety crimson with a white centre.

Auriculas grow well in John Innes No. 2 and preferably in a 3½in (9cm) clay pot. If you can get hold of the "long tom" type, so much the better, so that you can provide plenty of the drainage material so essential in growing good auriculas.

Cyclamen

The last remaining flowers of the cyclamen will be on the plants in April and the best plants can be selected for growing on again another year.

When there is no danger of frosts (you can still get them as late as April and May), place the cyclamen outside in a shady place and just give enough water to keep the compost moist.

They can remain in the old compost while the "resting" period is over and then, in about three or four months' time the old compost can be teased away to bare the roots. Pot on in a 3 or 3½in

Auricula 'Old Irish Blue'.

257

Ornamental plants under glass

Colour guide on page 242

Alpine Auricula.

Cyclamen persicum.

(7.5–9cm) pot using an "open" type compost and place in the cold frame. An occasional syringe of clear tepid water will soon have the new growth appearing, and when the roots have got hold of the new compost strongly, the plants can be moved into their final sized flowering pot.

Plunge the pots in a few inches of ashes or grit sand to keep them moist, which will keep them in good condition prior to moving into their flowering quarters. And — a little tip concerning cyclamen — when removing dead flowers, give the stem a sharp pull and this will leave a clean wound on the corm and prevent die-back.

Seed sown last August will have provided plants ready for their next potting. Use a peat based compost or a loam medium with a liberal helping of leaf mould.

Cinerarias

Still, one of the most eyecatching of pot plants, the cineraria is always worth growing.

Although a strong looking plant, they soon show resentment to conditions that do not suit them. Miss an occasion with the watering and the leaves drop like tatty rag and more often than not, never fully recover.

They dislike bright sun. Set them out under the greenhouse benching with just

Cyclamen decora.

the sidelights of the glass to ground
structure providing the light. Not the
ideal place for making the greenhouse
attractive, but it gives you some idea of
the cinerarias choice of conditions. So,
find a shady spot in the greenhouse or fix
up a piece of shading material if you
haven't a natural spot.

Keep the plants away from draughts.
They do not require a lot of heat but
detest the wind blowing around them.
Keep the compost just moist and an
occasional balanced liquid feed will keep
them perky.

April is the time to start the main batch
of seed sowing. At the end of the month
you can bring the seeds on in a cold frame
using one of the soilless or John Innes
seed composts. Keep the trays or pots of
seeds covered with a piece of glass and
newspaper until germinated and when
big enough to handle, pot them on into
2½in (6.5cm) pots and then put them in
the cold frame with the pots plunged in
weathered ashes.

There are many fine strains providing
for medium and dwarf plants with a great
colour range.

Early Flowering Spring Glory is a
mixed strain with large flowers on a
dwarf compact plant. It will flower by
mid-December from a May–June sowing.

A little taller is **Triumph Mixed** with
broad petalled, colourful flowers covering a wide range.

Cineraria.

Ornamental plants under glass

Colour guide on page 242

Calceolaria, 'Bubbles'.

One of the tallest is **Stellata Mixed Star** with star-like flowers in a colourful range.

Grandiflora Monarch Mixed has large striking flowers on a strong compact plant.

A few pots of each will give a varied and colourful display over a long period.

Calceolaria

The calceolaria has an exotic appearance, but is one of the easiest of all pot plants with a wonderful range of colour and ideal for mass planting on the staging. Mid-June throughout July is the best time for seed sowing. The seedlings should be potted on in their young stage using a well drained compost which should be pressed firmly.

Pot on in stages to 6 or 7in (15–18cm) pots. The plants will flower after around eight months from sowing. They relish overhead spraying with clear water until near the flowering stage when a drier atmosphere should be maintained.

Coleus

Coleus, with its attractive foliage colour in a range of greens, red, bronze, cream and gold are always worth space in the greenhouse. A few well grown specimens mixed with other subjects, will give the right overall look needed to decorate the greenhouse bench.

Sow seeds from February onwards, selecting the best colours for potting on when two or three leaves have developed. The best coleus are the hybrid named varieties obtained from a specialist from which cuttings can be taken to increase stock. Regular pinching of the growing tips to encourage breaks are essential in building up a well balanced plant. The plants will grow well in either a loam based or soilless compost.

Polyanthus

No subject earns its keep more than the polyanthus. A lovely pot plant with the added bonus that, after flowering under glass the first year, it will give several seasons of outdoor colour each spring from the same plant after bedding out.

April is the best time to sow seed to build up strong plants for flowering in the early months of next year. A cold greenhouse or frame offers ample protection to propagate the seed which can be sown in one of the peat based composts.

Don't worry if the seedlings are late showing through or are uneven in germinating. A little time and patience, plus

Polyanthus bedded out.

a spot shaded from the strong sun, is ideal for raising the seedlings.

Once the seedling leaves are big enough to handle comfortably, they can be moved on. A good idea is to prick them out into a tray of peaty compost which can be kept moist until the plants have built up a good root structure and can be potted on.

There is no need for an intermediate size pot. Pot on straight into a 4½ to 5in (11.5–12.5cm) pot using Levington or a John Innes type that has been supplemented with an extra helping of peat. Don't crock the pots. A layer of moist peat in the bottom will keep the polyanthus much happier. Keep the

plants in a shady place outside with an occasional spray of liquid derris to keep aphis at bay, and to combat the slugs, try to plunge the pots into a bed of weathered ash. This, apart from checking the slugs, also provides the nice cool root run so essential for growing good polyanthus. A few attentions to the odd points will be rewarded when the plants are in bloom under glass early in the year.

There are several fine varieties suitable for growing in pots, amongst them **Suttons Triumph** in a lovely range of white, yellow, pink, red, blue or mixed colours with a height of around 10in (25cm).

More dwarf in habit but with good sized and colourful blooms, **Pacific**

Dwarf Jewel comes in mixed colours that include many of the recognised polyanthus shades.

Hursts Early Dwarf Pacific Strain has been especially bred for its bright colour range, large trusses of bloom and a dwarf habit ideal for pot plant work.

Blackmore and Langdon — famous for their polyanthus breeding — have two ideal pot plant strains, the well known **Langdon's Blue** and a mixed range of attractive colours.

One strain that has been introduced recently by Suttons is "**Lemon Punch**", a dwarf polyanthus in lemon-yellow shades and long flowering in pots and the open ground.

261

Ornamental plants under glass

Colour guide on page 242

Gold lace polyanthus.

Primula acaulis, Snowball.

Primula elatior.

Primulas

These beautiful, delicate flowered plants are in fact, some of the easiest greenhouse plants to grow.

Primula obconica is about the easiest of all, tolerating more mis-management than most but still putting on a brave show of bright and colourful blooms. But it has one drawback. It can give some people an irritating skin rash.

It is easily raised from seed sown in March, April and May, ideally being grown on in a shaded cold-frame before bringing into the greenhouse.

P. malacoides has neat foliage and spikes of delicate flowers ranging from white to crimson. It is best raised from seed sown in June or July, in a well-drained compost. It is almost hardy, so should be grown in cool conditions.

P. kewensis has rich, yellow flowers in late spring and early summer. Seed should be sown in March.

P. sinensis is not as widely grown as it should be. Its attractive, single flowers in lavender shades, make it a fine pot plant. Again, this is best raised from seed sown in the early spring.

Salpiglossis

Salpiglossis is a lovely subject — in white, yellow, bronze and orange through to deep violet. The best plants are those raised from seed sown during August which will give a display in winter and early spring.

Move the young seedlings when in their third leaf stage and leave them in the cold frame until the end of October. Keep potting the plant on when the pots are full of root and give support with split canes or twigs.

Schizanthus.

Schizanthus

Schizanthus, "the poor man's orchid" is another delightful subject that is so easy to grow. Several months' flowering can be had from successive batches of seed sowing.

Sow from August onwards and prick out into boxes when the seedlings are large enough to handle. About ten weeks after sowing they will be ready for a 3in (7.5cm) pot using a not too strong compost. John Innes No. 1 will be sufficient at the early stage, the aim being to build up a compact plant. They can be finally potted on into pots up to 7in (18cm) in diameter depending upon the size of plant required. Use a final potting compost of John Innes No. 3 or Levington.

Streptocarpus

Streptocarpus is a wonderful plant and the best strains are from the named hybrids which can be increased each year by leaf cuttings. The last ten years has seen a great improvement in varieties bred by the specialists in a great colour range, although a sowing of seed can often produce something that little bit extra.

Seeds can be sown at any time of the year but a sowing in July and the following February will produce a successive batch of flowering plants.

The streptocarpus enjoys a shady spot and will not mind being under the foliage and shade of other subjects. The seed is exceptionally fine, almost like dust, so when sowing just press them into moist, peaty compost and don't cover them. Levington compost is an ideal medium. When the plants are reaching the flowering stage, they will appreciate a weekly liquid feed of a balanced fertiliser.

Schizanthus make fine pot plants.

Ornamental plants under glass — cacti

Colour guide on page 244

WHAT is the secret of flowering your cactus plants? Certainly there is no closely guarded mystery known only to a select few. The most important thing is to grow the correct species. There are many cacti that will flower in about three years from seed, while others will flower only after twenty years or more. The other important factor is adopting the correct growing technique to assure, as far as possible, that your plants will have a reasonable chance of flowering.

Cultivation

It must be remembered that all cacti are plants that, in nature, are subjected to a high light intensity, if not direct sunshine, throughout almost every day of the year. Obviously, we cannot create such ideal conditions in this country, but we should go as far as possible in this direction by growing them in the best light available.

A greenhouse, with plenty of ventilation during the warm weather, is the best situation and will give the plants every opportunity of producing flowers. For growing cacti indoors you must use the sunniest position for your plants. A south facing bay window is the best as this will give the nearest approach to the all-round and overhead light which is so necessary.

Seedlings and young plants need to be kept growing for as much of the year as possible with only a couple of months in a dry and dormant state. This necessitates a heated greenhouse or room, where a minimum of 45°F (7°C) should be kept through the winter.

The growing medium may be either a conventional John Innes compost with the addition of extra peat and grit, or a soilless compost such as Arthur Bowers (Cactus Formula). Whichever material you use, it will be necessary to feed with a general fertiliser a number of times during the season — once a month from May to September.

Correct watering is another very vital factor in the successful cultivation of cacti. You may apply the water overhead, into the rim of the pot or by capillary action from the bottom of the pot. The important thing to remember is that the compost should be thoroughly soaked at each watering and then left to dry out completely.

Propagation

Propagation of cacti can be by division, offsets or seed. Some *Mammillarias* will produce rooted offsets which can be detached easily and potted up singly. This also applies to *Notocactus ottonis*, many *Lobivias* and *Echinopsis*

A collection of cacti.

and most of the *Rebutias*. This is certainly a quick method of producing new plants, but is very limited in the range of species. Many of the best flowering cacti produce few, if any offsets and must be propagated from seed.

Cactus seed should be sown in a very fine medium. Many gardeners find Arthur Bowers ideal for this purpose. The medium should be moist but not wet when the seed is sown and the seed should be sprinkled evenly over the surface and pressed gently into the medium, but not entirely covered.

The container(s) should be placed into a heated propagator with the thermostat set at 75°F (24°C). The propagator should be in a shaded position or covered with a couple of layers of fine net. Good viable seed can be expected to germinate in any time between one week and six weeks.

The growing medium should be kept moist at all times but never soggy and saturated with water. Drying out of the medium can result in the tiny hair-like roots withering even before the cotyledons have been formed.

The seedlings should be watered regularly with a liquid feed added to the water. Systemic insecticide and fungi-

At this stage it is ready for potting on.

Ornamental plants under glass — cacti

Colour guide on page 244

Use a loop of paper to handle cacti.

cide should be used as necessary to guard against mealy bug, sciara fly and damping off.

Pricking out into seed trays should be done when the plants are between ¼in and ½in (6–13mm) in diameter. Growing cacti from seed is a time consuming job and needs a lot of patience and experience before really satisfying results can be expected. Most cacti are very slow growing and none can be expected to flower in much under three years.

What to grow

When choosing your seeds from a catalogue, look for *Rebutia*. All species will produce flowers in 3 to 5 years. The genus *Rebutia* has a number of divisions and other generic names may be encountered such as *Aylostera*, *Digitorebutia* and *Mediolobivia*.

Most of the genus *Copiapoa* require many years to reach flowering size, but C. *humilis*, C. *pepiniana* and C. *hypogea* can be flowered in 3 to 4 years.

With a few exceptions it is possible to flower *Gymnocalycium* within four years, but avoid G. *saglione* and G. *cardenasianum* which will take 10 years or more.

The genus *Lobivia* can be relied upon to flower as young plants and will produce blooms ranging in colour from white, yellow and orange to deep red.

Several *Notocactus* will flower when small, particularly N. *ottonis*, N. *pampeanus*, N. *concinnus* etc, but N. *leninghausii* and N. *schumannianus* will certainly keep you waiting a long time for the first flower.

In the range 3 to 5 years to flowering size, any *Parodia* should oblige and most of the *Mammillarias* will also flower within this time, although many species have quite small flowers. M. *zielmanniana* is a particularly good flowering plant having deep violet flowers.

Finally, among the easy-to-flower are certain species of *Echinocereus*. Look for E. *pulchellus* and E. *fitchii* but in general avoid the others if you are looking for quick flowering species.

A last word of advice. It is best to buy small plants that are in flower or show flower remains. They should produce their flowers every year without fail. If they do not, then look to your cultivation for the reason — don't blame the plant!

Cuttings

Colour guide on page 242

THE rooting of cuttings is too often surrounded by unnecessary mystery. Many inexperienced gardeners are offered conflicting advice. They end up having to decide whether to root in pure sand, John Innes compost, peat and sand or Vermiculite. Whether to cut the stem beneath a node, straight across or on the slant. Whether or not to use hormone powder or whether to slit the end of the stem and insert a grain of wheat ("when the wheat germinates it will help the cutting to root")!

The fact is, *no-one ever rooted a cutting*. All we do is keep the cutting alive and healthy until it forms roots itself. Any method which satisfies this need can be effective. It is true that cuttings can be in such condition that they root readily, and we can further provide conditions which encourage them to root quickly and prolifically — but it is the cutting itself which does the rooting!

With such realisation all we need to do is employ the simplest method of keeping cuttings alive and in healthy condition whilst promoting the reasonably speedy development of an adequate number of roots.

Compost

The medium in which cuttings are to be rooted needs to be retentive of moisture, aerated and free of harmful organisms. John Innes Seed Compost is a suitable medium, but open it up further by adding one part of peat and one part of horticultural sand to every four parts of seed compost, to give a preparation equally balanced in loam, peat and sand.

The advantage of using loam-based mediums is that they provide needed nutrients to developing roots, and they promote the formation of a generally "tougher" root system than inert mediums such as peat and sand.

Cuttings can be rooted in trays, round the edge of 3½in (9cm) pots or in a bed made up on the greenhouse staging. In the interests of simplicity, dispense with containers and root in a bed on the greenhouse staging, and as we shall see without the aid of a propagator.

Heated staging

The temperature of the compost is important. At 40°F (4°C) rooting will take as long as eight weeks, and at 50°F (10°C), a month, whilst at 60°F (15°C) cuttings will root in just over two weeks.

The desired bottom heat can be provided by an electric cable heater or by a paraffin heater positioned under the staging. By far the best method is to use a cable heater, thermostatically controlled at 60°F (15°C).

Hoya carnosa

267

Cuttings

Colour guide on page 244

Prepare a whole staging as a propagation bed by overlaying it with asbestos sheeting with a 4in (10cm) surrounding board. The cable runs up and down the asbestos at spacings of about 3in (7.5cm). This is overlaid with builder's sand to a depth of some 2in (5cm) with a rod-type thermostat in the sand about ½in (13mm) over the cable.

The sand is kept moist to disperse the heat. To avoid excessive evaporation a sheet of polythene is laid over the sand. The rooting compost is simply placed on the polythene sheeting to a depth of 2in (5cm). The polythene should be pierced at 4in (10cm) spacings to provide for drainage. In addition to facilitating the rooting of chrysanthemum cuttings, this staging can be used for bringing on backward stools, germinating seeds, and later for tomato plants in small pots.

Taking and trimming

Ideally, cuttings would be in active growth at the time of removal from the stools, and sufficiently fresh to enable them to be snapped off cleanly with the fingers to the desired rooting length of about 1½in (4cm). Fresh cuttings will root more freely than those which are dormant and hard.

In other cases cuttings will need trimming to length with a razor blade, but with the knowledge that, unless the blade is cleansed after every cut, the sap from one cutting will be passed on to the next, together with any diseases.

A straight cut across the stem to the desired length is all that is needed. It matters not whether it is above, below or between leaf joints. What must be avoided is the bruising of the ends of the stems, which can be the case if cuttings are trimmed with scissors. Bruised stems will rot and the cutting will be lost.

Hormone powders speed rooting where cuttings are on the hard side, and they certainly increase the number of roots formed. For this reason dip the bottom 6mm of the stems in hormone rooting powder before inserting them in the compost.

The dipping of cuttings in insecticide and/or fungicide is undesirable. Such practice can damage growing tips and in some cases cause them to become blind.

Insertion

Cuttings should be spaced some 2in (5cm) apart, which in the case of standard seed trays will give 28 cuttings to the tray. The advantage with trays is that when the cuttings have rooted the tray can be removed from the cable-heated staging and placed in cooler quarters to postpone the need for potting up. Where cuttings are rooted in a bed on the staging they need to be potted up soon after rooting to avoid excessively rapid growth.

Propagators are not necessary for rooting chrysanthemum cuttings. Indeed, they are undesirable. If cuttings are prepared and inserted in the manner sug-

gested, with gentle bottom heat, the temperature of the greenhouse itself can be as low as an economic 40°F (4°C), with normal ventilation provided, and the cuttings will still root in the periods mentioned. The big advantage with this method is that cuttings do not soften during rooting. They come through propagation as hard in foliage as when they entered it.

Watering

One has read many times that rooting cuttings should not be watered too frequently. This advice concerns propagators. With the open-staging method watering is virtually fool-proof and simplicity itself.

After a batch of cuttings has been inserted they are literally flooded in with a drenching from a fine-rosed watering can, and this soaking is repeated every three days until the freshening of the tips shows that rooting has taken place. Then water is applied less liberally and at longer intervals.

This method is simple and effective, with virtually 99% success!

The time to insert cuttings? An average timing is fourteen weeks ahead of the stopping date. This is calculated to have plants in nice stopping condition when the stop falls due.

Indoor plants

Colour guide on page 246

NOT since the Victorian era have so many people given plants house room. During the last decade, there has been an explosion of ideas on how to display plants, using anything to put them in from a disused fishtank to a fashionable jardiniere.

Indoor gardening is an especially important pastime, as everyone young or old can take part. Best of all, it includes people who do not boast an outdoor garden, or are housebound. Growing any plant is very rewarding, especially when, after it has been lovingly nurtured from seed or cutting, it flowers or fruits. Apart from this personal satisfaction of growing plants (or maybe just keeping them alive!) they give any room that "jungle freshness!"

Choosing plants

The majority of plants sold in garden centres and florists, under the heading of houseplants, are grown for their foliage. This is because they have more value for long term display, than the short lasting "flowering plants". When choosing plants for a specific purpose, there are certain features to look for. For instance, if you are choosing plants for a bottle garden they should be slow growing and not have too rampant a root system. They must also be tolerant to the high humidity that will build up, especially in sealed containers. Choose plants with leaves that have a variety of texture and colour, which will create interest. Similar care must be given when choosing plants for bowls and troughs, although they do not need to be quite so small, as they are not restricted by the height of a container.

Select plants which are neat and compact, avoiding one-sided, leggy plants. If while you are rummaging around for a nicely shaped plant, clouds of white fly appear and, on closer inspection the leaves are covered with scale etc, buy something else. It is important to buy plants which are as free of pests and diseases as is possible. Otherwise, when these little creatures are let loose in your house, they will go forth and multiply on all your other house plants.

When trying to decide what type of plant to grow, think of how you want to display it. For instance, a hanging basket planted with tall, bushy plants will not be quite so effective as one which includes trailing plants. If you have toddlers that tend to have a quick nibble of your plants occasionally, avoid those which have thorns, poisonous sap or stinging hairs. There are not many houseplants with these "dangers", but it is always worth checking.

Indoor plants

Colour guide on page 246

A collection looks better grouped closely.

Small pots can be put together in larger bowls.

Bowls

The container you use should have a depth of at least 3–5in (7.5–12.5cm) for the roots to be able to develop sufficiently. Preferably plant with slow growing species, as the bowl would soon become overcrowded. Regular thinning may be necessary and the larger plants will need replacing. As there is a lot of competition in a small space for water, it should be checked daily. The compost should be kept moist and not saturated, as there is not usually anywhere for the excess water to drain as most attractive bowls have sealed bases.

Plants that could be used are:
'Spider plant'' — *Chlorophytum*
''Croton'' — *Codiaeum*
''Ivy'' — *Hedera*
''Prayer plant'' — *Maranta*
''Pepper plant'' — *Peperomia*
''Aluminium plant'' — *Pilea*
''Ribbon ferns'' — *Pteris*

Bottles

It is not necessary to use the traditional carboy for your bottle garden. Any reasonable size of bottle can be used to make a garden. They do not necessarily have to have a lid, but if they don't, regular watering will be necessary. Due to plants breathing, condensation builds up in sealed containers thus making them self-watering. They should be placed in a well-lit situation and not in full sun, to

Remember to water them all.

prevent an excess build up of condensation. The plants you choose must be suited to the height and width of the bottle. In a small bottle no more than 2–3 plants should be considered.

"Bottle gardening" tools, which can be made by tying any household spoon, fork and cotton reel to long canes, are necessary when planting bottles which have a narrow neck. These require a lot more patience and skill to plant, than a bottle with a neck wide enough to plant by hand. To place the compost neatly in the bottom of the bottle use a paper funnel. Choose small plants, such as rooted cuttings, that will pass through the neck without damaging them.

It is very important to remove any dead and diseased leaves as they would increase the risk of infection, which could cause them to rot. This will be more of a problem in sealed containers, which have the ideal conditions (warm and wet) for fungal infection. If you remove the lid occasionally to reduce the temperature and humidity, the risk of attack should be reduced.

Plants that could be used are:
"Snakeskin plant" — *Fittonia*
"Maidenhair fern" — *Adiantum*
"Aluminium plant" — *Pilea*
"Pepper plant" — *Peperomia*
"Spider plant" — *Chlorophytum*
"Baby's tears" — *Helxine*
"Mother of thousands" — *Saxifrage*
"Sedge" — *Carex*

A bottle garden.

Indoor plants

Colour guide on page 246

Bark trough garden.

Logs and bark troughs

In the wild, some plants grow supported in the nooks and crannies of tree trunks and branches. Their roots absorb the moisture required from the atmosphere, which is usually very humid in the tropical rain forests where they grow. Rather than grow such plants in pots, it is much more interesting to try and create the most natural habitats possible. This can be done by wrapping the roots in sphagnum moss, to conserve moisture and, tying them to artificial trees

made from branches, or placing them in free standing trough-shaped pieces of bark. Hollowed logs, either home made, or those that can be bought specifically as blue-tit nesting boxes for the garden, can be used in a similar way.

Growing plants in this way requires no more maintenance than normal. Keeping the compost moist is the most important job and watering should be done daily, using a fine mist sprayer. A liquid feed should be applied regularly as there are no nutrients in sphagnum moss. The

selection of plants that can be grown in this way is fairly small compared with pot grown plants. A good selection of the "bread and butter" species are usually available from your local florist or garden centre.

Plants that could be used are:
"Birds-nest fern" — *Asplenium*
"Staghorn fern" — *Platycerium*
"Tank plants" — *Bromeliads*
Orchids, which are generally a more specialist interest, may be used, although they do not have the all year round

272

interest that the other suggestions have. But, if you are keen enough to grow them in your greenhouse, why not bring them into the house at flowering time and tie them to your artificial trees or plunge them in your trough.

Plant needs

It is important to try to achieve as near to the plants' natural conditions as possible. Light, of course is essential, but the degree of it required, depends upon the plants' natural place of origin. Those found in shady forest conditions, obviously need less light than those growing on open moorland. Therefore, a knowledge of the plants' habitat is not only interesting, but important if you are to get the best out of them. The circulation of air around the leaves is essential, but they must not be sitting in draughts.

In the end it is the temperature in your room that really limits your choice of plants. The majority of rooms are heated to a temperature of about 50–70°F (10–20°C) while they are occupied, but this is not always a constant temperature. The temperature generally falls considerably at night. Therefore, when choosing a plant, if you are unsure of its requirements, seek advice. It is always better to buy young plants for a room where the temperature is not quite ideal, as they find it easier to establish than mature plants that have been grown under glass.

General maintenance of plants should include cleaning the leaves. This is done not only for the sake of appearance, but also to remove the dust, which will block the plants' 'breathing pores''.

The amount of water to give a plant, is often the most difficult thing to decide. It is best to keep the compost just moist, and not saturated. In the winter particularly, let the compost dry almost completely before giving it a really good soaking. Watering should be done preferably in the morning to allow the plant to dry out during the rest of the day. The plant should not be left sitting in a saucer of water, as it would cause the compost to become putrid.

A proprietary brand of liquid feed should be applied regularly, to build up healthy plants. The leaves of some plants should be sprayed lightly on warmer days, especially in centrally heated rooms which can be extremely dry. This will create a humid atmosphere around the plant and prevent it from wilting, which is often caused by loss of moisture through the leaves, rather than drought. Other treatments that may be necessary are pruning, staking, pest and disease control and potting.

Calathea Zebrina.

Indoor plants

Colour guide on page 246

Aspidistra.

WHEN choosing a plant have clear in your mind the room that you are going to put it in. The factors of that room should influence or limit your choice. Although it is necessary that all plants have air circulating around them, very few are tolerant of draughts. Therefore if you are choosing a plant for the hall or the landing avoid those which would be damaged by cold draughts.

Light

The next question you would need to ask yourself is whether or not there is enough light. Rooms that have small windows, that face NE or NW or are heavily shaded by your garden plants will receive very little light, again limiting your choice. The majority of plants prefer a well lit room, but very few can tolerate direct sunlight. South, south east and west facing rooms provide the best light, but it is unwise to place a plant on a window ledge unprotected by a net curtain or blind from direct sunlight. This is especially important on a south facing window ledge as the plants would scorch. They are best moved from the window mid day until early evening, during the summer months. Plants should also be moved from the windowsill on cold nights so that they do not suffer from cold or even frost damage, which can happen, especially if they are trapped between the curtains and the glass. They can also be damaged when you close the curtains if they brush against the plants causing bruising or even snapping of the leaves and stems. Avoid placing plants on a TV or a shelf above a radiator as the degree of temperature fluctuation will be greater.

Humidity

The natural habitats of many of our common house plants are tropical rainforests and jungles. Therefore, many find it difficult to adapt and grow well in the dry atmosphere of centrally heated houses. *Bromeliads* or "Tank plants" are excellent for dry, centrally heated rooms, as they store their own moisture in their "vases" which are made up from their leaves. There are many ways by which we can overcome the problems created by the lack of humidity fairly easily. Some plants such as *Saintpaulias* and ferns grow particularly well in warm, moist rooms such as the bathroom. If the temperature in your bathroom fluctuates and is fairly cool, choose a warmer room and cover the plant with a bell jar or make a bottle garden. Growing groups of plants in bowls, troughs etc creates a "microclimate" where the atmosphere immediately around the plants is more moist than that of the room. Extra humidity can be created by standing plants in trays of pebbles which can be wetted without the plant roots sitting in water. Alternatively, plunge the pot in moist peat. Climbing and trailing plants require staking for support. Use a sphagnum covered pole, which when regularly sprayed to keep it moist will create a humid environment around the leaves. These are especially useful for plants which have aerial roots.

Top dress

During the winter months plants put on very little growth therefore, it is best to wait until the spring to re-pot. But this does not mean that you should overlook the compost altogether. Scrape any moss and weeds that have grown on the surface and the hard crusty skin of compost which sometimes develops. Top-dress with fresh compost which has fertilisers incorporated. As the winter growth is negligible compared with the summer, feeding with NPK is not so important. Nitrogen especially should be cut out altogether as the resulting growth would be soft and weak.

Watering

It is equally important to cut down on watering in winter. It must only be done when the compost feels fairly dry, but do not allow it to dry out completely as many soilless composts can be difficult to re-wet. Generally, the water tends to drain between the side of the pot and the shrunken rootball. It is then necessary to stand the entire pot in a bowl of water and, leave there only as long as the air bubbles rise up from the surface of the compost. Do not leave any pot standing in a saucer of water as the compost will become sour due to the loss of oxygen and the roots may rot off. It is often suggested that some plants should be watered from the base. Do not sit them in a saucer of water as it is easy to forget them and the problems already mentioned will occur. Place the pots in about 1 in (2.5cm) of water in the kitchen sink until the top of the compost is just moist. It is then unlikely that you'll forget them. There are available a variety of capillary watering systems that are so designed for use in the house. These will prove invaluable for gardeners who often enjoy weekends away from home. If you constantly lose plants due to watering difficulties try growing them in a hydroponic unit. This is a method whereby the plant is not grown in compost but is anchored in the pot by clay granules. The roots sit in a nutrient solution which is

Monstera deliciosa.

Indoor plants

Colour guide on page 246

Asparagus plumosa.

topped up when the indicator falls below the level. Because the plant is sitting in "water" there is a greater degree of humidity around the plant than with the usual method, therefore plants tend to grow well especially in centrally heated rooms.

Pruning

Pruning, if at all necessary, is not usually a major part of house plant care, as the majority of plants we grow tend not to require shaping. Usually the overall shape is gained by pinching out the leader to produce a bushy plant or removing any side shoots for a straight stem. Only when a plant has become spindly in growth is "pruning" required. The principles are the same as for any other pruning ie cutting out all the old wood and removing crossed branches. By pruning to a bud facing in the direction where you want the shoot to form, you can create the shape desired. It is usually done in winter when there is little sap flow, but any "weeping" wounds can be stopped by sealing them with charcoal powder.

Pests and diseases

Pests and diseases should not be that common on your house plants if they are healthy and well grown. Some plants are more prone to attack than others, therefore you should keep a special eye on them. Once they become infested it won't be long before colonies of whitefly etc will be eating out on another favourite plant. If you choose to use a chemical control, make sure that it will not damage the plants that you are going to spray. Always read the instructions clearly and take any necessary precautions specified. The majority of diseases that attack plants are caused by fungi. They usually attack weak, unhealthy plants that are growing in poor conditions. Apart from rectifying the growing conditions use a chemical fungicide. Warm and wet conditions are ideal for fungi development, therefore it is always worth checking regularly, bottle gardens etc, for any signs of attack. Remove any dead leaves and flowers as they are a source of infection.

WHICH plants to choose for your rooms that are: 1 — Cool and shady. 2 — Warm and shady. 3 — Well lit, but with no direct sunshine. 4 — In full sun most of the day. 5 — Not heated during the day in winter. 6 — Centrally heated.

1 This type of room is usually facing NE or NW and is therefore always in slight shade but, has the advantage of having a constant temperature.

Plants that grow well at a minimum winter temperature of 45°F (7°C) and are tolerant to full shade are: "Ribbon ferns" — *Pteris*, these are fairly easy plants to care for and require not much more than a regular watering all year round. They need feeding monthly during the summer and plunging in moist peat or gravel to keep up the humidity. The *Asparagus ferns*, which are not really ferns but members of the Lily family, also suit these conditions and require very much the same conditions as the Ribbon ferns.

To grow the "biggest *Aspidistra* in the world" why not find it a spot in this room. Keep the plant happy by giving it a monthly feed and a moderate watering all year round. Polish the leaves regularly and it really will deserve the pride of place.

Philodendron, "the sweetheart vine" will do well in cool conditions if kept a little on the dry side. Feed from April–August and re-pot in spring. Pinch out the tips for more bushy growth and train round a sphagnum covered pole or trellis.

2 In a warmer, shady room where the minimum temperature is at least 50°F (10°C) there is a greater range of plants to choose from. Many will require a more humid atmosphere, therefore why not grow them in containers or troughs whereby a "microclimate" will be created.

No houseplant collection is usually complete without the ubiquitous "Rubber plant" — *Ficus elastica*. They are fairly easy to care for but will not tolerate draughts, therefore don't sit them too near a window or door. Keep just moist in winter and water freely in summer.

If your preference is a more graceful plant that is still just as robust as the "Rubber Plant" try a "Swiss Cheese plant" — *Monstera deliciosa*. Its requirements are not unlike those of the "Rubber Plant" but, more attention to staking is necessary. They are best grown round sphagnum covered poles which when sprayed will increase the humidity around the leaves. "Prayer plant" — *Maranta* and "Pepper plants" — *Peperomias*, too grow well in warm, moist, shady conditions. Both are suitable for bottle gardens but, *Peperomias* especially need to be watched closely for fungal attack which will cause them to rot if conditions are too cool. They should be watered well during the growing season and sparingly in winter.

Sansevieria.

Indoor plants

Colour guide on page 246

Hedera canariensis.

Hedera helix.

3 For your north facing window choose plants that will tolerate a great deal of light, but no direct sunlight.

Cyclamen is a good example and, is probably about the most popular pot plant grown for winter flowering. An even temperature of around 50°F (10°C) is required during the flowering period, when they should be well watered and fed at fortnightly intervals. It is important to try and keep the corm and young buds dry. Remove any dead flowers and leaves from the corm to prevent fungal attack and eventual rot.

Pot grown *Primulas*, the most common being *polyanthus* and *obconica* are equally as attractive as *Cyclamen* but a little easier to care for. In winter the temperature should not exceed 50–54deg F (10–12deg C) as higher temperatures would shorten the flowering season and, cause the flowers to fade. The compost should just be kept moist, preferably use rain water.

Two versatile houseplants suitable for hanging baskets, troughs and bowls are: "Spider plant" — *Chlorophytum* and "Ivies" — *Hederas*. They both tolerate most conditions and do especially well on a north facing windowsill. They should be kept just moist throughout the year, especially *Chlorophytum* which has succulent roots. *Hederas* can also be trained quite effectively on a trellis.

Chlorophytum elatum varigatum.

4 Rooms that are usually in full sun for most of the day, face east-south-east to west-south-west. They provide good light conditions that suit many types of plant, especially flowering species, but can also be very dangerous as temperature fluctuation is at its greatest. In very strong sunlight there is very little humidity and unless the plants are screened by a net curtain or blind they will become badly scorched and shrivelled.

One of the most attractive of all foliage plants that are very easy to grow are *Coleus*. There is a whole range of colours from buff through yellows and reds to crimson. Good light is necessary for the leaf colours to develop. They need a minimum temperature of 50°F (10°C). Water well during the growing season, easing off in winter.

If you want a flowering plant that will give you a full summer season of pleasure, don't look any further than *Regal Pelargoniums*. They really will enjoy basking in the sun on your window sill. They prefer a dry atmosphere and, although they require watering often during the summer they should be allowed almost to dry out in between applications.

A flowering plant that never fails to intrigue is the "Shrimp plant" — *Beloperone*. It is easily grown and, is best

Calathea ornata.

Indoor plants

Colour guide on page 246

Philodendron.

Mimosa pudica.

Citrus.

situated in a sunny spot where it will be encouraged to produce the showy shrimp-like, pinkish bracts that surround the flowers. To produce a compact, bushy plant, cut hard back in February. Maintain a temperature of 50°F (10°C) and, water moderately all year round.

5 For rooms that are not heated during the day in winter, choose hardy plants that will tolerate a minimum temperature of 40–50°F (4–10°C) such as:

Aspidistra — "Cast Iron plant"
Fatsia japonica — "False castor oil plant"
Ficus pumila — "Creeping fig"
Saxifrage stolonifera — "Mother of thousands"
Setcreasia — "Purple heart"
Cissus antartica — "Kangaroo vine"

6 In centrally heated rooms, where the temperature is thermostatically controlled and is therefore more stable, more plants can be grown successfully.

Usually the atmosphere is very dry, which makes them especially suitable for growing Cacti and succulents. Also plants which have fleshy root systems or are bulbous are equally successful.

"Mother in law's tongue" — *Sansevieria*, would be a good choice but avoid overwatering which would inevitably lead to root rot and finally death. If you like Exotics, try *Hoya carnosa*, a heavily scented, vigorous flowering climber. It is most effective trained round wire hoops or canes.

CULTIVATION DETAILS OF SOME POPULAR ORNAMENTAL PLANTS

Botanical Name	Common Name	Colour	Temperature	Propagation	Remarks
Aphelandra	Zebra Plant	Striped leaves	60–65F 15–18C	Cuttings	Moderate watering in winter
Azalea indica	Indian Azalea	Various	60–70F 15–20C	Cuttings	Likes plenty of water
Begonia rex	Fan Plant	Coloured foliage	55–70F 12–20C	Seed, leaves	Avoid draughts
Beloperone guttata	Shrimp Plant	Pink	50–65F 10–18C	Seeds, cuttings	Needs plenty of light
Brunfelsia calycina	Paint Brush	Various	60–65F 15–18C	Seeds	Prefers semi-shade
Calceolaria	Slipper Plant	Various	50–65F 10–18C	Seeds	Long flowering
Cineraria	Cineraria	Various	50–65F 10–18C	Seeds	Avoid draughts Water carefully
Cyclamen	Butterfly Flower	Various	45–65F 7–18C	Seeds	Avoid wetting the tuber
Dieffenbachia	Dumb Cane	Foliage	60–70F 15–20C	Cuttings	Likes warmth and moisture
Dracaena terminalis	Flaming Dragon	Coloured leaves	60–65F 15–18C	Cuttings	Good drainage essential
Ficus elastica	Rubber Plant	Foliage	55–75F 12–23C	Cuttings	Stands central heating
Fittonia	Snakeskin Plant	Foliage	50–65F 10–18C	Cuttings	Likes warmth and moisture
Fuchsia	Lady's Ear Drops	Various	45–70F 7–20C	Seed, cuttings	Likes plenty of water
Euphorbia pulcherrima	Poinsettia	Scarlet bracts	60–70F 15–20C	Cuttings	Winter show
Hedera	Ivies	Green and gold	40–70F 4–20C	Cuttings	Prefers semi-shade Water freely in summer
Grevillea robusta	Silky Oak	Foliage	45–65F 7–18C	Seeds	Thrives in sun or shade
Monstera deliciosa	Cheese Plant	Foliage	50–70F 10–20C	Cuttings	Easy and large flowering
Maranta kerchoveana	Prayer Plant	Spotted foliage	55–70F 12–20C	Division	Repot frequently
Neanthe bella	Parlour Palm	Foliage	50–65F 10–18C	Division	Semi-shade
Philodendron	Sweetheart Plant	Cream on pink spathes	65–75F 18–23C	Stem cuttings	Semi-climber
Pilea cardierei	Friendship Plant	Foliage	65–75F 18–23C	Seeds, cuttings	Water carefully
Rhoicissus	Grape Ivy	Evergreen climber	65–75F 18–23C	Cuttings, seed	Likes light and good drainage
Saintpaulia	African Violet	Various	55–70F 12–20C	Seeds, leaf cuttings	Water moderately in winter
Sansevieria	Mother-in-Law's Tongue	Foliage Insignificant flowers	55–65F 12–18C	Division	Easy
Solanum capsicastrum	Winter Cherry	Red berries	55–65F 12–18C	Seed	Cool conditions
Spathiphyllum	White Sails	Attractive foliage	65–75F 18–23C	Seed, division	Likes a humid atmosphere
Streptocarpus	Cape Primrose	Various	50–70F 10–20C	Seed	Prefers semi-shade
Tolmiea menziesii	Pick-a-Back Plant	Foliage	40–60F 4–15C	Division	Lime-free soil
Tradescantia	Wandering Sailor	Coloured leaves	45–65F 7–18C	Cuttings	Keep in dull light

Index

A

B

C